100 Masterpieces of the 20th Century
from the collections of the Centre Pompidou

Centre Pompidou

ISBN: 978-2-84426-468-8

Publisher number: 1425

Copyright registration: September 2010

Front cover (left to right), details from:

Man Ray, *Le Violon d'Ingres*, 1924

Amedeo Modigliani, *Portrait de Dédie*, [1918]

Martial Raysse, *Made in Japan - La grande odalisque*, 1964

René Magritte, *Les Marches de l'été*, 1938

100
Masterpieces of the 20th Century

Foreword

To choose a hundred masterpieces from among the collections of the Centre Pompidou is evidently not an easy thing to do, and one that cannot help but raise many questions. Products of the twentieth-century avant-gardes, these works are the fruit of artistic procedures that sometimes aimed not only to challenge the authority of the museum but also to put into question the very idea of a masterpiece. What meaning can it have, when art is now constituted by a continuous breaking with any form of tradition? Can one speak of a masterpiece when such notions as beauty, rule and craft have lost all relevance?
The question is so complex and so rewarding that the Centre Pompidou-Metz – which joins Beaubourg as a space for the public display of the vast collection of the Musée National d'Art Moderne, the largest collection of modern and contemporary art in Europe, and one of the two biggest in the world, alongside the Museum of Modern Art in New York – took it as the subject of its inaugural exhibition in Spring 2010, entitled, precisely, "Masterpieces?", which interrogated the notion and its relevance to modern and contemporary art.
But to these fascinating theoretical considerations must be opposed the wider public's need for signposts, for points of reference, and this all the more as the history of twentieth-century art is often not as well known as it might be, and can appear, at first sight, to be forbiddingly complex a fragmented and chaotic story that is furthermore still being written, in which themes or tendencies that seemed firmly established can be transformed before our eyes.
It was to meet this legitimate desire for understanding that this book was conceived, imposing on us the difficult task, fraught with intellectual uncertainties as it might be, of selecting a hundred major works to provide a key to the understanding of twentieth-century art in all its strength and vitality.
These works were selected from among the collections of the Musée National d'Art Moderne for their importance to the history of art – as judged by their influence and their reception by viewers, critics and academics – and also as worthy examples of the work of the key artists of modernity.
Like all selections, of course, this choice has its own measure of the arbitrary, and with it comes a dose of the unexpected and perhaps unexpectable, giving the result its relish and testifying to the genuine spirit in which this delicate exercise was conducted – a promise, I hope, of the pleasure that awaits the reader.

Alain Seban
President of the Centre Pompidou

Preface

Any choice of a hundred works from a collection as rich and extensive as that of the Musée National d'Art Moderne is bound to be arbitrary. The bequests of studio contents and the in-depth holdings of certain major artists that are one of the glories of the collection could hardly be reflected, and very many artists of great note have necessarily been excluded.

The multidisciplinary character of the Museum is likewise under-represented, as is contemporary art. Consciously incomplete, turning its attention here and there among periods and movements, among artists of differing degrees of importance, this selection offers only a glimpse of the collection through a number of works that might be considered among its highlights. Certain outstanding ensembles, like André Breton's studio wall, or the Atelier Brancusi, simply could not be left out. Other works from the Museum's more or less abundant holdings of such figures as Duchamp, Matisse, Picasso or Mondrian have been chosen for the light they cast on the artist's work as a whole.

Without the determination of the Museum's successive directors and their curatorial teams, together with the support of the public authorities, this remarkable collection could not have come into being. Even more important, however, has been the generosity of the many donors who, through the six decades of the Museum's existence, have given the collection its own distinctive personality, with all its strengths and weaknesses. A museum's collection grows by successive strata, these owing as much to political events and national cultural policy as to the acts of generosity of individuals or groups – notably in our case a Society of Friends of the Museum now more than a century old. If the creation of a museum is above all, in Europe at least, a matter of political decision, the development of its collections largely depends on private persons, animated for the most part by a duty of memory. A concern to pass an artist on to posterity, to reinforce a presence, to fill a lacuna; but also to fulfil a civic role by offering to the community a cultural good acquired by purchase, gift, or inheritance: these are some of the motivations that have led individuals to present works to the Museum or in other ways to support their acquisition.

To this may be added the initiatives of collectors, dealers, or indeed the creators themselves, in seeking to promote or reinforce the presence of contemporary artists, so setting them in a context, a conspectus in which past meets present.

Three phases may be distinguished in the history of the Musée National d'Art Moderne. Successor to the Musée du Luxembourg, founded in the early nineteenth century to show living French artists, and its later pendant, the Jeu de Paume, opened in 1932 and devoted to contemporary art from abroad, the Musée National d'Art Moderne finally opened at the Palais de Tokyo after the end of the Second World War. Its first director, Jean Cassou, a poet and thinker in close contact with artistic circles, endeavoured to fill the shocking gaps in the national collections by seeking gifts or purchases on favourable terms from the many artists who then lived in Paris. This first period saw the establishment of a firm foundation, with the acquisition of major works by Matisse, Bonnard, Braque, Delaunay and Picasso, among many others.

With the creation of the Centre Beaubourg, renamed the Centre Georges Pompidou after the death of its chief inspirer, the Museum's collection found itself radically reshaped. Opened in 1977, the Centre Pompidou was a multidisciplinary institution focused on the heritage of modernity and on contemporary creation. The Centre's architecture would do a great deal to popularise the museum experience and so promote access to modern art. The Museum was now also able, finally, to concentrate on the crucial absences in its collection, to open itself to international art, to American art more particularly, and to deliberately engage with its own time by offering a place to contemporary artists. Some of the great figures in modern art, still scandalously unrepresented, now entered the collection: De Chirico, Hausmann, Magritte, Malevich, Mondrian, Pollock, each with indisputable masterpieces, while essential contemporaries like Beuys, Warhol, Johns, Fontana or Klein joined them with works equally carefully selected.

Another novelty was the range of disciplines covered. Long absent from the Museum, photography now took its place among the arts, occupying an ever more important place in the collection. The moving image, in the form of video and experimental film, was accorded equality with earlier forms. The collection thus grew at an extraordinary rate.

In 1993 the Museum embarked upon a new phase in its history as it became the Musée National d'Art Moderne – Centre de Création Industriel, as the centre for industrial design that had until then been an independent department within the Centre Pompidou joined with the Museum to form a new institution. The most important result being that architecture and design, until then well represented among Centre's exhibitions but largely absent from the collections, are now among the disciplines collected and conserved by the Museum.

In general, the ongoing quest for new works has allowed the Museum to reflect new trends while also consolidating its existing holdings. The André Breton collection offers an interesting illustration of the policy at work, as it finds itself reconstituted over time through the acquisition of major Surrealist works that once belonged to it.

It is then a strikingly rich museum, and one in constant development, that is presented in highly condensed form here. It is our hope that this book will prompt readers to explore the collection in detail, coming to know the many artists who pioneered new ways of seeing and making – sometimes long misunderstood – and in so doing paying an appropriate tribute to all those who have helped make it what it is today.

Alfred Pacquement
Director, Musée national d'art moderne –
Centre de création industrielle

Catalogue

Vassily Kandinsky · Pierre Bonnard · Henri Matisse · Georges Rouault · Piet Mondrian · Maurice de Vlaminck · Constantin Brancusi · Raymond Duchamp-Villon · Julio González · Raoul Dufy · Francis Picabia · Kasimir Malevitch · Paul Klee · Pablo Picasso · Fernand Léger · Georges Braque · Amedeo Modigliani · Luigi Russolo · Sonia Delaunay · Jean Arp · Raoul Hausmann · Marcel Duchamp · Marc Chagall · Kurt Schwitters · Le Corbusier · Giorgio De Chirico · Man Ray · Max Ernst · Otto Dix · Alexandre Rodtchenko · Joan Miró · André Breton · Alexander Calder · René Magritte · Luis Buñuel · Alberto Giacometti · Jean Dubuffet · Hans Bellmer · Mark Rothko · Salvador Dalí · Willem De Kooning · Barnett Newman · Victor Vasarely · Frida Kahlo · Balthus · Francis Bacon · Louise Bourgeois · Jackson Pollock · Nicolas de Staël · Pierre Soulages · César · Joseph Beuys · Marc Riboud · Jean Tinguely · Raymond Hains · Pierre Alechinsky · Yves Klein · Cy Twombly · Arman · Andy Warhol · Yaacov Agam · Jasper Johns · Niki de Saint Phalle · Gerhard Richter · Dan Flavin · Ben · Martial Raysse · Georg Baselitz · Daniel Buren · Jean-Pierre Raynaud · Vito Acconci · Bruce Nauman · Annette Messager · Christian Boltanski · Jean Nouvel · Jeff Wall · ORLAN · Philippe Starck · Martin Parr · Anish Kapoor · Andreas Gursky · Peter Doig · Xavier Veilhan

1906

Les Arbres rouges
[Red Trees]
Oil on canvas
65 × 81 cm
Purchased 1947 - AM 2673 P

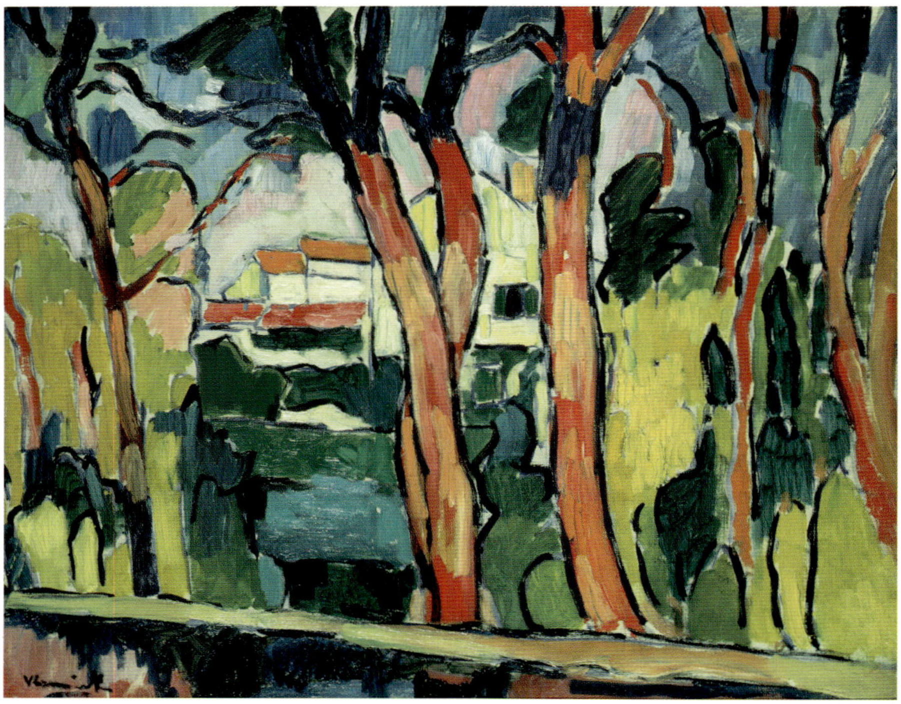

Maurice de Vlaminck

1876, Paris (France)
1958, Rueil-la-Gadelière (France) †

The Van Gogh retrospective at the Berheim-Jeune gallery in 1901 acted as a revelation to Vlaminck. From 1904, he began creating works characterised by the use of pure colours, as though freshly squeezed from the tube.
By exhibiting his paintings alongside those of Derain and Matisse at the 1905 Salon d'Automne, he participated in the advent of Fauvism, which structured space and forms through colour, to the detriment of draughtsmanship.
Les Arbres rouges harks back to Cézanne in its schematic construction. The verticality of the tree trunks lends a vigorous rhythm to the composition of the canvas. The forms are geometrised; the uniform blocks of colour with their black contours juxtapose starkly contrasting reds and greens. The intensity of the colours also contributes to the singular treatment of light, in which the *chiaroscuro* is not emphasised by deep shadows but by fluid bluish swatches of colour •

Raoul Dufy

1877, Le Havre (France)
1953, Forcalquier (France) †

Born into a family of musicians in Le Havre, Dufy studied art in Paris, producing works initially imbued with Impressionism. Having discovered the works of Matisse, he joined the ranks of the Fauvists in 1905. He was a keen observer of places of entertainment such as regattas and casinos and, in the 1930s, of lavish official functions, and developed a significant byline decorating interiors, public spaces, theatres and ceramics. Dufy managed to transcend the 'society' aspect of these subjects, however, thanks to his qualities as a draughtsman and colourist.
Here, he picks up the theme of flag-decked streets, dear to the Impressionists (Manet, Monet, Van Gogh) as well as his Fauvist peers (Braque, Derain, Marquet, Vlaminck). This painting represents 14 July celebrations in a street in Le Havre. It shows a less powerful chromatic range than a number of contemporary Fauvist works, but its density and economy of means are quite remarkable. By reducing the range of colours Dufy lends them profound intensity, accentuated by the painting's schematic construction. The geometric colour blocks of the flags, placed in the foreground, hinder the perspective created by the façades of the buildings. Some of the flags betray a hint of movement, in a fluctuating play on effects of transparency. The Bastille Day celebrations become a pretext for exploring new ways of expressing form, colour and movement •

1906

La Rue pavoisée
[Street with Flags]
Oil on canvas; 81 × 65 cm
Bequeathed by Mrs. Raoul Dufy, 1963 - AM 4113 P

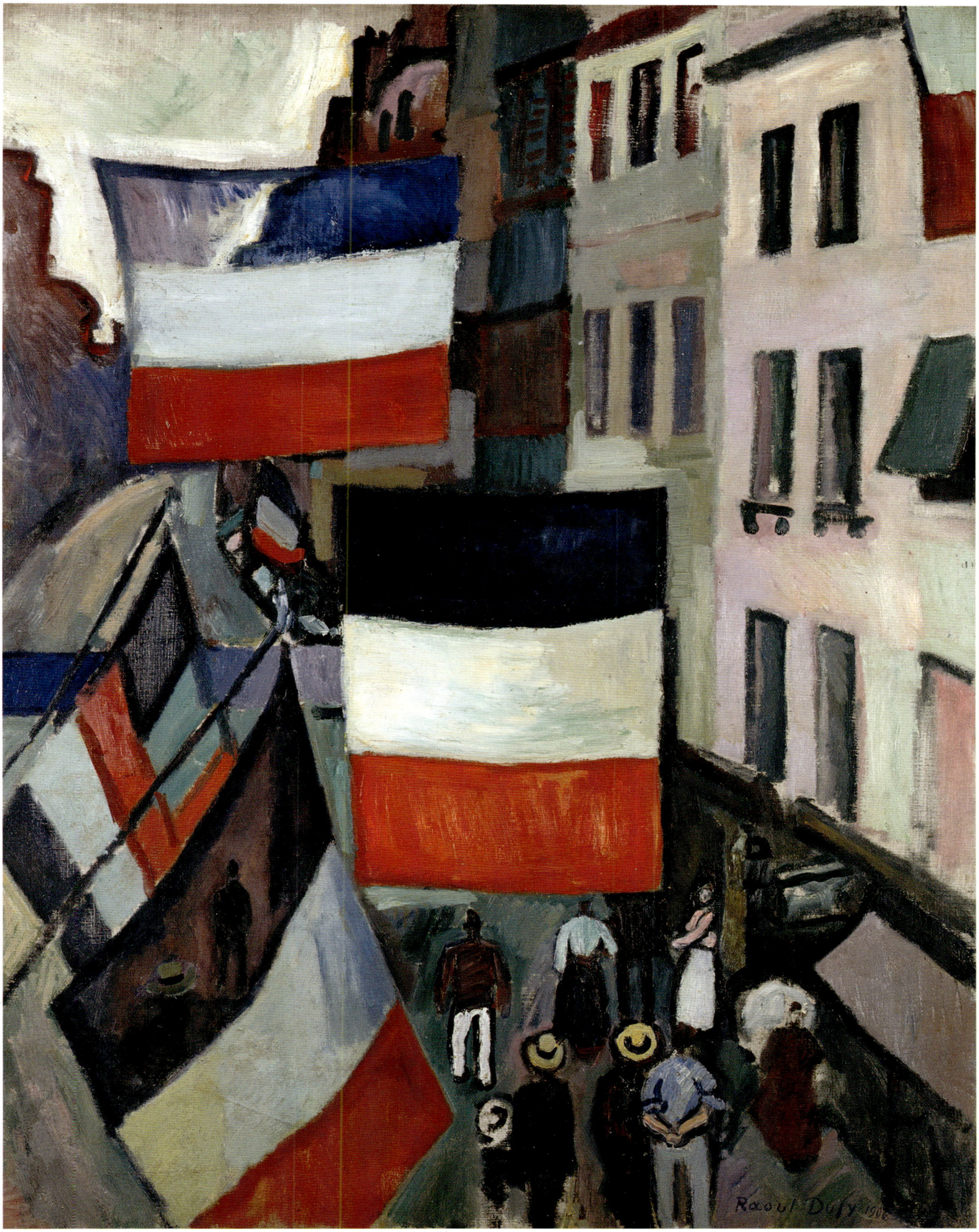
Raoul Dufy

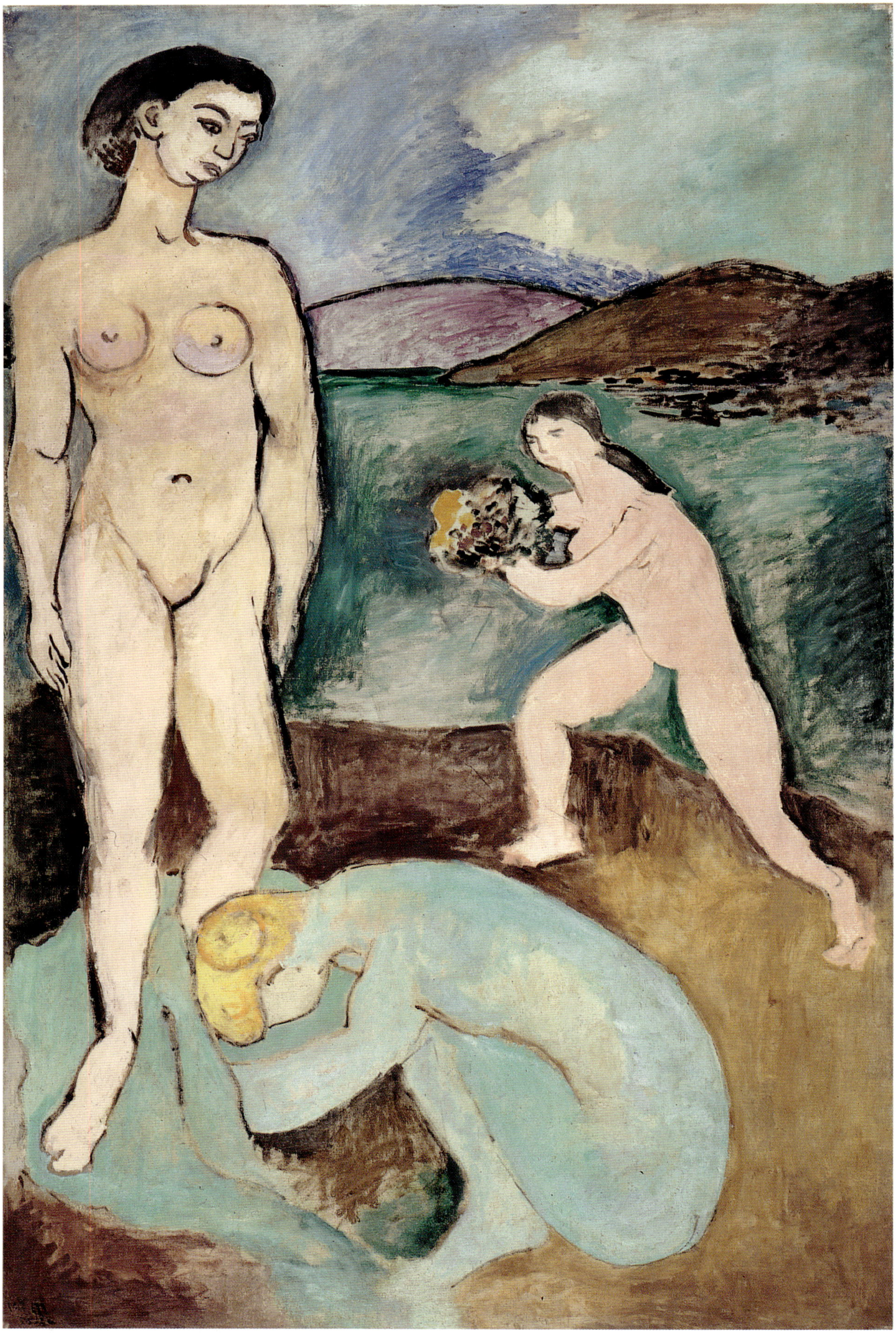

Georges Braque

1882, Argenteuil (France)
1963, Paris (France) †

Braque first trained as a painter-decorator under his father, a painting contractor, before moving to Paris in 1900 to study at the Humbert academy. Struck by the Fauvist paintings shown by Matisse and Derain at the 1905 Salon d'Automne, he became a fervent proponent of this art form, which exalts colours, giving them a free rein in constructing forms and space. Braque spent the winter of 1906–1907 in L'Estaque, a little harbour near Marseille where Cézanne had painted a number of views in the 1870s. It was there that he developed a series exploring "the influences of light, of atmosphere, [...] the effect of rain reviving the colours".
At the beginning of his stay, he depicted this road, flanked by majestic trees and overlooking the sea. Everything was on hand to make the light of the South of France radiate across the canvas: a schematic construction, the refined juxtaposition of colours, bursting with vibrant contrasts, the subtle variations of the brushstroke, alternately relaxed and taut.

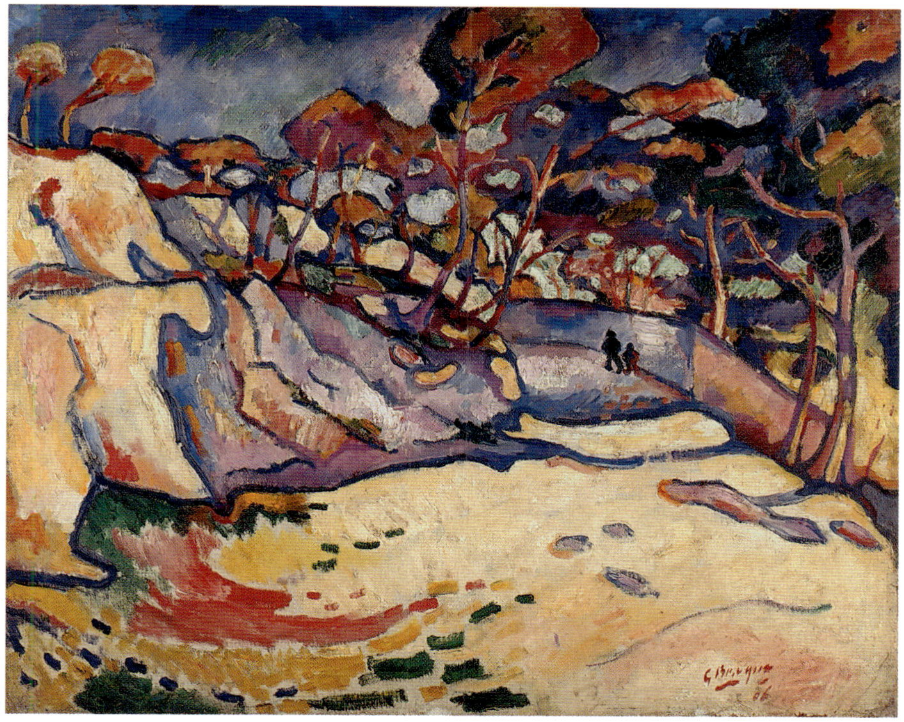

During his second visit to L'Estaque in the autumn of 1907, Braque created a new series of paintings with geometrised forms and a palette confined to warmer hues. The works produced by Braque on his return to L'Estaque in 1908, which were first shown in Paris that same year, were panned by the art critic Louis Vauxcelles, who deplored this "terrible simplification", which reduced everything to "cubes" •

1906

L'Estaque
Oil on canvas
60 × 73.5 cm
Accepted in lieu of tax, 1982 - AM 1982-98

[1907]

Le Luxe I
[Luxury I]
Oil on canvas
210 × 138 cm
Purchased 1945 - AM 2586 P

Henri Matisse

1869, Le Cateau-Cambrésis (France)
1954, Nice (France) †

The work and personality of Matisse dominated the first half of the twentieth century. Unlike his contemporary Picasso, however, Matisse was searching for "an art of balance, of purity and serenity, devoid of worrying or depressing subject matter". Matisse first studied law, becoming a solicitor's clerk, and only began drawing while recovering from an illness. Following a lengthy period of training, he created a furore at the 1905 Salon d'Automne with his Fauvist works. Following this episode, he shot to fame as leader of the "cage of wild beasts" [fauves in French] but his Fauvist period was only short-lived.
Le Luxe I belongs to the cycle of Matisse's first major compositions devoted to the traditional Golden Age theme, together with *Luxe, calme et volupté* [Luxury, Tranquillity and Pleasure] (1904) and *Le Bonheur de vivre* [Joy of Life] (1906). Although his three bathers hark back to the academic genre of the nude, Matisse moved away from the Impressionist and Fauvist styles, seeking his inspiration from the decorative uniform colour blocks dear to Puvis de Chavannes, who advocated a return to the simplicity of the characteristic frescoes of the Italian Primitives. The fluid, stylised aspect of the body contrasts with the faces, which illustrate the painter's interest in the primitive arts. *Le Luxe I* marks a transitional phase between the large charcoal drawing on cardboard, also in the Museum's collections, and the more accomplished version of this same theme, *Le Luxe II*, held at the Statens Museum for Kunst in Copenhagen •

1907-1908

Grand nu

[Large Nude]

Oil on canvas; 140 × 100 cm
Accepted in lieu of tax from
Alex Maguy-Glass, 2002 -
AM 2002-127

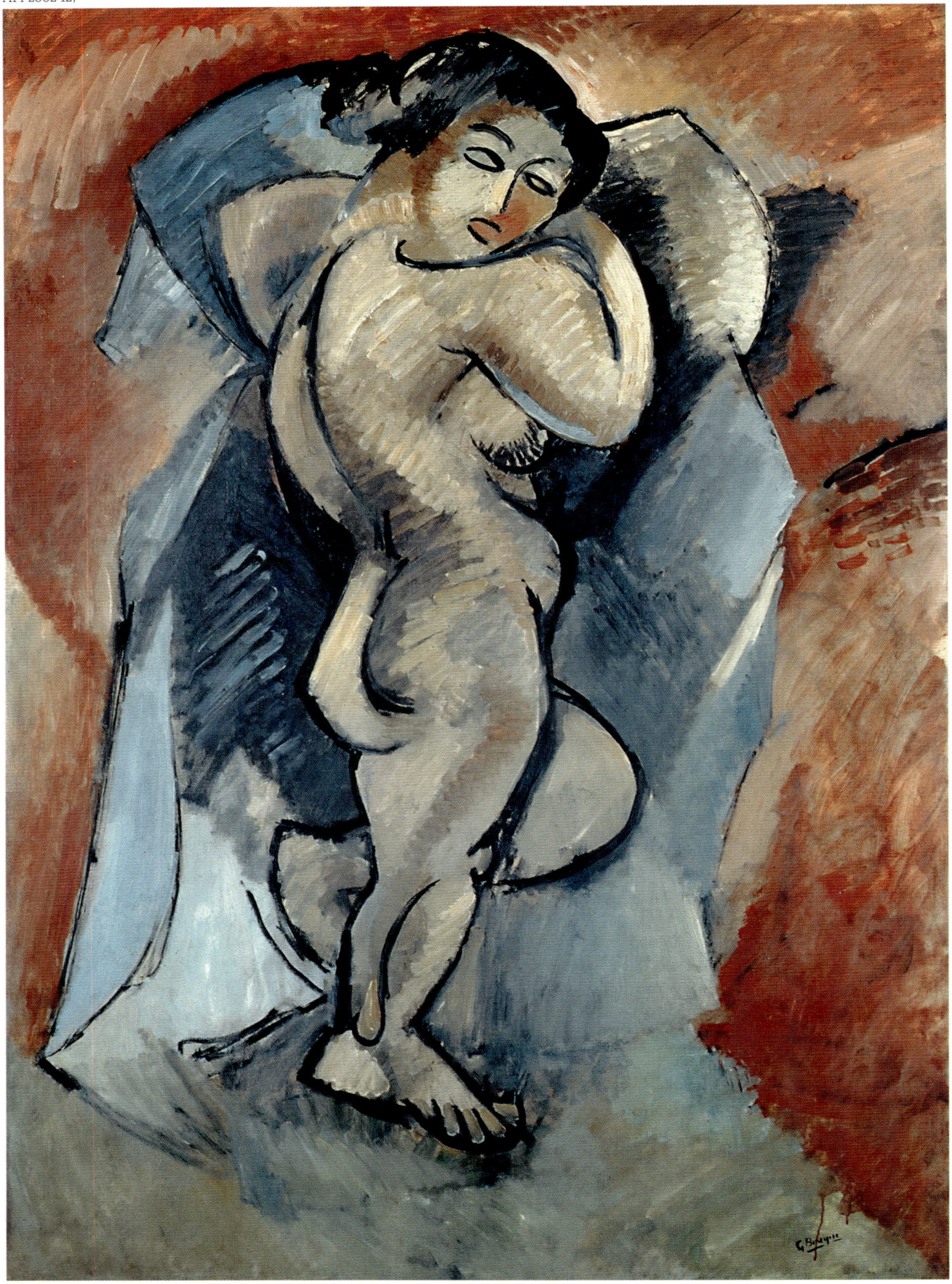

Georges Braque

1882, Argenteuil (France)
1963, Paris (France) †

This painting with its imposing dimensions marks a cornerstone in the emergence of Cubism, created and brought to fruition by Braque and Picasso between 1907 and 1914. On his first visit to Picasso's studio, Braque was struck by *Les Demoiselles d'Avignon*, which not only bore the stamp of Cézanne, but also drew on "Negro art" and Matisse's contemporary nudes. This discovery struck a chord with the research Braque himself was undertaking at that time, inspired by the model of Cézanne's bathers, which he had discovered at the 1906 Salon d'Automne. This *Grand nu* took several months to complete and instigated a totally original interplay between figure and background. The spatial ambiguity of the standing figure, whose face betrays the influence of "Negro art", suggests that it could just as easily be construed as a recumbent figure or be viewed from above. The mystery is compounded by the forms situated behind the model – do they depict a doorway framing the posing model or the folds of classic drapery? In June 1908, Braque left to spend the summer in L'Estaque and may well have taken the *Grand nu* with him in order to work on it. While he was there, he created a number of small compact canvases with geometrised forms which paved the way for the emergence of Cubism •

Pablo Picasso

1881, Málaga (Spain)
1973, Mougins (France) †

Taking the work of Cézanne as their starting point, Braque and Picasso drew up the rules of a new visual lexicon which simplified forms and accentuated volumes, reconstructing them through an assembly of open planes. In 1910–1911, their research culminated in the complex paintings of analytical Cubism. The motifs – figures, landscapes or still lifes – are broken up into small crystalline elements, in more or less geometric signs, with a reduced ochre and grey palette. The representation of *Le Guitariste*, entirely treated in layered, shimmering planes, borders on abstraction. Although the forms are pulverised into inter-connecting facets, the layout of the ridges ensures that the outline of the musician still remains legible.
From 1913, the reference to colours and real forms gradually reappeared with synthetic Cubism. Together with a less clear-cut fragmentation of planes, from 1912 this new stage was marked by more frequent recourse to collage and pasted papers, such as newspaper cuttings and wallpaper imitating other materials •

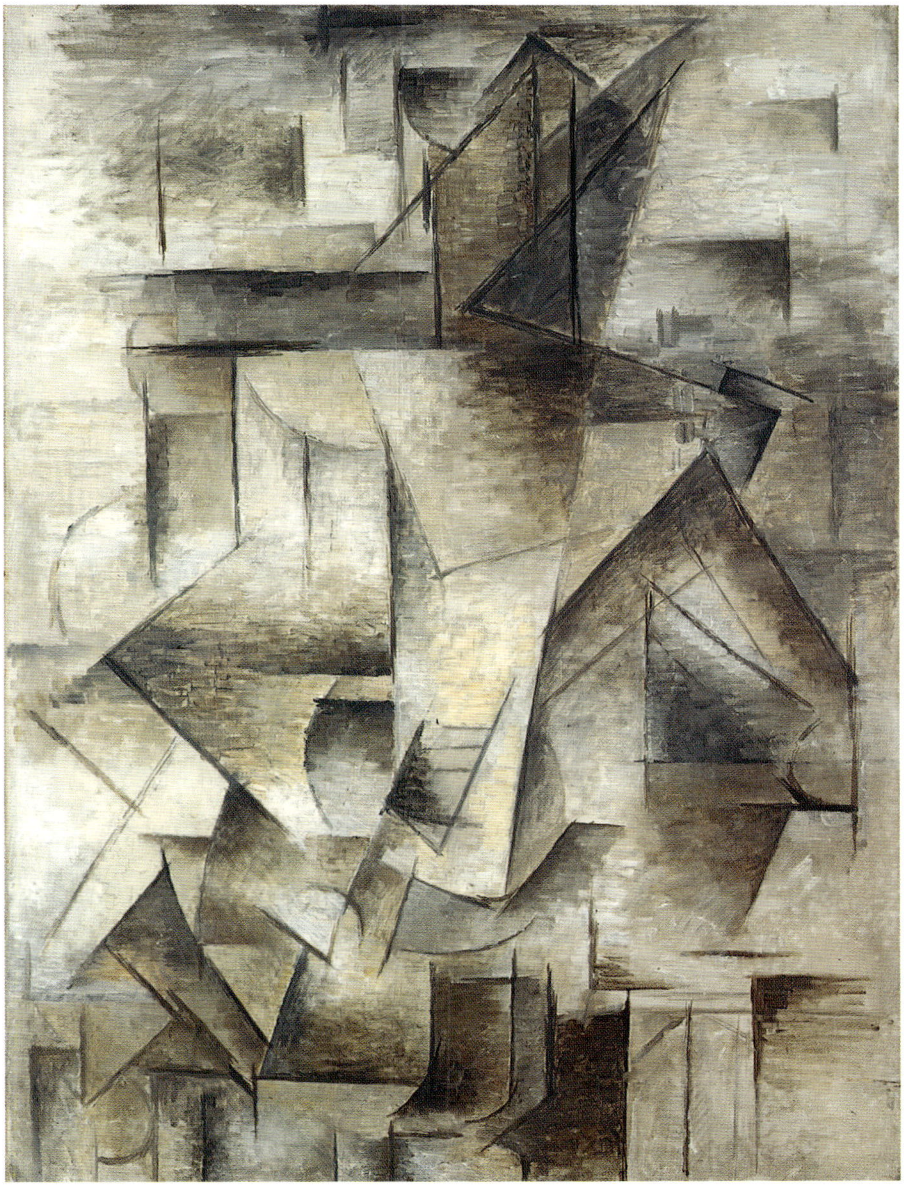

1910

Le Guitariste
[Guitar Player]
Oil on canvas; 100 × 73 cm
Donated by Mr. and Mrs. André Lefèvre, 1952 - AM 3970 P

1910

Improvisation XIV

Oil on canvas
74 × 125.5 cm
Gift of Nina Kandinsky 1966 -
AM 4347 P

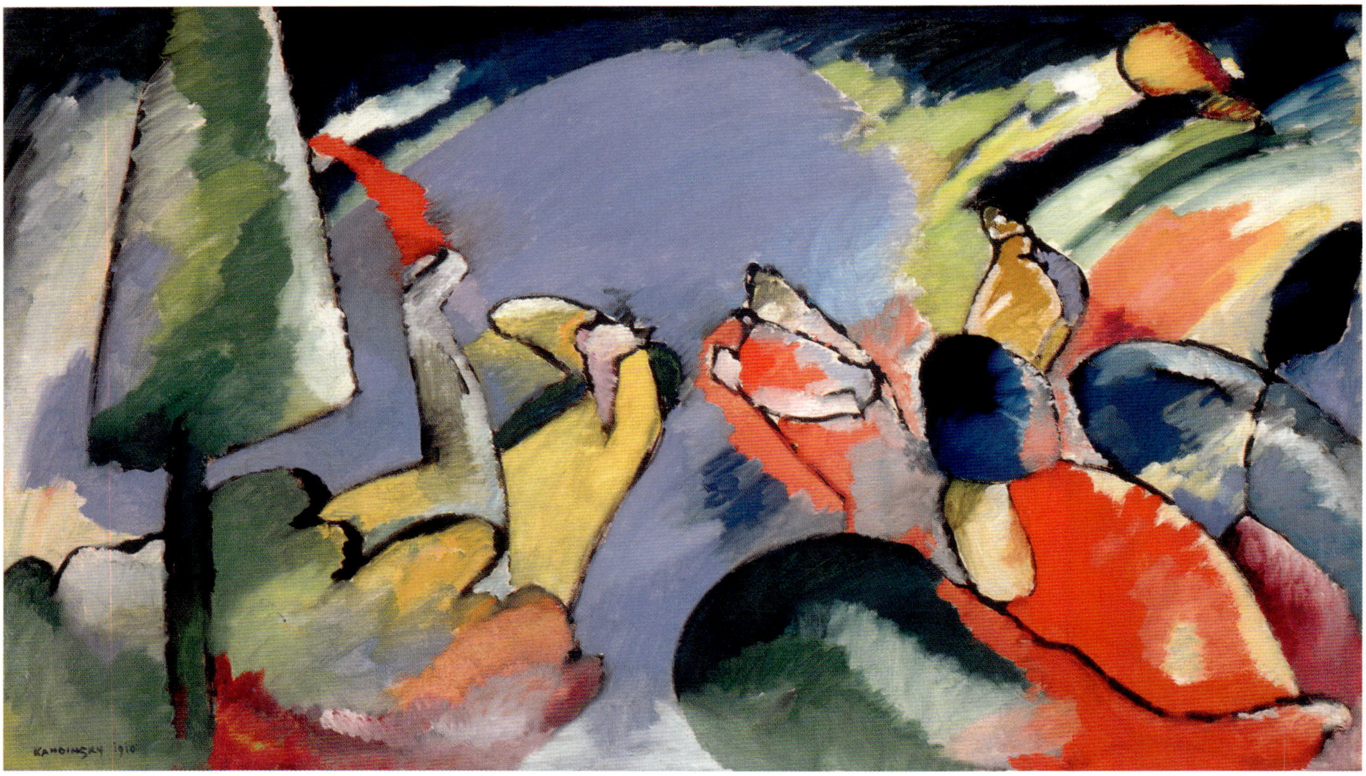

Vassily Kandinsky

1866, Moscow (Russia)
1944, Neuilly-sur-Seine (France) †

At the age of thirty, Vasily Kandinsky gave up his law career in favour of painting, which he studied in Munich in 1896. From 1906 – which he spent in Paris – until 1914, the painter developed an increasingly free approach to his signature themes: scenes inspired by Russian folklore or landscapes, sometimes featuring horsemen. *Improvisation 14* is contemporary with Kandinsky's first abstract watercolour and belongs to his period of burgeoning abstraction. In the foreground, a conical tree is the only clearly identifiable element in this landscape of vibrantly brushed colours, now only applied in oblique sweeps. The coloured mass of the mountains is interwoven with the multicoloured sky. The thick black contours which characterise the figures cease at times to define them. The dynamic collision of the various blocks creates an impression of tension. The increasing autonomy of the colours characterises these "symphonic" works, which demonstrate the significance of music to the painter (Kandinsky was close to Arnold Schoenberg, who broke free of the tonal system during the same period, paving the way for dodecaphonism). Kandinsky claimed that the true content of his paintings was of a psychological nature. It reflected "what the onlooker feels through the effect of the colours and forms". In 1912, *Avec l'Arc noir* [With a Black Arc], from which all figurative references have disappeared, established him as the master of lyrical abstraction •

Constantin Brancusi

1876, Pestisani (Romania)
1957, Paris (France) †

Constantin Brancusi hailed from the Carpathian Mountains, where woodcarving is an age-old tradition. Following his studies in Bucharest, the Romanian artist undertook a lengthy journey across Europe, often on foot. This brought him to Paris in 1904, where he worked briefly under Rodin. Although Brancusi's approach cannot be affiliated to a specific movement, the artist, inspired by African masks, sought new geometrisation and concision. The unfinished quality of his early figures could be seen as evocative of Rodin but unlike the older sculptor, Brancusi refused to impose his forms on matter: "It is the texture of the material itself that dictates the theme and form, both of which should emerge from the matter, not be imposed upon it from the outside." Like an intercessor, the artist thus attempts to reveal the "cosmic essence of matter". The model for *La Muse endormie* was Baroness Frachon, the subject of a number of Brancusi's portraits between 1908 and 1910. Here, however, the artist replaced the classic bust by a head lying on its side, removed from its body, much like a mask. The traits and expression have been pared down and a sensibility of extraordinary delicacy touches upon the surface of the mouth, eyes and hair. By means of the streamlined volumes, the sculptor lets the matter itself conjure up a being waking up to the awareness of the world •

1910

La Muse endormie
[Sleeping Muse]
Polished bronze
16 × 27.3 × 18.5 cm
Gift of Baroness
Renée Irana Frachon,
1963 - AM 1374 S

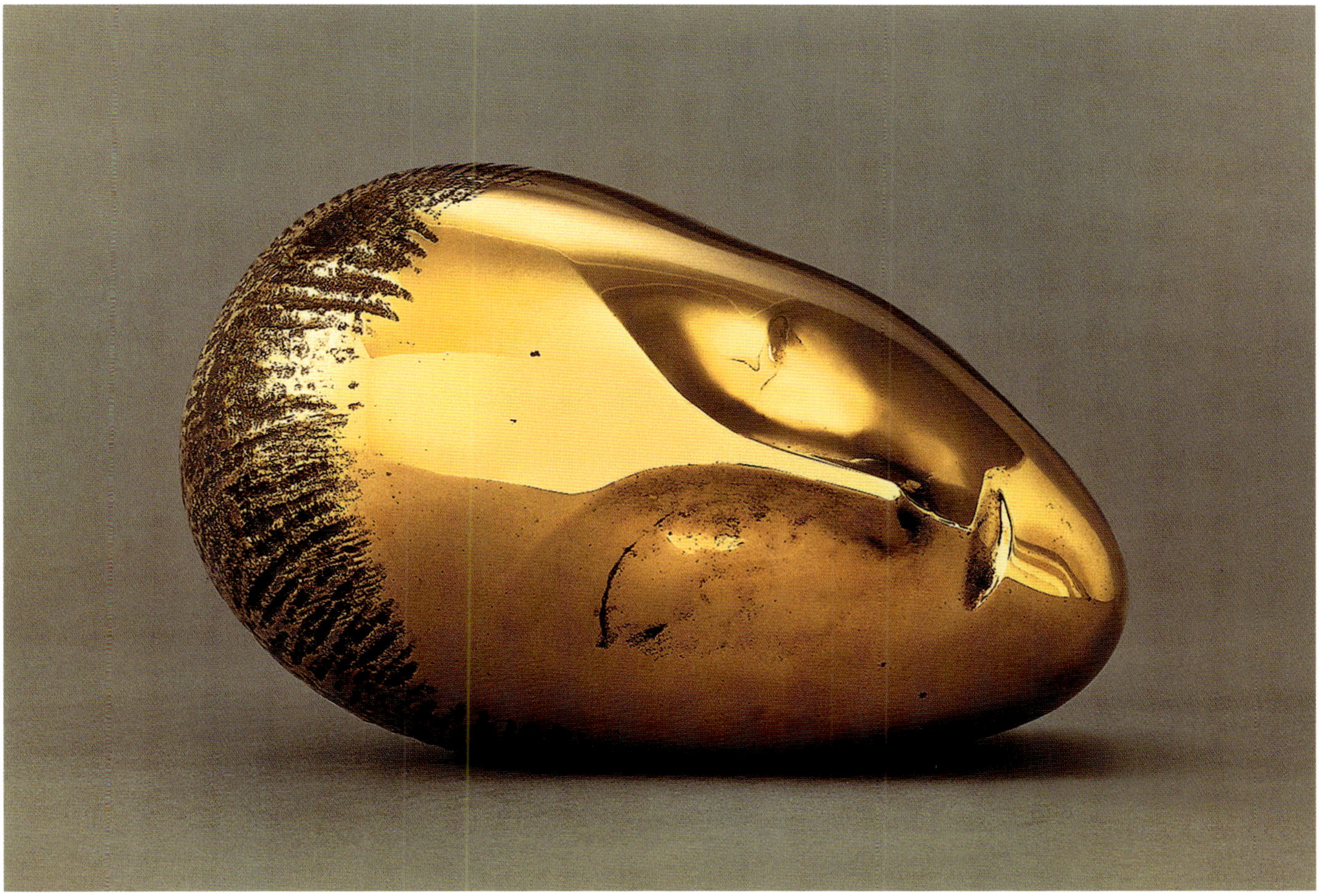

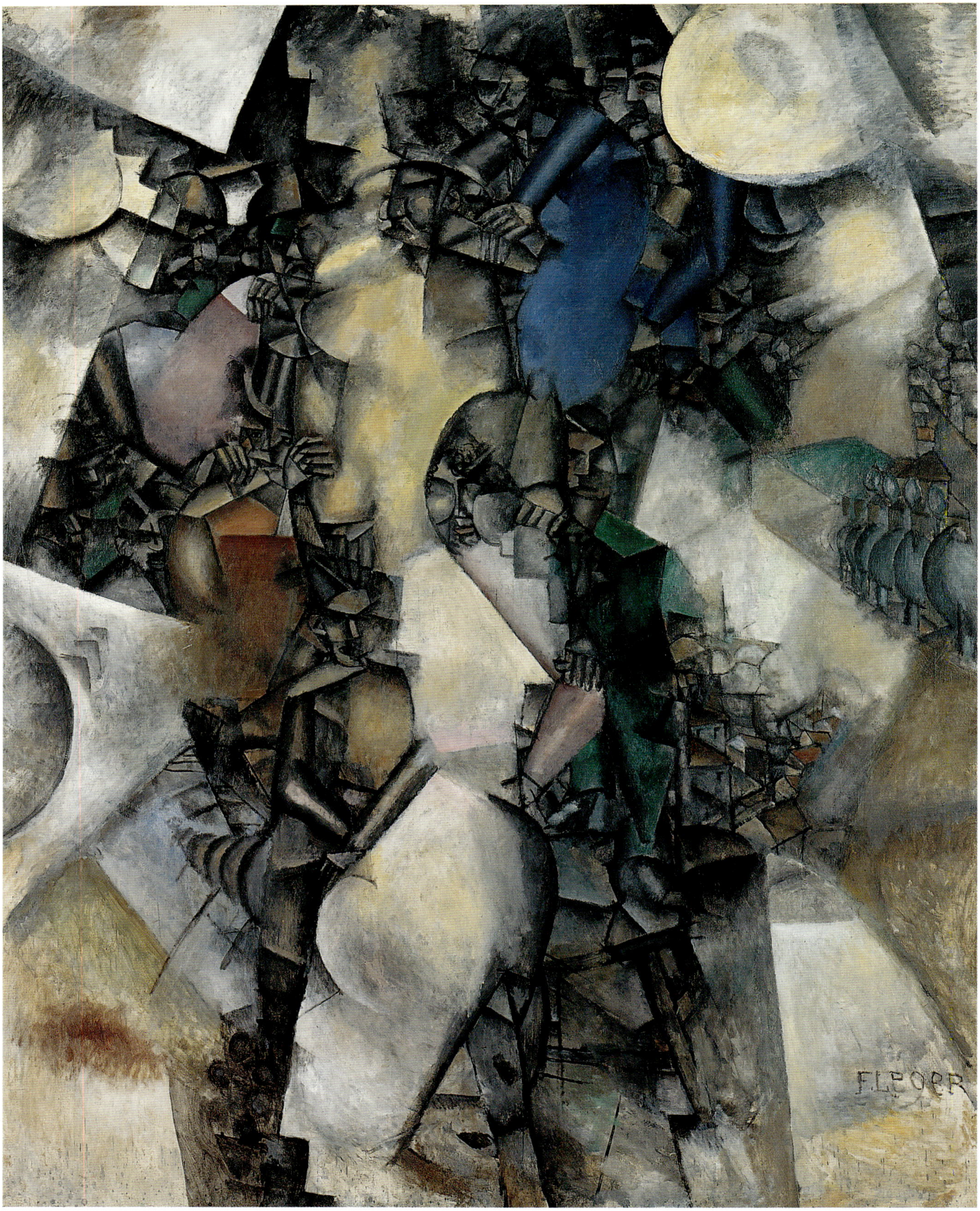
F.LEGER

[1911]

La Noce
[The Wedding]
Oil on canvas
257 × 206 cm
Gift of Alfred Flechtheim,
1937 - AM 2146 P

Fernand Léger

1881, Argentan (France)
1955, Gif-sur-Yvette (France) †

Fernand Léger studied architecture before turning to painting. His early canvases were inspired by Neo-Impressionism and Fauvism. From 1909, however, like Braque and Picasso, he adopted Cubism.
La Noce depicts a bride and groom and their wedding procession walking along a village street. The figures, depicted as mechanical elements, are closeted within a composition based on the law of plastic contrasts. Essentially static rectilinear and angular forms are juxtaposed with rounder cylindrical or conical shapes, which exude an element of dynamism. These contrasting forms introduce a whirling movement to the afocal composition, which is given the Cubist treatment through its multiplicity of vantage points.
Although the black-circled contours, angular or deformed faces and geometric monochrome interlocking surfaces evoke analytical Cubism, the composition, the dynamic movement Léger lends to the canvas as a whole and the uniform blocks of bright colour which punctuate the canvas are all derived from Futurism. In common with his friends the Delaunays and the artists of the Section d'Or [Golden Section], Léger was leading his art towards an Orphic form of Cubism, a more poetic Cubism which reinstated the fundamental role of colour •

Luigi Russolo

1885, Portogruaro (Italy)
1947, Cerro di Laveno (Italy) †

A musician and painter, Russolo was moving in Milanese Symbolist avant-garde circles when he met Marinetti, the founder and theoretician of Futurism. In 1909, this Italian poet published his *Manifeste futuriste* in *Le Figaro*. The text hailed the dynamism and energy of the modern world: "We declare [...] that all worn-out subjects must be swept away, to allow us to express our dizzying life of steel, pride, fever and speed." Alongside Marinetti and other painters (Carrà, Boccioni, Severini and Balla), Russolo launched himself into the Italian Futurist adventure.
The car and speed were inherent in the Futurist aesthetic. The composition of *Automobile in corsa* synthesised the visual and auditory resonance of a car in full motion. The representation of the machine itself, "more beautiful than the Victory of Samothrace", is eclipsed by the plastic rendition of speed. The outline of the vehicle, rendered by "force-lines", which multiply the sharp angles following a single axis, overturns the entire space. In the background, the collapsing buildings seem to be sucked into the wake of colours. Everything is combined to convey the powerful acceleration of the engine and its vibrations •

[1912-1913]

Automobile in corsa
[Dynamism of a Car]
Oil on canvas
106 × 140 cm
Gift of Sonia Delaunay,
1949 - AM 2917 P

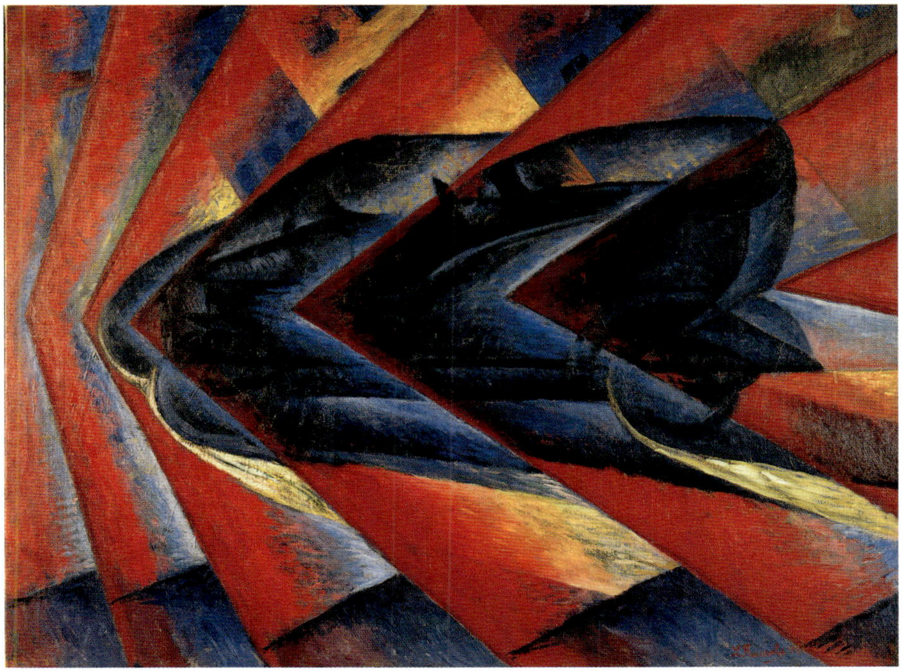

1913

Udnie
Oil on canvas
290 × 300 cm
Purchased by the State, 1948
Attribution, 1949 - AM 2874 P

Francis Picabia

1879, Paris (France)
1953, Paris (France) †

In 1913, the Armory Show in New York introduced the American public to European modern art, and to Cubism and Futurism in particular. Through his excesses and resounding proclamations, Francis Picabia was one of the figureheads of this whole turbulent avant-garde movement. On his return to France, stimulated by the hustle and bustle of the city and by its power, he painted a series of works whose dimensions and dynamism illustrated this fascination with the energy of a "city standing". One of these, the monumental *Udnie*, brought about a synthesis of Orphic Cubism and Futurism.
As indicated by its sub-titles, *Jeune fille américaine*; *Danse*, its subject was inspired by the dancing of a young Polish actress observed aboard the liner Picabia took to New York. Although *Udnie* borrowed its dynamism from Futurist painting, its "mechanical" aspect conjures up the contemporary works of Marcel Duchamp, a close friend of Picabia's. Picabia perceived art as a rebus which has been stripped of all its anecdotal content. As he put it, "art is a successful attempt to externalise inner thoughts or feelings by projecting subjective, emotional and mental states on to the canvas" (1913). Although the dance theme filters through the overlapping metal petals of *Udnie*, its pictorial space, with its spiralling movement, appears above all to represent a metaphor of the elasticity of memory •

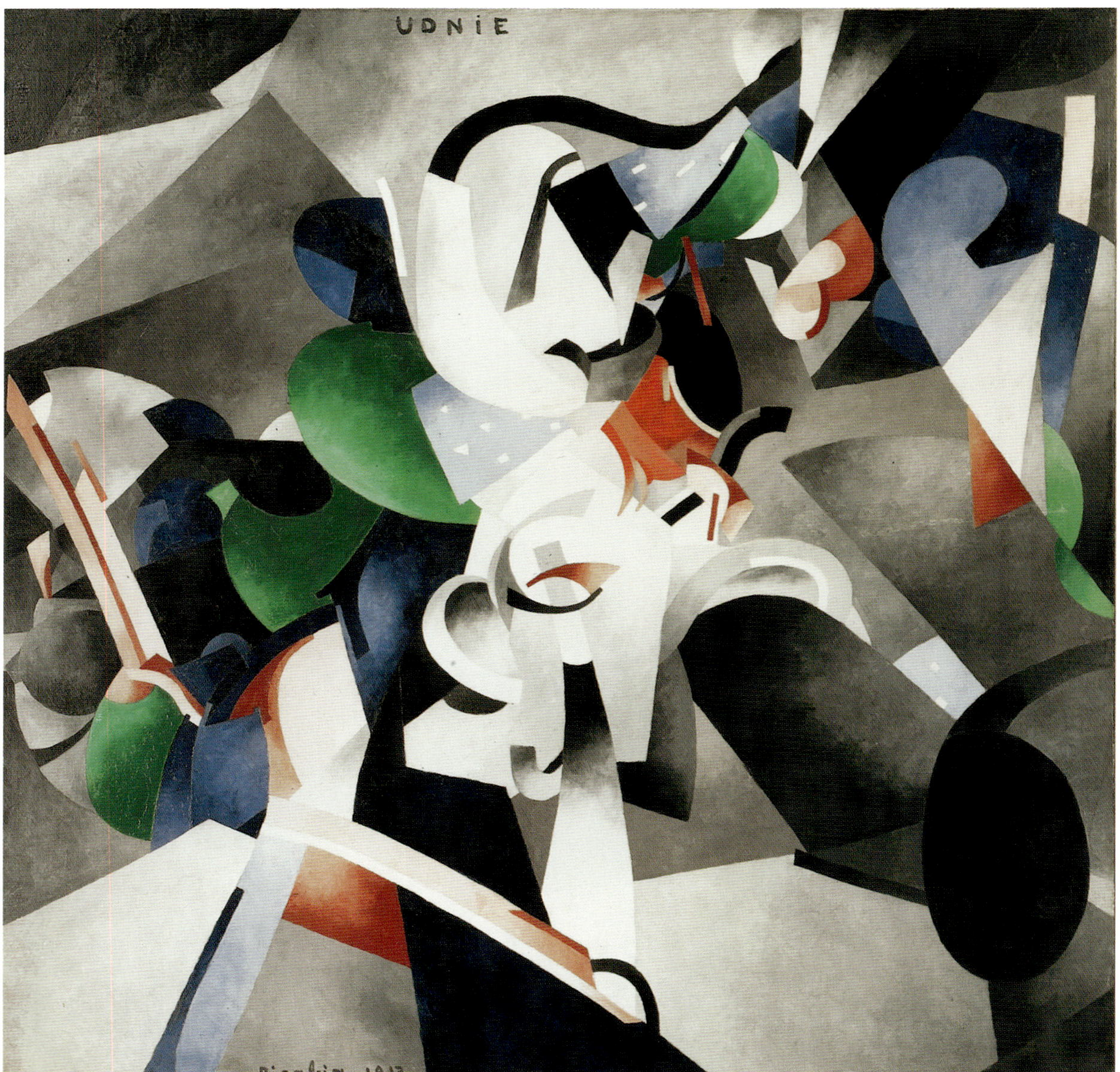

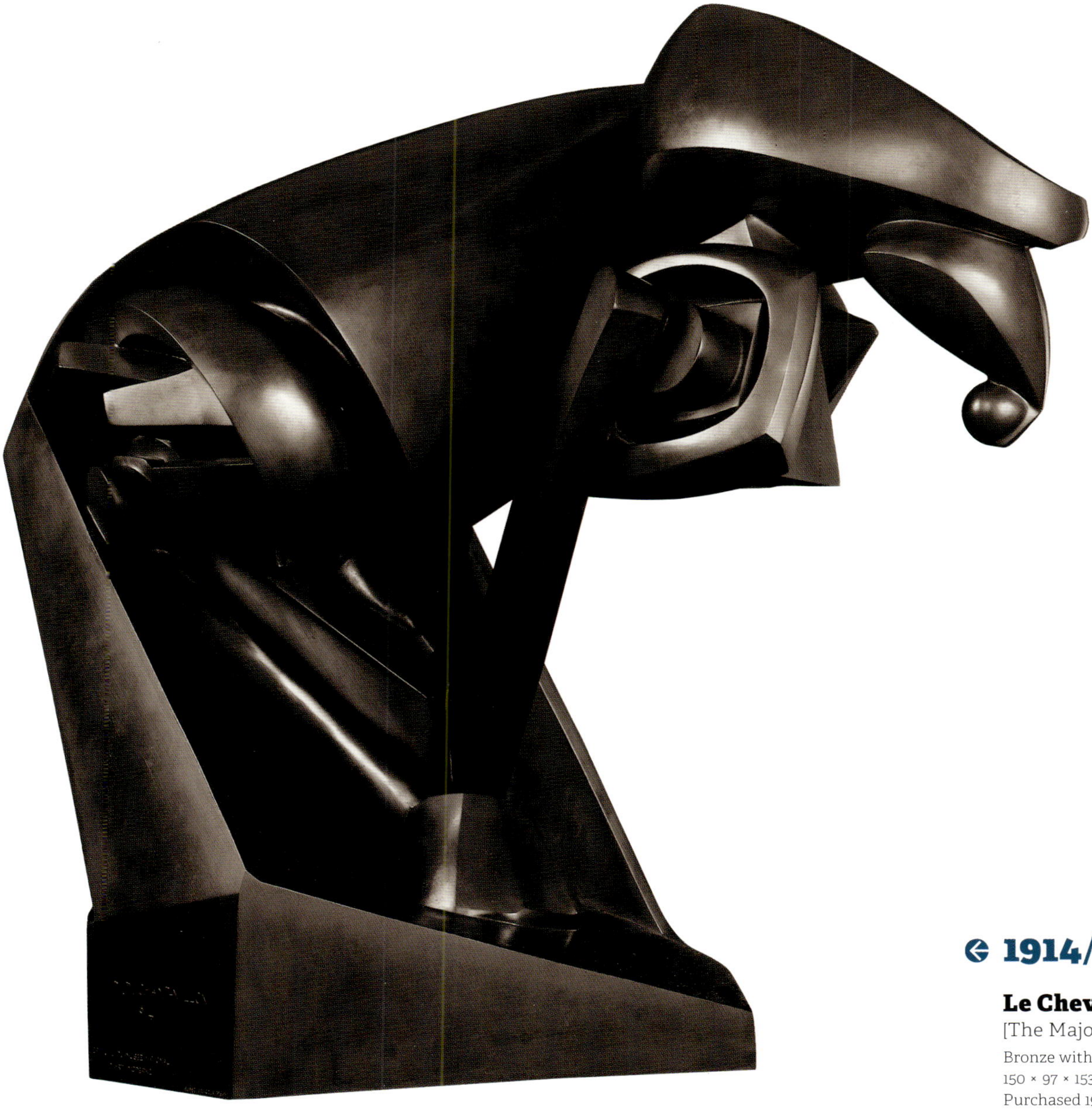

1914/1976

Le Cheval majeur
[The Major Horse]
Bronze with black patina
150 × 97 × 153 cm
Purchased 1976 - AM 1977-206

Raymond Duchamp-Villon

1876, Damville (France)
1918, Cannes (France) †

Raymond Duchamp-Villon was born into a cultured, middle-class family. Forced to give up his medical studies because of a serious illness, he turned to sculpture. Although Rodin's influence can be perceived in his early works, from 1910 his interest in Cubism led him to reduce and stylise his volumes, while seeking to retranscribe the movement.
With his brothers Jacques Villon and Marcel Duchamp, he ran the Puteaux Group and took part in the Section d'Or [Golden Section], two movements that played a seminal role in launching Cubism. He was called up in 1914 as an auxiliary doctor but managed to keep working as a sculptor. Prepared by a series of plasters, *Le Cheval majeur*, represented here by a posthumous bronze enlargement, depicts the fusion between animal and rider. Its form, which could be taken as an illustration of the expression "steam horse", is rendered by vigorous interlocking volumes, some rounded, some rectilinear, conjuring up rods and pistons. The animal's force is expressed in a plastic form akin to the creations of Boccioni, whose sculpted work, shown in Paris in 1913, finds an echo in the works of Duchamp-Villon. *Le Cheval majeur* melds together vital and mechanical forces, while epitomising a synthesis between Cubism and Futurism, the main avant-garde movements of the early 1900s •

Vassily Kandinsky

1866, Moscow (Russia)
1944, Neuilly-sur-Seine (France) †

Recognised as one of the pioneers of lyrical abstraction, Kandinsky was a painter and theoretician. His essay *Du Spirituel dans l'art* [Concerning the Spiritual in Art] (1910), analysed the links between painting and music and examined the expressive value of forms and colours. Cold, mystical blue is contrasted with warm, aggressive yellow and peaceful green...
The composition is dominated by a powerful red spot. To Kandinsky, this colour had psychological value – it "acts from inside, like a colour bubbling with hectic, ardent life" – and also harks back to the Russian *isbas*. This chromatic nucleus stabilises the explosion of a multitude of vigorous iridescent forms, sumptuous and multicoloured. Structured around the arches of a bridge or by the central black line conjuring up the double summit of a mountain, these elements create a shapeless, organic world, delving into the conflictual relationship of colours. Kandinsky's precise geometric forms, on the other hand, appeared in 1922, when he began teaching at the Bauhaus school of art and architecture. Created in Weimar in 1919 by Walter Gropius, it was influenced by Russian Constructivism and de Stijl and targeted a "synthesis of the arts" between painting, design and architecture. To Kandinsky, studying the autonomous and expressive character of the spot, the line and the plane tied in with the elaboration of a new lexicon, in which geometrical figures played a crucial role •

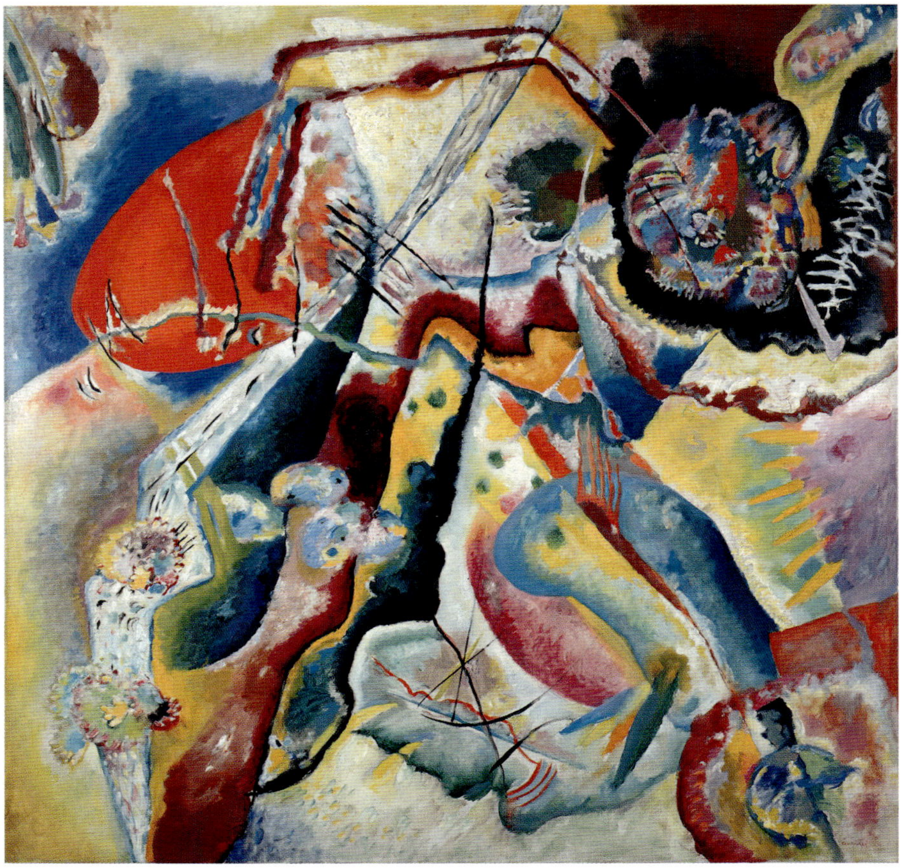

1914

Bild mit rotem Fleck
[Painting with Red Spot]
Oil on canvas
130 × 130 cm
Donated by Nina Kandinsky, 1976 - AM 1976-863

[1914]

Intérieur, bocal de poissons rouges
[Interior with a Goldfish Bowl]
Oil on canvas
147 × 97 cm
Bequeathed by Baroness Eva Gourguaud, 1965 - AM 4311 P

Henri Matisse

1869, Le Cateau-Cambrésis (France)
1954, Nice (France) †

In 1913, Matisse moved back to 19, quai Saint-Michel, one floor below the studio he had occupied a few years earlier. In 1917, the "new sensations" the painter had experienced during his visits to Tangiers, which resurfaced on his return to this familiar environment, triggered a series of works revolving around the theme of the artist's studio. In this canvas, one finds all the characteristic freshness and exuberant, striking vitality of Matisse's art. Around the geometrical forms of the high window and goldfish bowl, a composition subtly condenses effects of opacity and transparency (the light reverberating from the Seine, the panes, the aquarium). The omnipresence of blue, bold and covered with other colours, unifies the composition, based on the interplay of picture within picture and on the contrasts of planes, and removes the duality between interior and exterior. This space, layered and analysed in successive coloured planes, illustrates the influence of Cubism on Matisse's work between 1914 and 1918 •

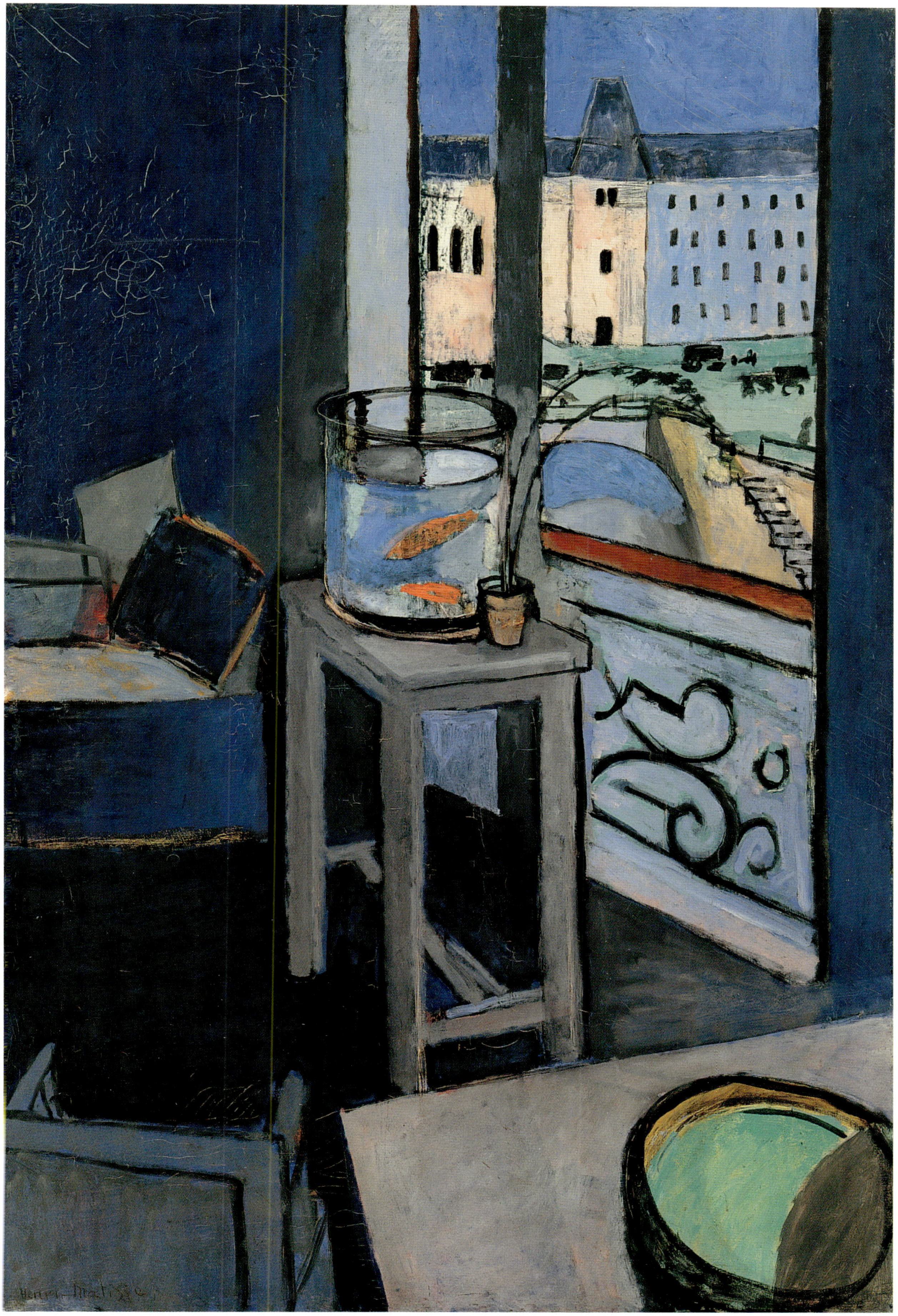
Henri-Matisse

Sonia Delaunay

(born Sarah Stern, later Terk)

1885, Gradizhsk (Russia)
1979, Paris (France) †

1914

Prismes électriques
[Electric Prisms]
Oil on canvas
250 × 250 cm
Purchased by the State, 1958;
attribution, 1958 - AM 3606 P

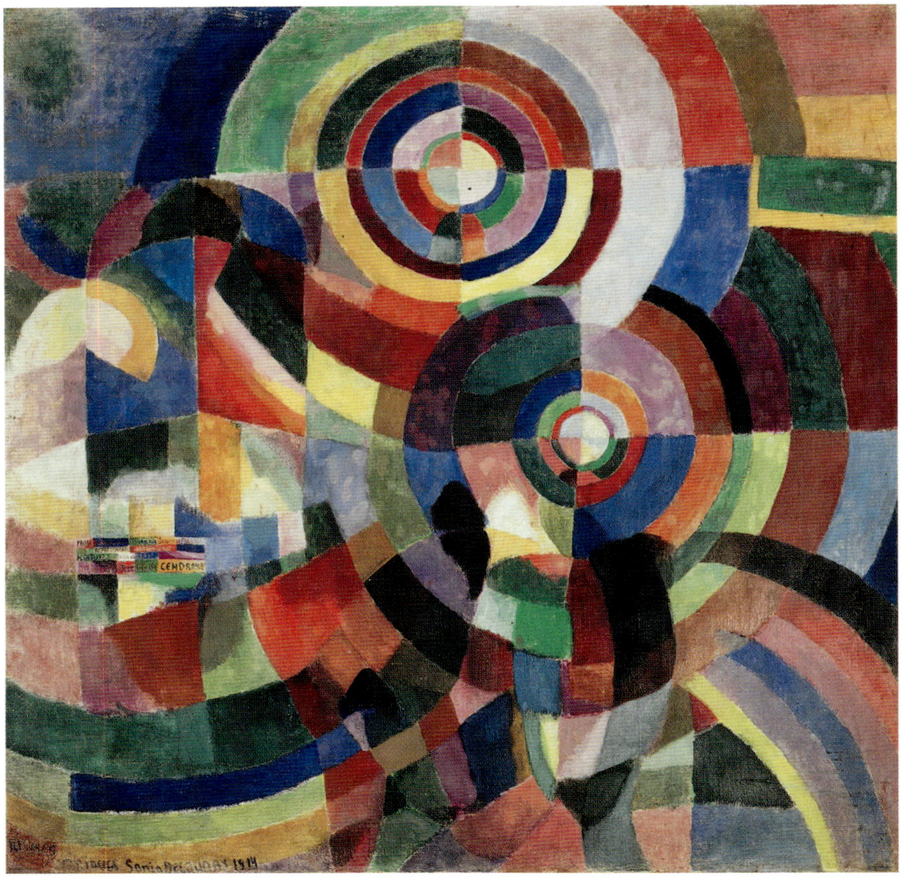

Following a select cosmopolitan education in St Petersburg, Sonia Terk left Russia to study art in Karlsruhe. In 1905, she moved to Paris. Her Fauvist, Primitivist period came to an end in 1909 when she met Robert Delaunay. Side by side, they chose to follow the path of Cubism, then launched themselves simultaneously into a more abstract form of research, termed "Orphic Cubism" by Guillaume Apollinaire. The "law of simultaneous contrast", based on the scientific treatise by Chevreul, enabled the Delaunays to implement the inherent dynamism of colour itself. The optic nature of their poetic Cubism formed a striking contrast with the static analysis of the object advocated by other Cubists. From 1912, Sonia Delaunay began to depict colour in accordance with this principle. In *Prismes électriques*, the ephemeral variations of light emanating from electric globes are represented by coloured discs. The colours of the prism, applied in silken, transparent drips which take over the entire space, become the sole subject-matter of this vast square canvas. Only the cartridge on the left stands out. This is a reference to Sonia Delaunay's collaboration with Blaise Cendrars on *La Prose du Transsibérien et de la petite Jehanne de France*, "the first simultaneous book", which conjures up a correspondence between words and colours by juxtaposing them on the page. This monumental work, an exhilarating expression of the infinity of perceptive space, is a celebration of urban life and the poetry of modernity •

Giorgio De Chirico

1888, Volos (Greece)
1978, Rome (Italy) †

1914

Portrait prémonitoire de Guillaume Apollinaire
[Premonitory Portrait of Apollinaire]
Oil and charcoal on canvas
81.5 × 65 cm
Purchased 1975 - AM 1975-52

On his arrival in Paris in 1911, Giorgio de Chirico joined the circle of painters and poets gravitating around Guillaume Apollinaire and his magazine *Les Soirées de Paris*. Back in 1913, the poet had been struck by the "strange" and "surprising" nature of De Chirico's work. The painter's metaphysical world was to become a major reference in Surrealism. De Chirico has produced an enigmatic composition in this picture, its false realism heralding the advent of Surrealism. The space, cordoned off by sharply inclined planes, creates a "dark box", its elements evoking the painter's interest in the world of dreams and the imaginary. In the foreground, a classical plaster bust, its sight obscured by dark glasses, symbolises the inner vision of the poet, his capacity to see beyond the visible world. On the right, the moulds represent a lyre and a fish, the iconographical attributes of Orpheus, the ancient poet with whom Apollinaire had been compared. Finally, a target drawn on the temple of Apollinaire's shadow shows the precise spot of the shrapnel wound the poet was to receive in 1916.
De Chirico gave this premonitory portrait to Apollinaire, who reproduced it as the frontispiece of his first collection of calligrams •

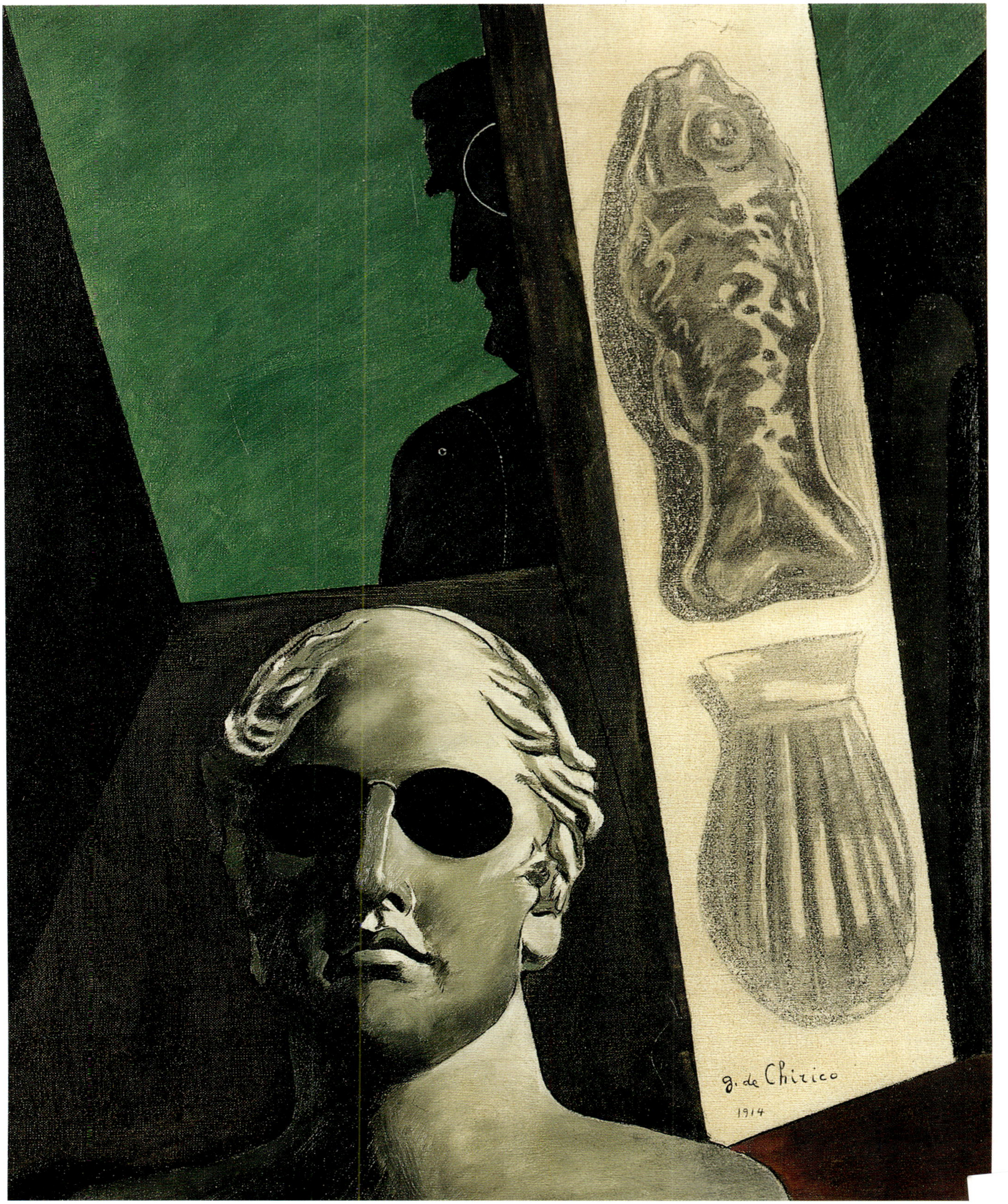
g. de Chirico
1914

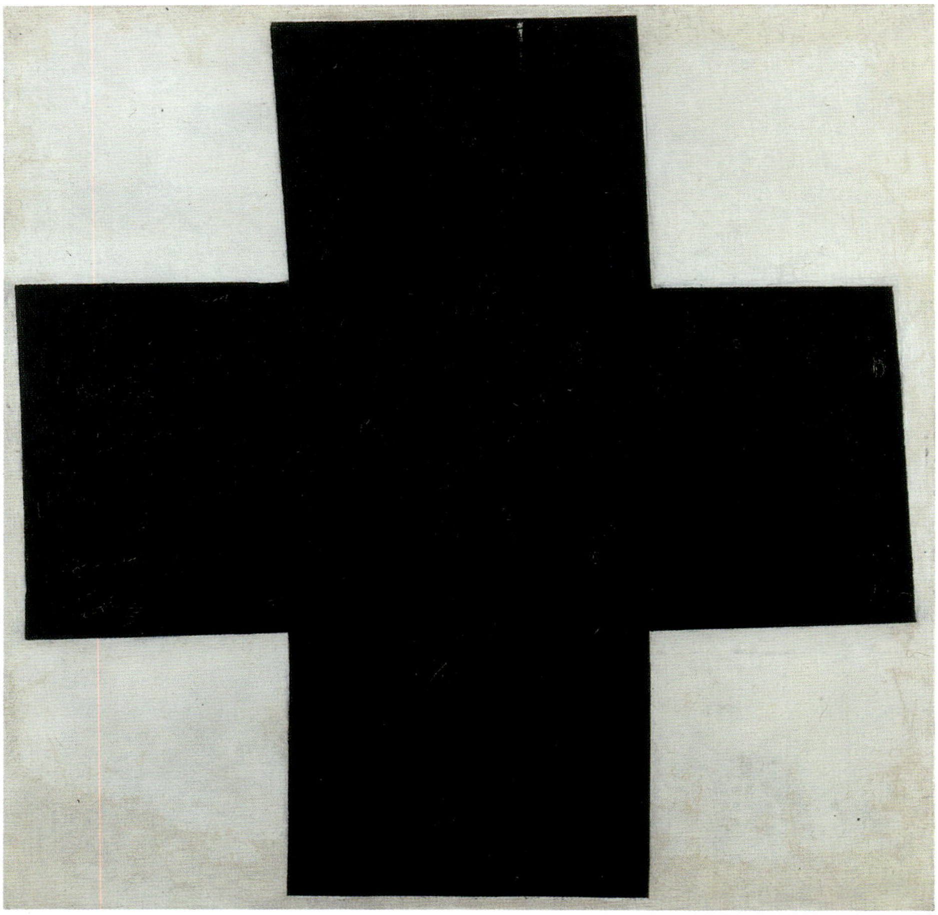

1915

Croix [noire]
[(Black) Cross]
Oil on canvas
80 × 80 cm
Gift of the Scaler Foundation and the Beaubourg Foundation, 1980 - AM 1980-1

Kasimir Malevitch

1879, Kiev (Russia)
1935, Leningrad (USSR) †

[Kasimir Malevich] Trained at the Kiev School of Art, Malevich settled in Moscow in 1904, where he began painting in Impressionist vein. From 1907, Fauvist and Cubist innovations began to influence his works. The radical nature of his approach, based on transcending illusionist representation, really came to the fore in 1913, when he introduced a "black square" into the sets and costumes created for Mikhail Matiushin's Cubo-Futurist opera *La Victoire sur le soleil* [Victory over the Sun]. Two years on, this black square became an independent pictorial entity, which Malevich showed in Petrograd alongside other abstract paintings, including *Croix noire*, at the first major event devoted to the Russian avant-garde.
Far from being a static, rigid, strictly orthogonal form, *Croix noire* is vibrant with the driving force created by the distortion of its two arms. The work epitomises Malevich's "suprematism", based on the supremacy of pure colour. In this "non-objective" art, which abolishes the realism of objects, the forms stem from the square: the circle (obtained by rotation) and the cross (the division of a square into two rectangles, one of which pivots at a 90° angle). Symbolising the collapse of the traditional world of objects, and their mimetic representation, the icon of *Croix noire* only depicts the reality of the painting in a cosmic space •

➔ 1917/1964

Fontaine
[Fountain]
White earthenware covered in glazed ceramic and paint
Rrose replica, 1964, produced by the Schwarz gallery, Milan
63 × 48 × 35 cm
Purchased 1986 - AM 1986-295

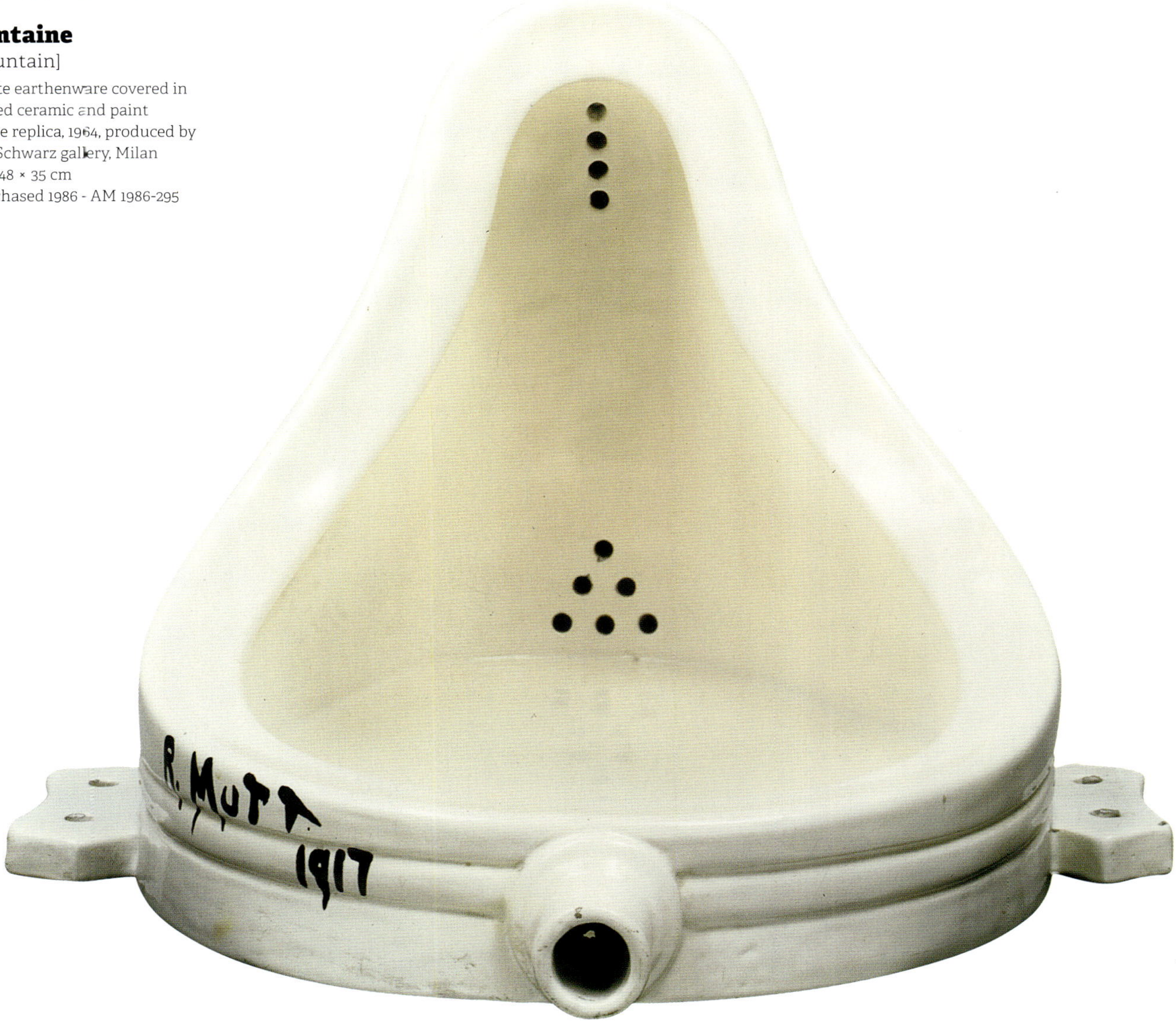

Marcel Duchamp

1887, Blainville-Crevon (France)
1968, Neuilly-sur-Seine (France) †

Duchamp came to Paris to join his older brothers, the artists Jacques Villon and Raymond Duchamp-Villon, when he was only seventeen. He got to know a number of Cubist painters, such as Picabia, and created a furore in 1912 with his *Nu descendant un escalier* [Nude Descending a Staircase]. The work was repudiated by the Cubists, who judged it too close to Futurism in its way of expressing movement, and had it removed from the Salon des Indépendants. At that stage, Duchamp turned away from "retinian" painting. To mark his rejection of the traditional canons of art and beauty, from 1914 he put his name to a series of manufactured objects, which he bought and displayed as completed sculptures. With these "ready-mades", the object replaced the sculpture, the artist choosing unilaterally to elevate it to the status of work of art. In 1917, Duchamp showed this painted porcelain urinal in New York, where he had been living since 1915. He signed it with the name of the manufacturer, "R. Mutt" and christened it *Fontaine*. The object, chosen with irony, was not only banal but provocative. Duchamp ultimately gave up any real activity, circumscribing it to his writings or stances, and may thus be considered the father of conceptual art •

1917

Double portrait au verre de vin
[Double Portrait with a Glass of Wine]
Oil on canvas
235 × 137 cm
Gift of the artist,
1949 - AM 2774-P

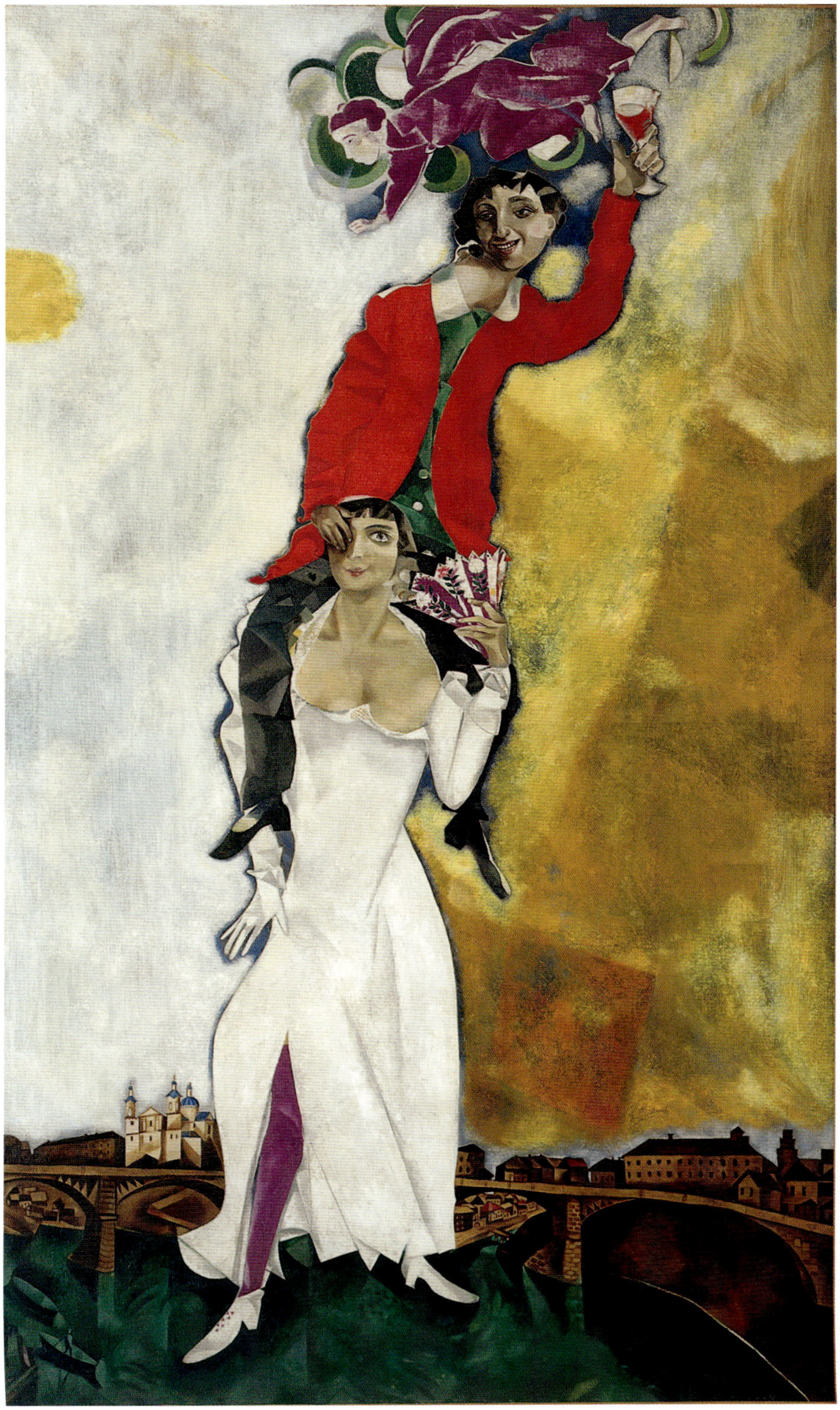

Marc Chagall

1887, Vitebsk (Russia)
1985, Saint-Paul (France) †

Born into a family of Jewish shopkeepers in Vitebsk, Chagall demonstrated his drawing talent at a young age. Having studied painting in St Petersburg, he arrived in Paris in 1910. In 1912, he moved into La Ruche, where he rubbed shoulders with the cosmopolitan circles of the Fauvist and Cubist avant-garde.
Double Portrait au verre de vin celebrates the union of the painter and his wife Bella Rosenfeld, whom he had married in 1915. In this composition which exudes exhilaration and joy, the couple are represented in the form of two giants striking an acrobatic posture. The duo do not seem remotely concerned by the celestial presence of the Angel of the Annunciation who has come to bless them – a figure deemed to represent their daughter Ida, who was born in 1916. In the background, one can see the steeples and bridge crossing the Dvina in Vitebsk, to which Chagall had returned in 1914 and where he remained, caught off-guard by the Revolution, until 1922, the year he left the USSR forever. Although Chagall assimilated the plastic innovations of his time, he never abandoned his painting with its chromatic intensity – Expressionist in nature yet dreamlike in spirit – nor his personal universe, fuelled by Russian Jewish reality •

[1918]

Portrait de Dédie

Oil on canvas
92 × 60 cm
Donated by Mr. and Mrs. André Lefèvre, 1952 - AM 3974-P

Amedeo Modigliani

1884, Livorno (Italy)
1920, Paris (France) †

Born into a middle-class family in Livorno, Modigliani turned to painting at the early age of fourteen. Initially attracted by Impressionism, he moved to Paris in 1906, where he frequented the Cubists and got to know Picasso, Gris and Apollinaire, among others. In Paris, the painter developed a style whose harmony and coherence were in stark contrast with the excesses of his Bohemian lifestyle. He produced a great number of nudes and portraits, in which one can detect the overlapping influences of Cézanne, Gauguin and even African art, in the faces particularly, which are at times represented like "masks", with hollowed-out almond-shaped eyes. The gracious linear quality of the smooth volumes and uniform colour blocks also conjure up the art of the Siennese Renaissance, an essential element in his artistic training. This portrait of Odette Hayden, the first wife of the Cubist painter Henri Hayden, is characteristic. In a neutral space, the model adopts a languishing pose, accentuated by the bent head and long flexible neck – a position that would border on Mannerism were it not relieved by the austerity of the black dress and the sad facial expression. Modigliani's early death and his companion's suicide fuelled the myth of the benighted artist, adding to the success of this art imbued with melancholy •

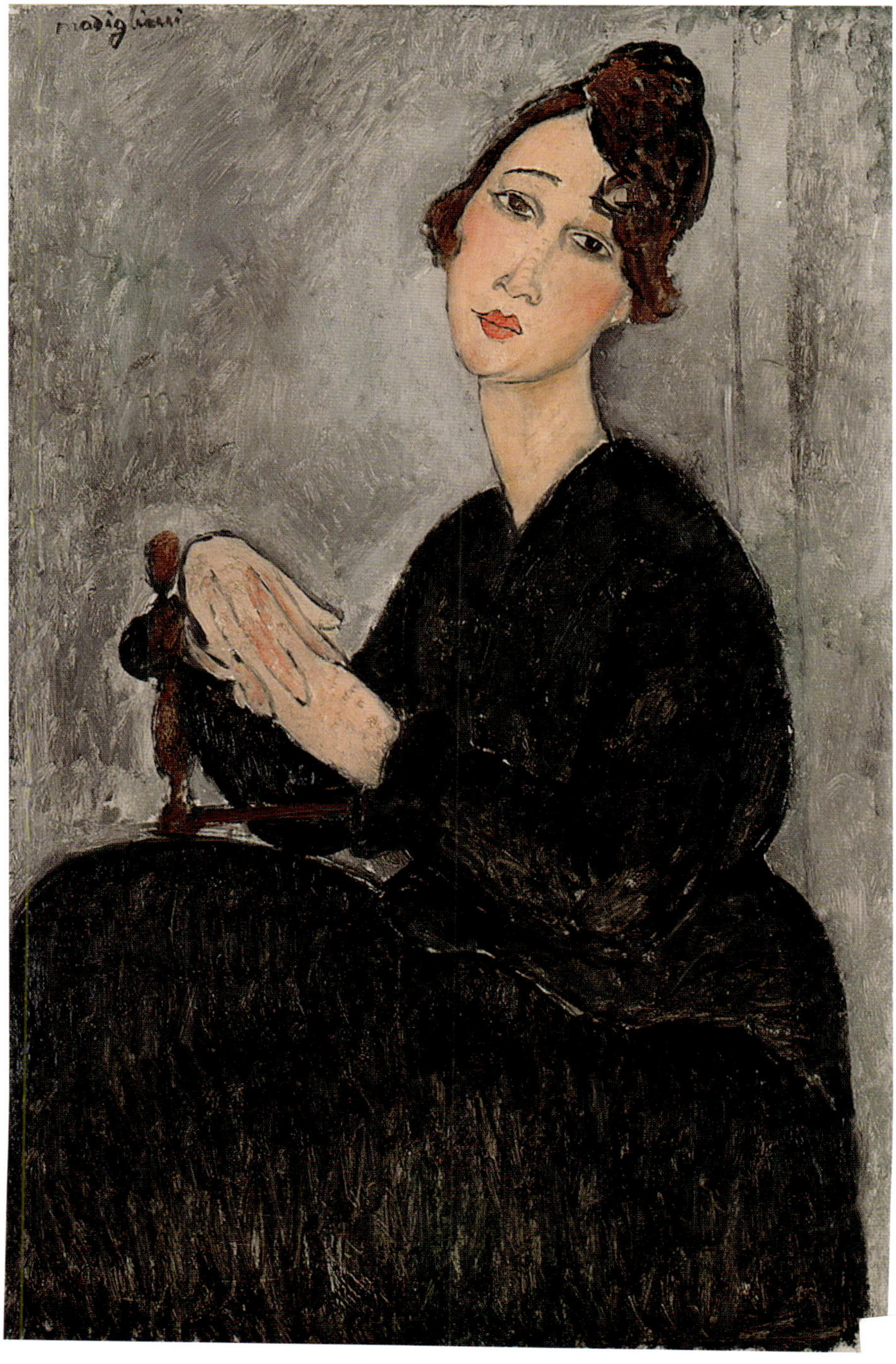

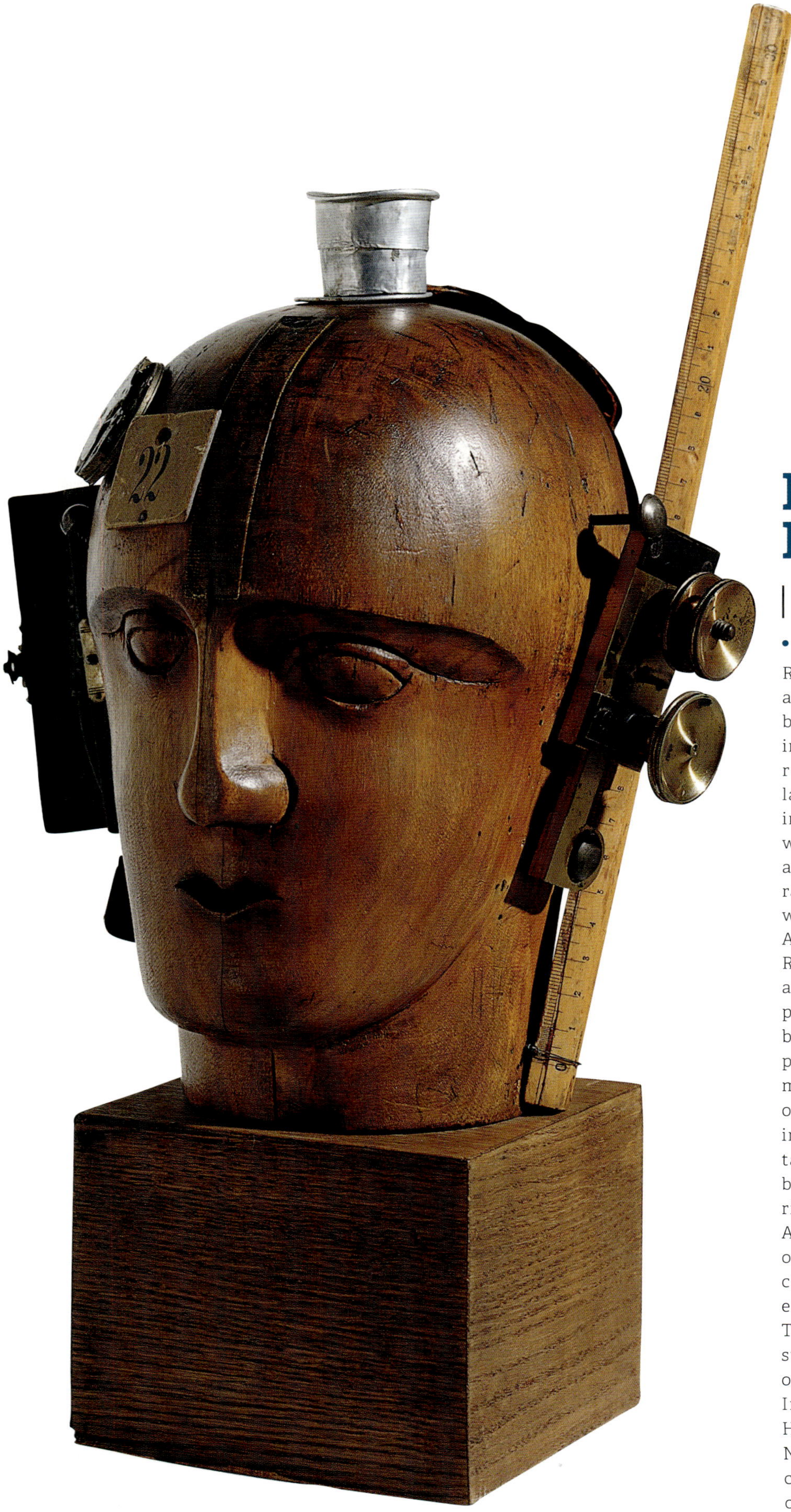

[1919]

Mechanischer Kopf
[Mechanical Head]
Barber's dummy, wood and miscellaneous objects
32.5 × 21 × 20 cm
Purchased 1974 - AM 1974-6

Raoul Hausmann

1886, Vienna (Austria)
1971, Limoges (France) †

Raoul Hausmann embarked on a career as an Expressionist painter before signing the Dada Manifesto in Berlin in 1918. This iconoclastic, revolutionary movement was launched during the First World War, in 1916, and marked a complete schism with the old world. Anti-military and anti-bourgeois, Dada criticised the rational world and traditional art with corrosive irony.

A painter, photographer and poet, Raoul Hausmann raised accident and chance to the status of an artistic process, using elements from the most banal reality as artistic media. In this particular assembly, he grafts a miscellany of objects on to the head of a wooden dummy: measuring instruments (a graduated ruler, a tape-measure), a wallet (affixed to the back), a jewellery case (in lieu of the right ear) and a registration number. According to him, "The average man only possesses the abilities that chance has stuck on to his skull, externally, but his brain is empty." This wooden mechanical head symbolised to Hausmann "the spirit of our time".

In 1933, he left Germany for good. His works were repudiated by the National Socialist regime, who considered them to be examples of "degenerate" art •

➔ 1923

Ubu Imperator
Oil on canvas
81 × 65 cm
Gift of the Fondation pour la recherche médicale, as a tribute to Mrs. Hélène Anavi, 1984 - AM 1984-281

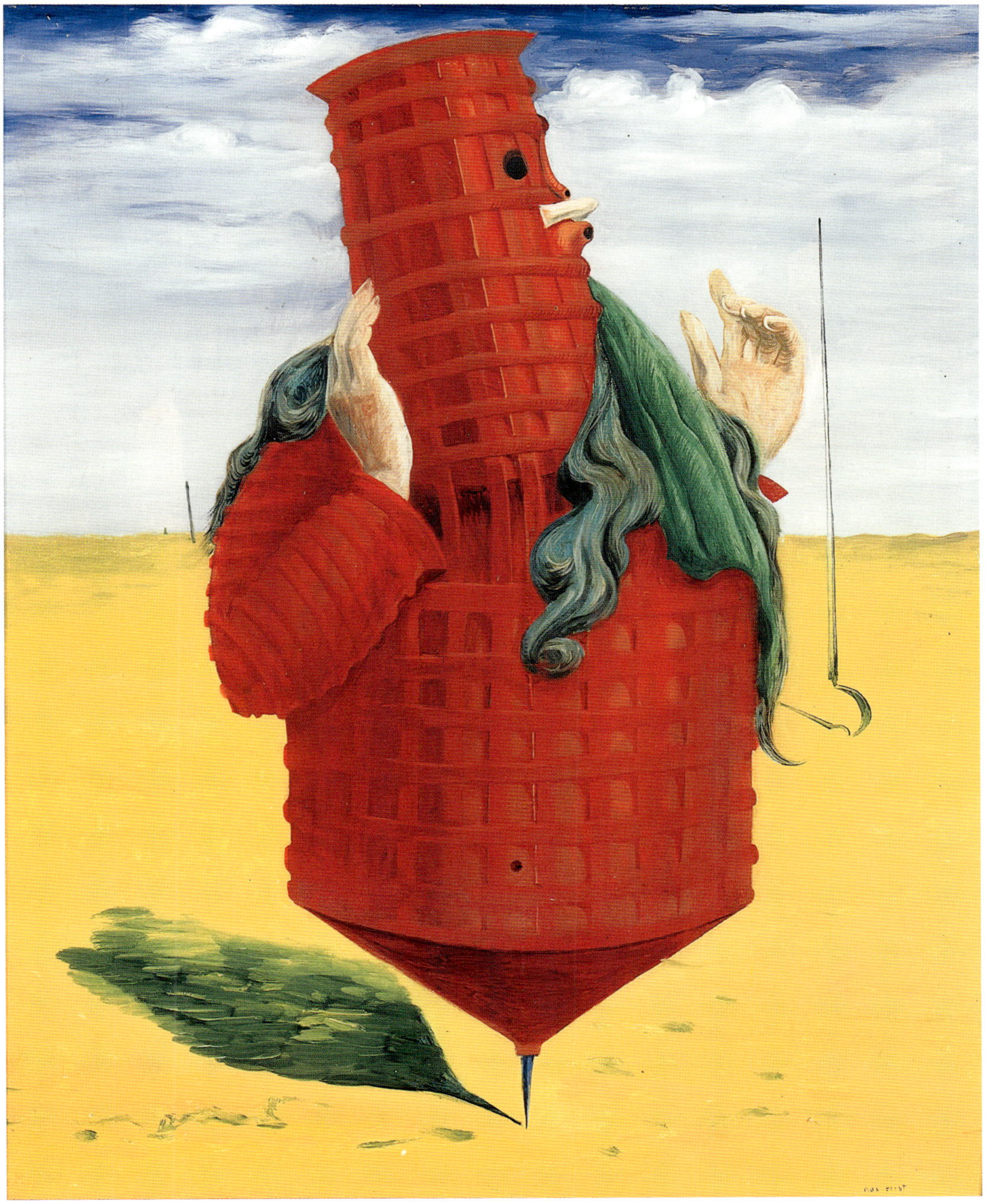

Max Ernst

1891, Brühl (Germany)
1976, Paris (France) †

In 1917, after studying philosophy and psychology, Max Ernst joined up with Dada in Cologne. He adopted a range of drawing techniques (*frottage*, *grattage*, decalcomania), revelatory of forms and meanings which delved into the subconscious. In 1922, the year André Breton announced the death of this subversive movement, Ernst moved to Paris, having already produced a number of important Freudian-inspired canvases. *Ubu Imperator* represents a wobbling, erratic spinning top with arms and long hair. The hybrid and combinatory shape halfway between object and human being epitomises the monstrous father-figure and rejects the buffoonery of all systems of authority. Balancing on its slender strut, Father Ubu takes on the shape of a frame similar to the moulds used in foundries to cast bronze equestrian statues, those pompous emblems of absolute monarchy. With this condemnation of the pride and fatuousness of authority, the entire gamut of traditional aesthetics is also turned into a target of ridicule •

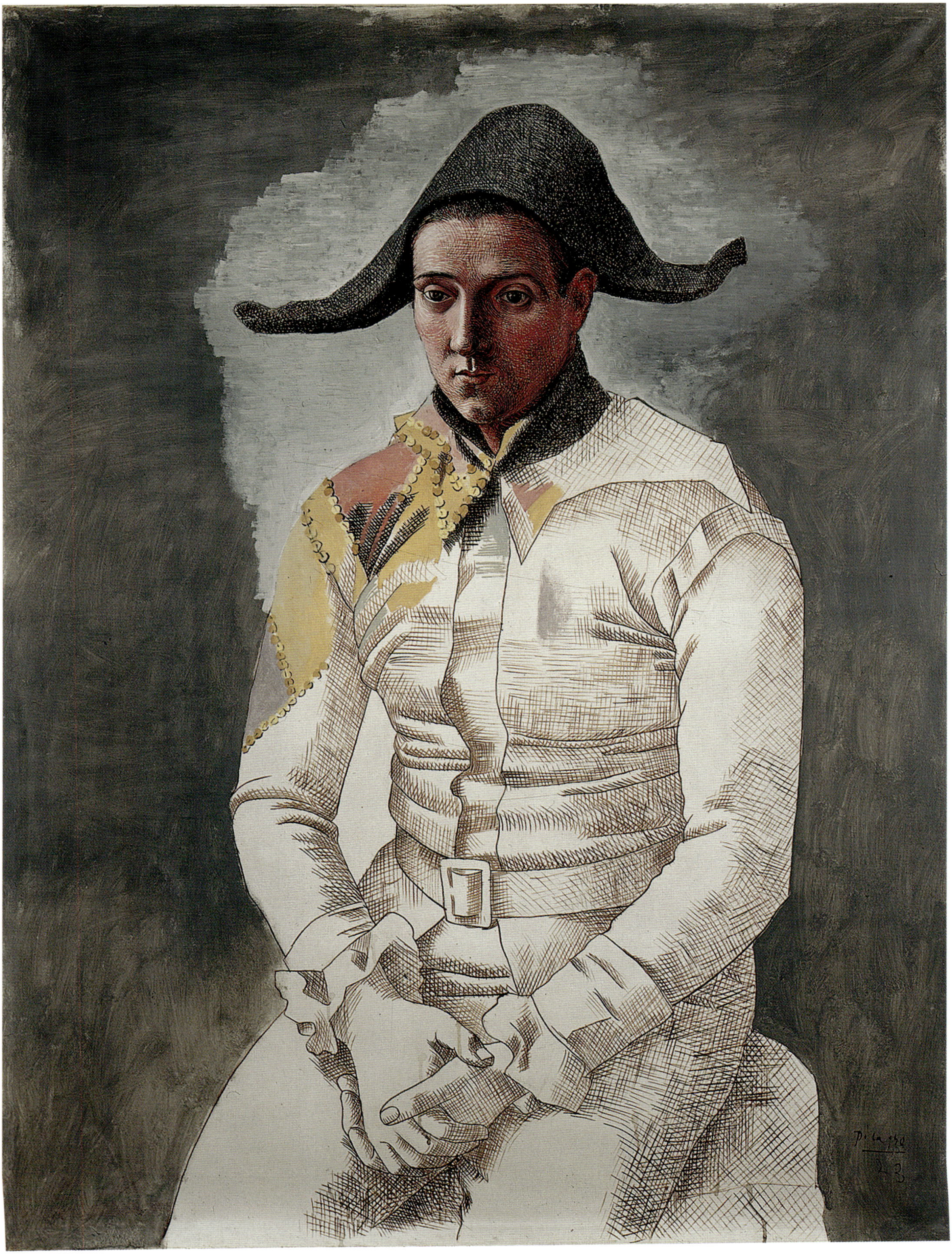
Picasso
23

1923

Arlequin
[Harlequin]
Oil on canvas
130 × 97 cm
Bequeathed by Baroness Eva Gourgaud, 1965 - AM 4313 P

Pablo Picasso

1881, Málaga (Spain)
1973, Mougins (France) †

While the inter-war years in Europe witnessed a burgeoning of abstract art, a number of avant-garde artists also began to hark back to a classicising realism. In France, Picasso, the master of Cubism, reverted to figurative art in 1915, with a series of Ingres-style portraits. A number of these demonstrated the artist's new interest in antique statuary, compounded by his visit to Italy in 1917 with Serge Diaghilev's Ballets Russes. The harlequin, which cropped up periodically in his work, from 1901 until his final years, epitomised his melancholic *alter ego*. The charm of this portrait posed by the Spanish painter Joaquín Salvado stems from the ambivalence between the precision of the line, its taut graphic quality akin to engraving, and the deliberately incomplete nature of the painting. Marking a break with avant-garde forms, this type of figurative portrait, characteristic of the "return to order" style, reflects, despite its reassuring nature, the anxiety and melancholia prevailing throughout Europe at that time •

Man Ray

1890, Philadelphia, PA (United States)
1976, Paris (France) †

On his arrival in France in 1921, Man Ray was soon drawn into the web of the Dadaists, and later the Surrealists. In 1924, in this singular image, an emblematic example of Man Ray's work, the body of Kiki de Montparnasse, the painters' muse at that time, has been transformed into a musical instrument by the addition of two sound holes. A reference to Ingres' talent as a violinist, this visual play on words calls on the famous painter's bathers to evoke the photographer's passion for his lover's body. Here he puts a new slant on it, demonstrating his playful attitude towards photographic techniques, which at the time were meant to revolutionise one's vision rather than reproduce the familiar. This was the period when the Surrealists, far from considering photography as a simple mechanical means of faithfully recording reality, began to call on it in order to draw out the various forms of subconscious and to annihilate the principle of reality itself. The idea of a phantasmagorical projection over reality thereby ingratiated itself into the photographic subjects themselves. Here, Man Ray also succeeds in engineering a shift from the aesthetics of the Dadaist revolt against classically beautiful painting towards the poetics of the strange, the fantastic and the quintessentially Surrealist dream, that Breton was to consecrate officially that same year in his *Manifeste du surréalisme* •

1924

Le Violon d'Ingres
[Ingres' Violin]
Silver salt print enhanced with graphite and Indian ink and pasted on paper
Gelatin silver print enhanced with graphite and Indian ink
28.2 × 22.5 cm
Purchased 1993 AM - 1993-117

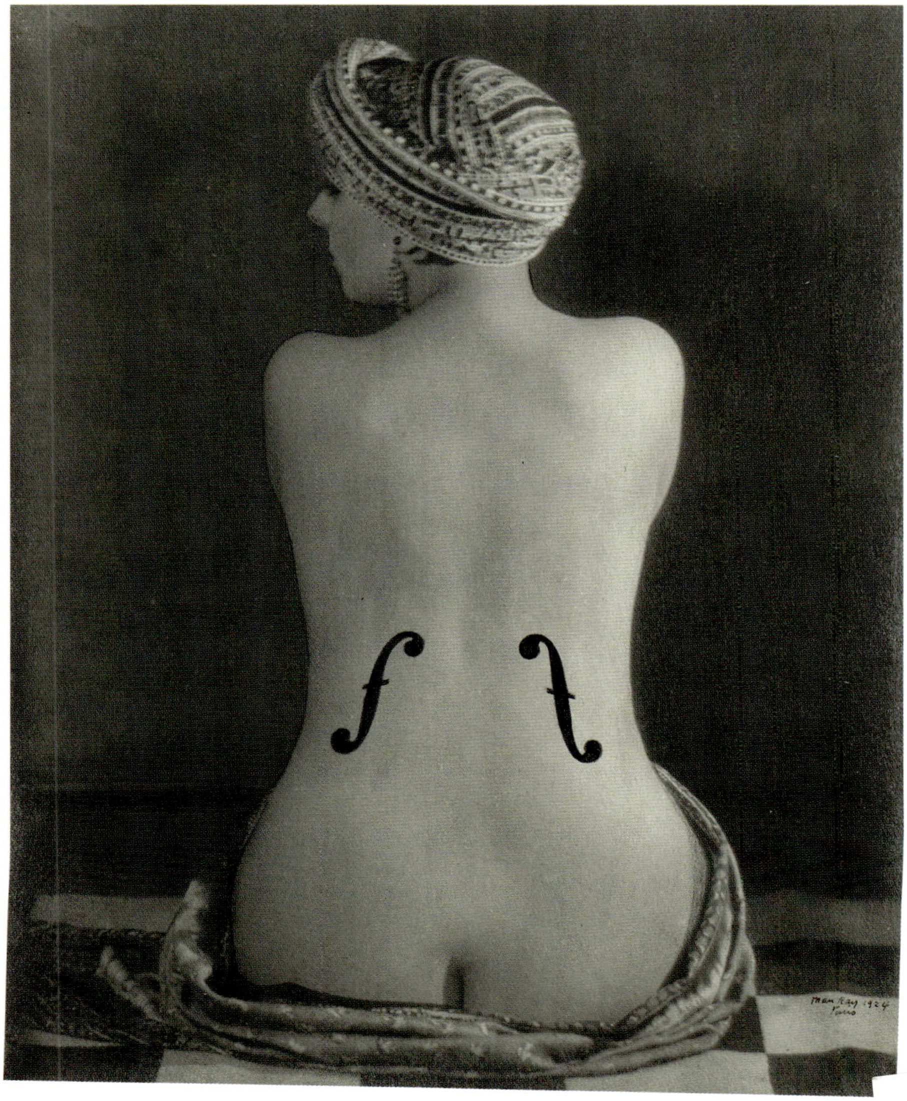

1927

Femme
[Woman]

Oil on plywood, wood, gold bronze paint
136 × 100 × 3.8 cm
Gift of Aube Breton-Elléouët and Oona Elléouët, 2003 -
AM 2003-580

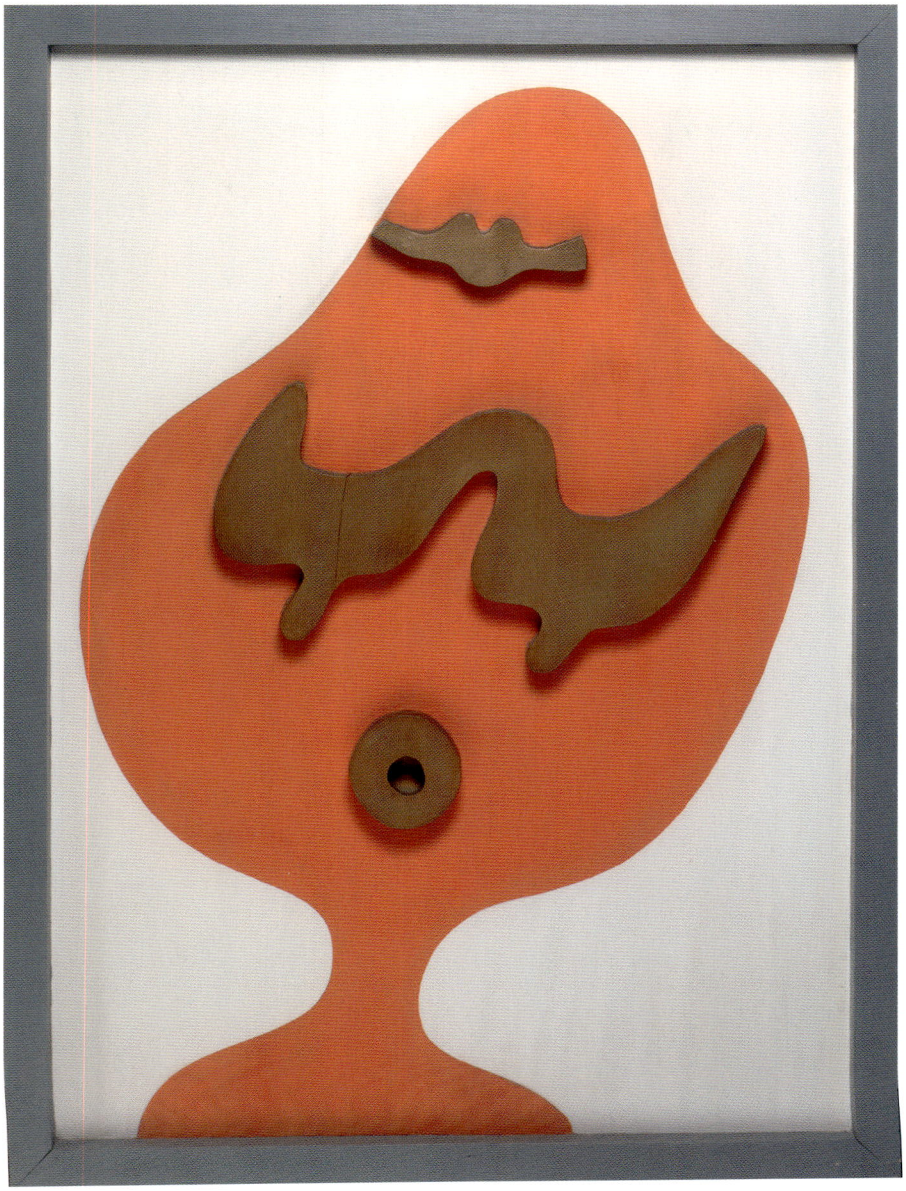

Jean Arp

1886, Strasbourg (France)
1966, Basel (Switzerland) †

Son of a German father and a French Alsatian mother, Arp studied at the Kunstgewerbeschule in Strasbourg and at the Kunstschule in Weimar before going to Paris and meeting Picasso and Apollinaire in 1908. Leaving there for Zurich, he was involved, with Tzara and others, in the explosive emergence of Dada in 1916. Then aligning himself with Surrealism, he showed his work at the movement's first exhibition, in Paris in 1925. "Art is Arp", Marcel Duchamp would say. Painter, sculptor and poet, in 1920 Arp began to explore his "object language" in mural reliefs more figurative in vocabulary.

Femme is one of Arp's reliefs in painted wood, their forms derived from bodily features (lips, eyes, moustaches...) or everyday objects (glasses, bottles...). Its scale, its form (suggestive of an inverted amphora) and its vitalist alphabet – with simplified mouth, breasts and navel echoing each other in curves and counter-curves – make it a monument to a myth of origin, a modern fertility idol recalling the generous forms of Aurignacian Venus figurines. "Moving ovals, symbols of the growth and metamorphosis of bodies", wrote Arp, whose reinvented representation of womanhood distinctly recalls the productions of the "primitive" artists admired by the Surrealists. Part of Breton's collection at his studio at 42 rue Fontaine, this joyfully innocent *Femme* there offered an echo to Miró's *Tête* and Picasso's *Figure*, both also created in 1927 •

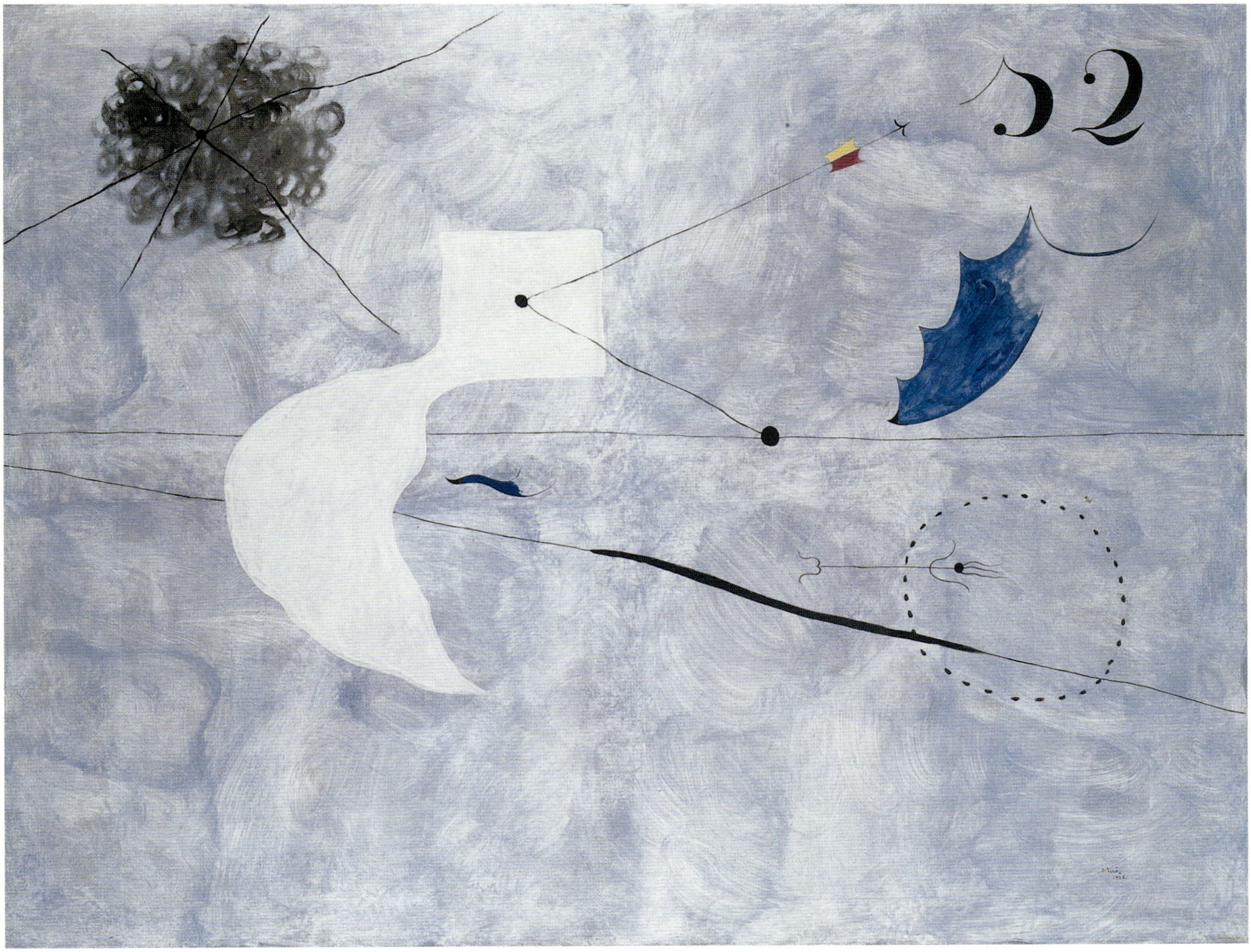

Joan Miró

1893, Barcelona (Spain)
1983, Palma de Mallorca (Spain) †

Joan Miró moved to Paris in 1920. There he got to know the Surrealists, and this played a decisive role in the inception of his "painting-poetry". From 1925, he began producing his "dream paintings"; *La Sieste* belongs to these. Blending the imaginary and the real, they are characterised by broad strokes of vast, almost monochrome backgrounds, predominant elements featuring scattered signs and meticulous calligraphic inscriptions such as letters, numbers, dots and lines. In *La Sieste*, the volatile, vibrant matter of the blue background, a blend of sea and sky, is bedecked with slender, flowing drawings. These stem from a methodical process of decantation of forms, as illustrated by two preparatory sketches. The first shows the accessories of a seascape at siesta time, with, as Miró indicates, "a sail, a woman swimming, a craggy mountain. The sun, the tongues of its rays, [...] a plane, [...], a group of dancers [...]. At the foot of the house, [...] adorned by a sundial [...], the woman is lying, asleep, daydreaming". In the final painting, some of these elements have been amalgamated to create symbolic configurations with elliptical forms: the square of the house with the sinuous outline of the sleeping woman, the peaks of the rocky summits, the top of the sail... Shifting pictograms paving the way for dreams, in the brightness of this poetic, magnetic lexicon, in which white and black, full and hollow, the precise and the shapeless are all perfectly balanced •

1925

La Sieste
[Siesta]
Oil on canvas
113 × 146 cm
Purchased 1977 -
AM 1977-203

➔ [1922-1966]

Wall from the studio of André Breton
255 objects, paintings and drawings
Accepted in lieu of tax, 2003 -
AM 2003-3 (1 to 257)

André Breton

1896, Tinchebray (France)
1966, Paris (France) †

Throughout his life, André Breton was an avid collector, motivated by an "irrepressible need for ownership", which he attributed to a longing to "appropriate the power of objects". Apart from the years he spent in exile in Marseille and New York, between 1940 and 1946, the creator and theoretician of Surrealism lived at 42 rue Fontaine from 1922 until his death in 1966. Over the years, he accumulated a vast number of objects and works of art in his apartment, particularly on the wall behind his desk: paintings, Oceanian, pre-Columbian and North American masks and artefacts, found objects, popular trinkets, stones, roots, butterfly boxes... These curios, which he picked up on walks, on visits to the studios of fellow-artists, at junk shops or antique dealers, triggered surprise and reflection, striking his "untutored eye, the primal eye, freed of all shackles". This collection encapsulates Breton's aesthetic philosophy and includes works by some of the artists he upheld: *Notre avenir est dans l'air* by Picasso (1912), *LHOOQ* by Picabia (1919), *Tête* by Miro (1927), *Femme* by Jean Arp (1927), *Boule suspendue* by Giacometti (1930–1931) and *Coin de chasteté* by Duchamp (1954/1963). The elements, meticulously laid out according to criteria of juxtaposition, accumulation or contrast, and designed to perpetuate an aura of strangeness, turned the wall into a real cabinet of curiosities, epitomising the Surrealist universe. Preserved by Breton's heirs for thirty-six years, this extraordinary collection was accepted in lieu of tax and entered the Museum's collections in 2003 •

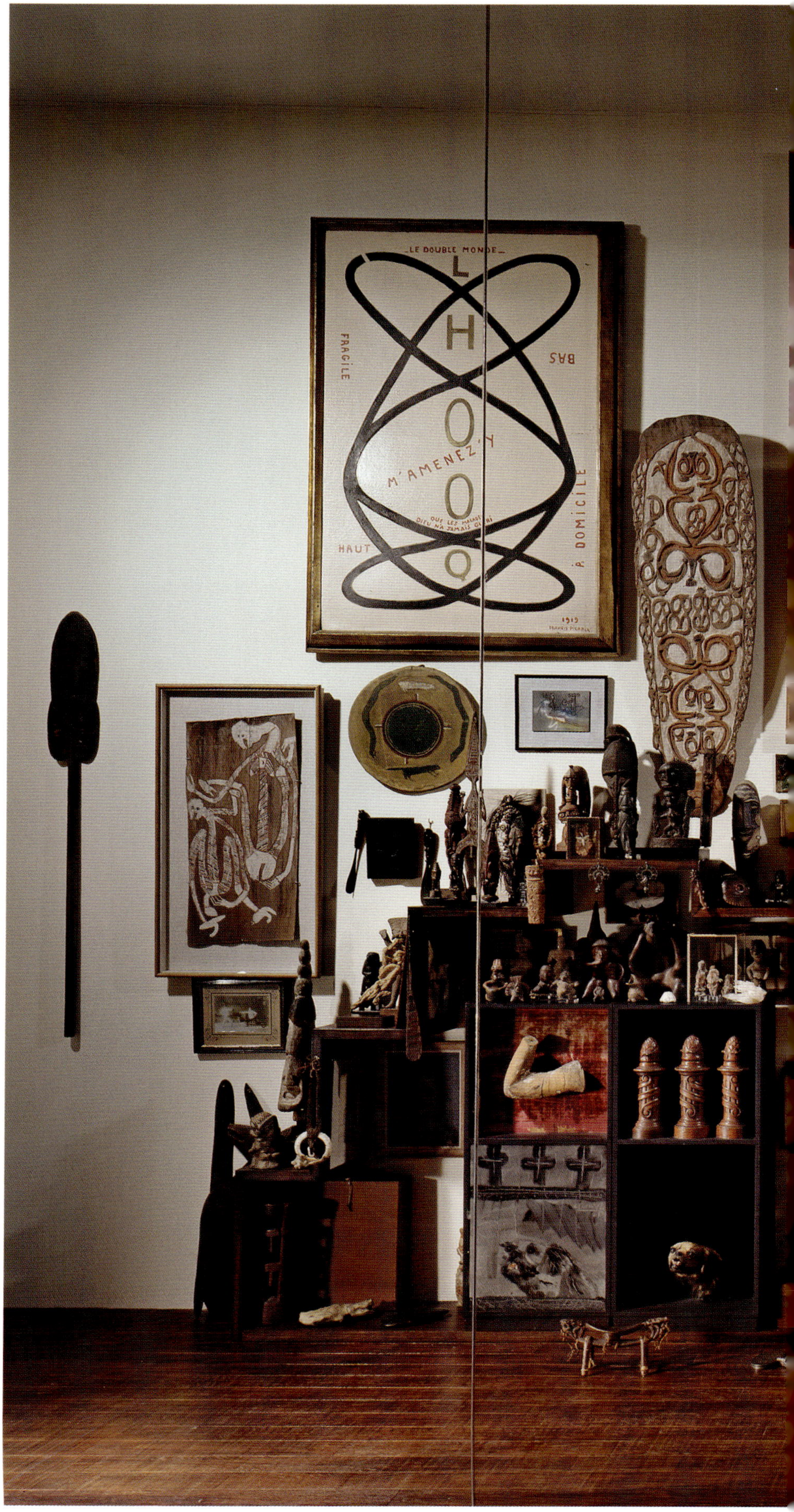

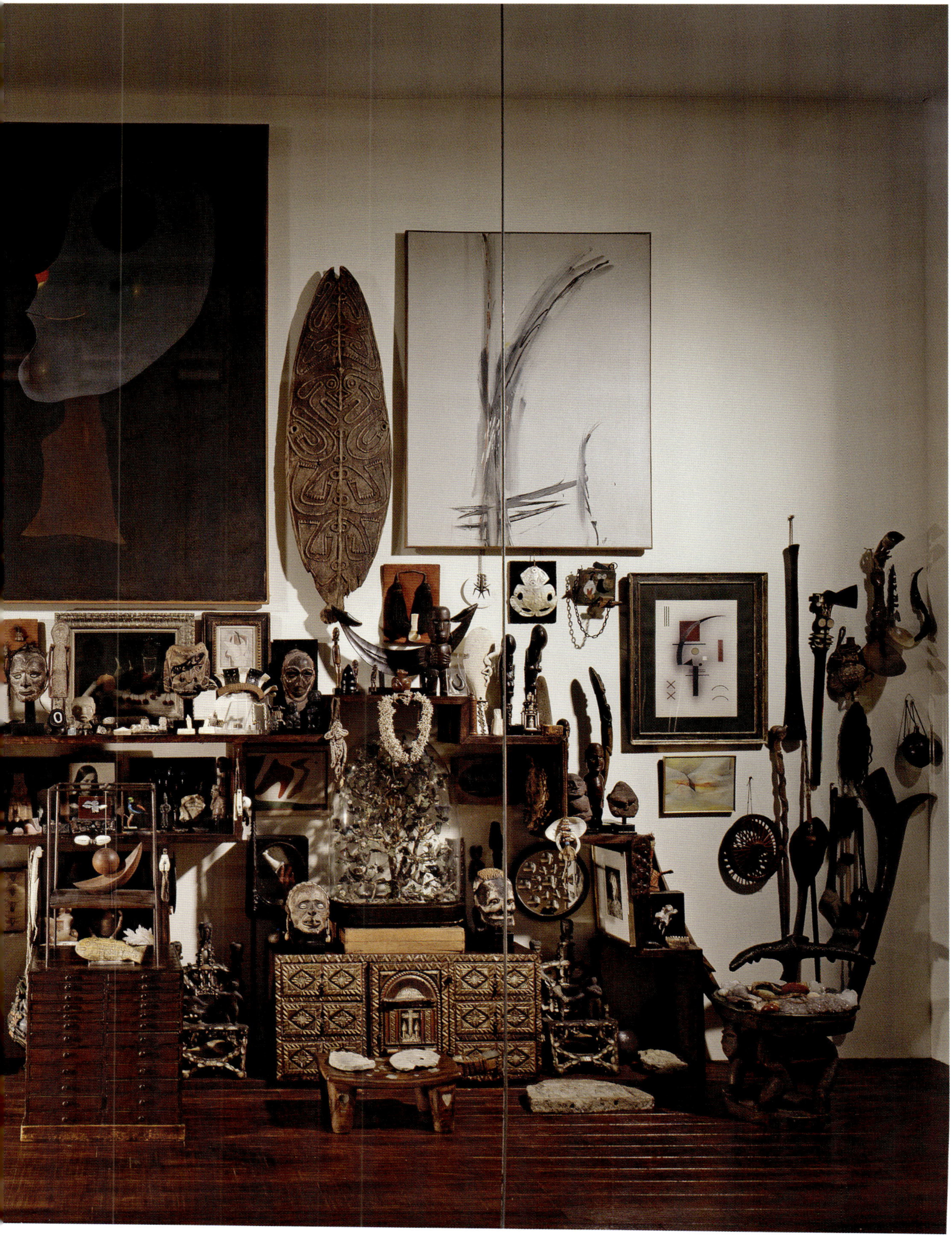

1926

Bildnis der Journalistin Sylvia von Harden
[Portrait of the journalist Sylvia von Harden]
Oil and tempera on wood
121 × 89 cm
Purchased 1961 - AM 3899 P

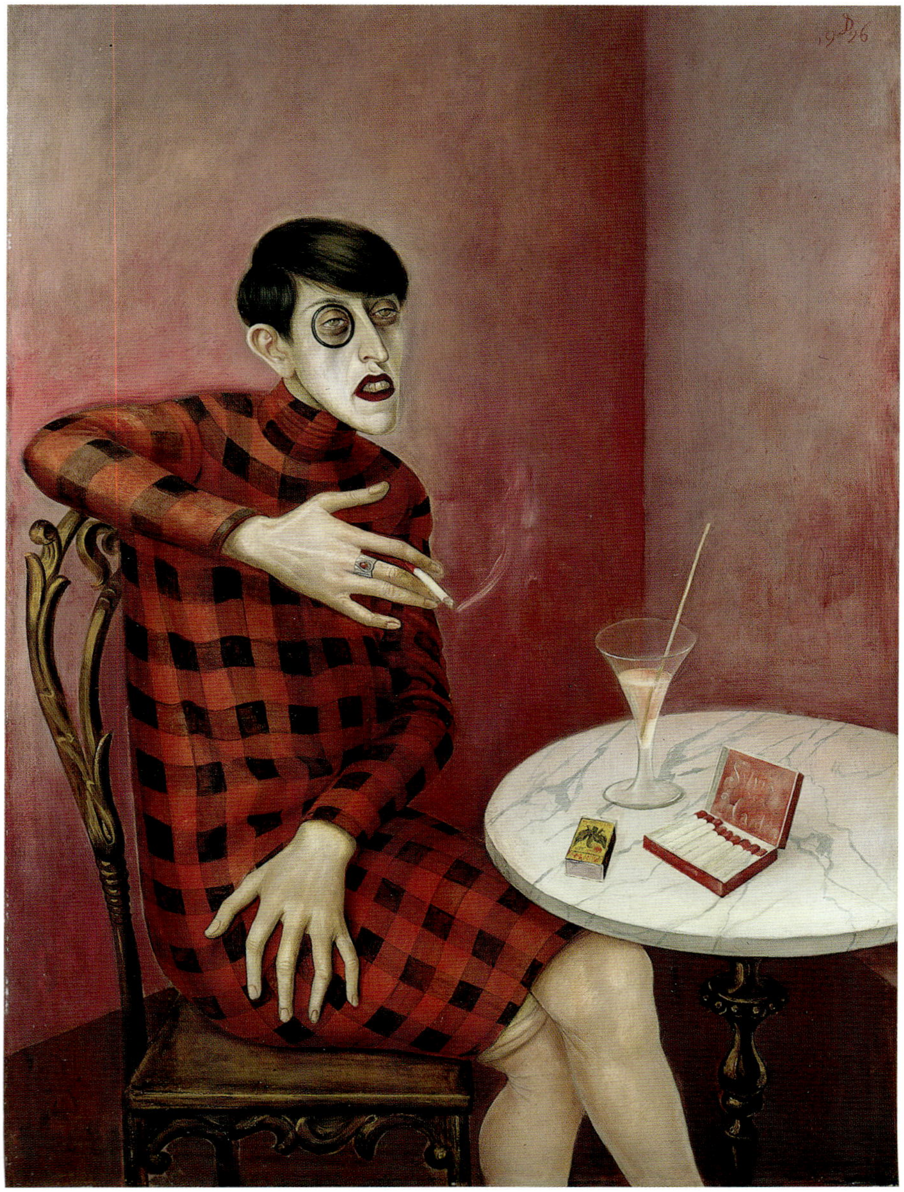

Otto Dix

1891, Untermhaus (Germany)
1969, Singen (German Federal Republic) †

Otto Dix moved to Berlin in 1925. On a visit to Italy, he became more familiar with Renaissance pictorial techniques and this experience strengthened his attachment to the legacy of early sixteenth century German artists, such as Grünewald, the Cranachs and Holbein. The use of oil paint and *tempera* on wood lent great precision to Dix's art. He took part in the exhibition "Neue Sachlichkeit" [New Objectivity], a critical realist movement which emerged in Germany in the early 1920s. Its members, sceptical witnesses of their own era, were determined to describe daily reality and its ugly aspects from an objective standpoint. They were keen observers of the city, with its excesses and frequently gruelling reality.
This caricature is a portrait of Sylvia von Harden, a journalist Dix had got to know at the Romanisches Café, the hub of Berlin's artistic and literary intelligentsia. Through this portrait of a butch-looking woman with a monocle and cigarette, the attributes of the emancipated intellectual woman in the 1920s, Dix offers up a sharp and scathing vision.
The journalist's nonchalant pose is anything but natural and her self-satisfied bearing is at odds with her rolled-down stocking.
This alliance between sobriety and caricature, precision and expression, made Otto Dix one of the dominating personalities of the New Objectivity movement in 1920s Germany •

1927

Composition à la main et aux chapeaux
[Composition with Hand and Hats]
Oil on canvas
248 × 185.5 cm
Accepted in lieu of tax, 1982 -
AM 1982-104

Fernand Léger

1881, Argentan (France)
1955, Gif-sur-Yvette (France) †

A Cubist painter whose "contrasts of forms" had gained him a recognised place in the pre-war avant-garde, Fernand Léger found his work transformed by the experience of the First World War. The world had changed, he noted: everything was more complex, everything went much faster. It was the advent of modernity that Léger sought to register when in 1924 he began a series of large still lifes whose inclusion of mechanical elements endeavours to do justice to modern life. Leger monumentalised ordinary manufactured objects – typewriter, accordion, umbrella, ball bearings – by rendering them in close up, using areas of flat colour.
The *Composition à la main et aux chapeaux* is the culmination of this series. The elaborate assemblage of diverse objects makes reference to Léger's *Ballet mécanique*, the "first film without a script," made with the help of Man Ray and Dudley Murphy in 1923–1924, in which he used close-up and a variety of fragmentation effects to generate a repetitive, rhythmic energy. Here Léger has divided the canvas into rectangular compartments, a succession of planes on which appear, without regard for scale or narrative, three hats, two aces, a face in profile, a pipe, four spoons, two life-belts, two bottles, a stamp... The grouping and repetition of these objects/pictograms again recall the rhythms of film. Right at the bottom, a hand holds up a bowler hat, most likely in an allusion to Chaplin, discovered by Léger, through Apollinaire, while on leave in 1916 •

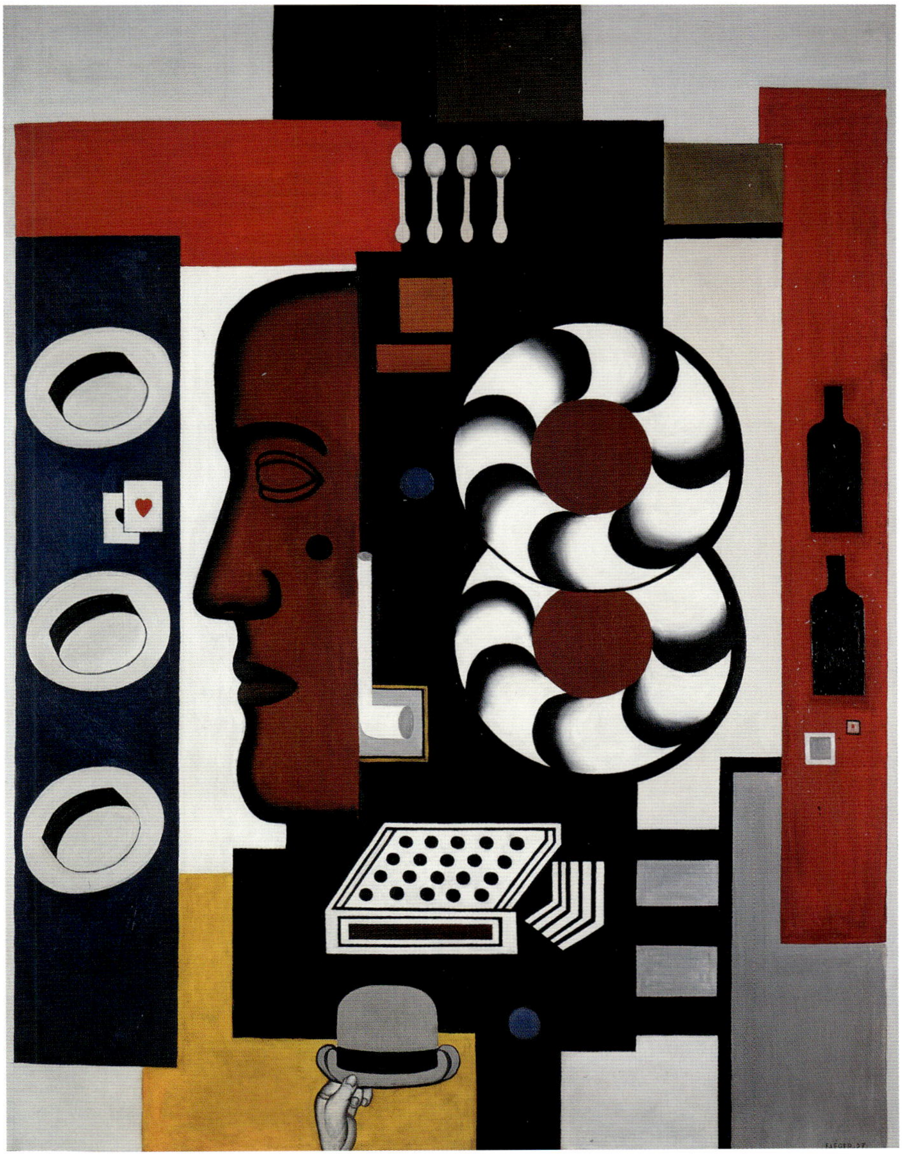

➔ [1928]

Joséphine Baker IV
Wire
100.5 × 84 × 21 cm
Gift of the artist, 1966 - AM 1518 S

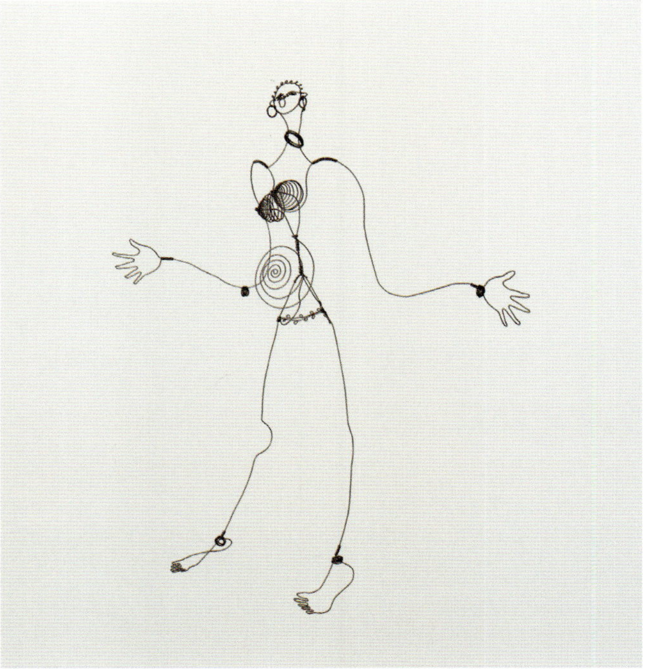

Alexander Calder

1898, Lawnton, PA (United States)
1976, New York, NY (United States) †

Calder was born near Philadelphia, where he studied engineering, before opting for an artistic career. In 1926–1927, in Paris, where he was living, he created *Cirque*, which comprised over one hundred wire figures. The world of entertainment and the circus were to become his signature themes. Between 1927 and 1929, the artist devoted a series of five sculptures to Josephine Baker (1906–1975), the "Black Pearl" of the Champs-Élysées Theatre's *Revue nègre*. This example could well be the fourth version. Suspended in thin air by a thread, the twisted, rolled wire figures, their empty, mobile forms resembling "drawings in space", strike different postures, evoking the exhilarating routine performed by the semi-nude dancer, her sole costume consisting of a ring of feathers or bananas around her waist. The ductility of the wire proved a perfect medium for the sculptor's sense of humour and caricature. His rapid thumbnail stroke captures the dancer's lanky pose, the spiralling form of her breasts and waist evoking the singular, quirky vivacity of her movements.
By grasping the equilibrium and vitality of the bodies, Calder is also experimenting with the possibilities of hollowed-out forms of metal sculpture, in much the same way as González and Picasso •

Constantin Brancusi

1876, Pestisani (Romania)
1957, Paris (France) †

An academically trained sculptor, Constantin Brancusi attracted the attention of Rodin at the Salon d'Automne of 1906. After only a month in the master's studio, however, the young Brancusi decided to leave, to pursue direct carving. In 1913 he began to carve wood to make bases for his other works, in a number of simple forms derived from Romanian rural architecture. Thus were laid the foundations for the series of *Endless Columns*, which he would develop over two decades, and for the organisation of space by vertical rhythm.
The first *Endless Column* dates from 1918. Consisting of three and then two modules of oak, it stood at first on a stone base, testimony to the changed status of a work that had equally lowly origins. Another *Endless Column* carved from a poplar tree at Voulangis in 1926 stood almost eight metres high before it was cut down. Then, not long before 1928, Brancusi made *Colonne sans fin III*, a shorter version somewhere between the two in width. At the same time, he modified the rhythm of the two other columns. The repetition of the motif – a pair of truncated pyramids or a rhomboid, depending on how one looks at it – produces an upward dynamic that the viewer is invited to prolong in imagination.
The infinite potential of the movement depends on the rhythmic qualities of the work and the harmony of its proportions.
The series would culminate in a monumental bronze version of 1937, installed in the open air as part of the Romanian military memorial at Tîrgu Jiu •

➔ [ante 1928]

Colonne sans fin III
[Endless Column III]
View of the Atelier Brancusi with *Colonne sans fin III* in the centre
Poplar; 301.5 × 30 × 30 cm
Bequeathed by the artist, 1957
AM 4002-118

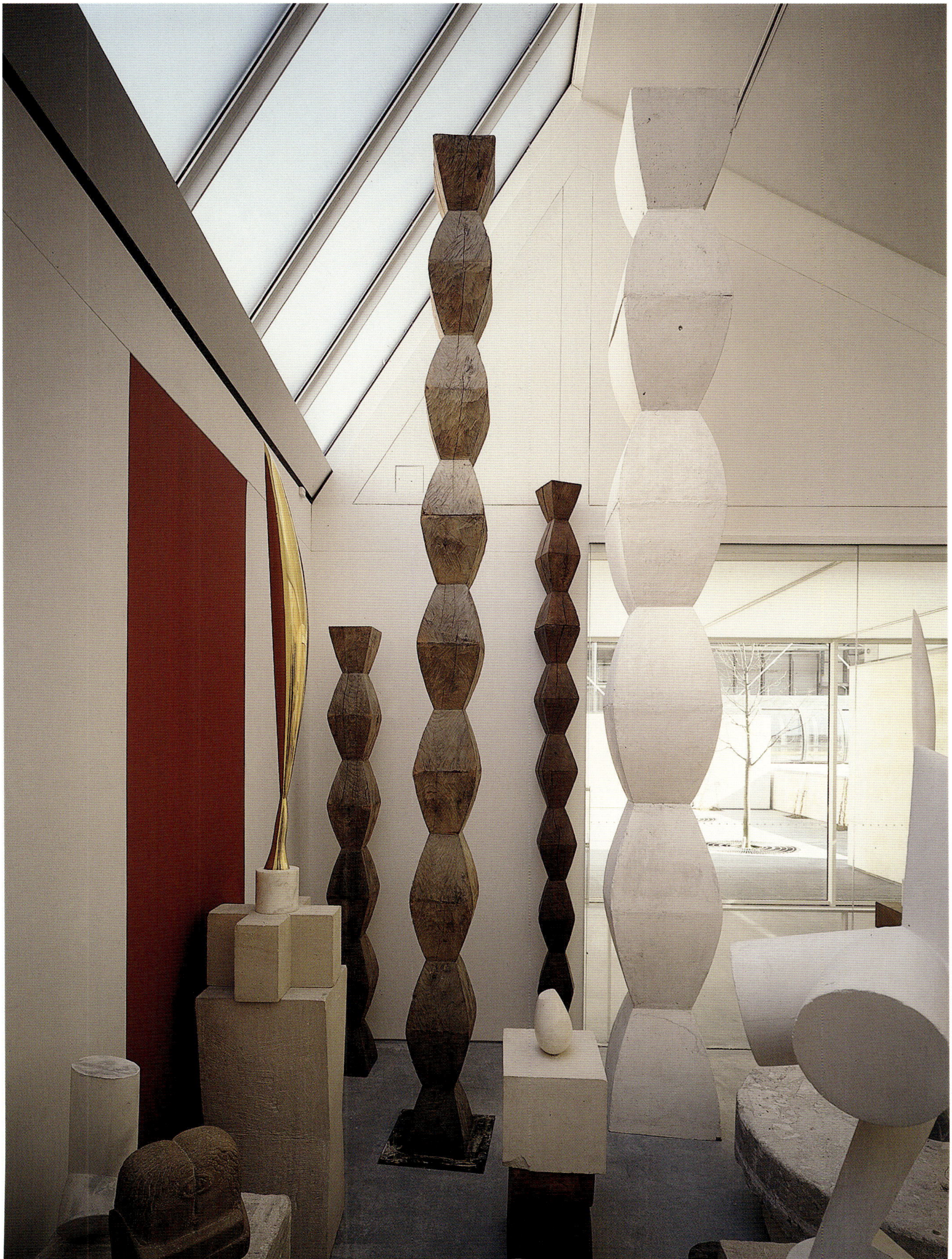

1930

L'Escalier
[Stairs]
Gelatin silver print
29.6 × 42 cm
Gift of Mulia Rodchenko, 1981 -
AM 1981-585

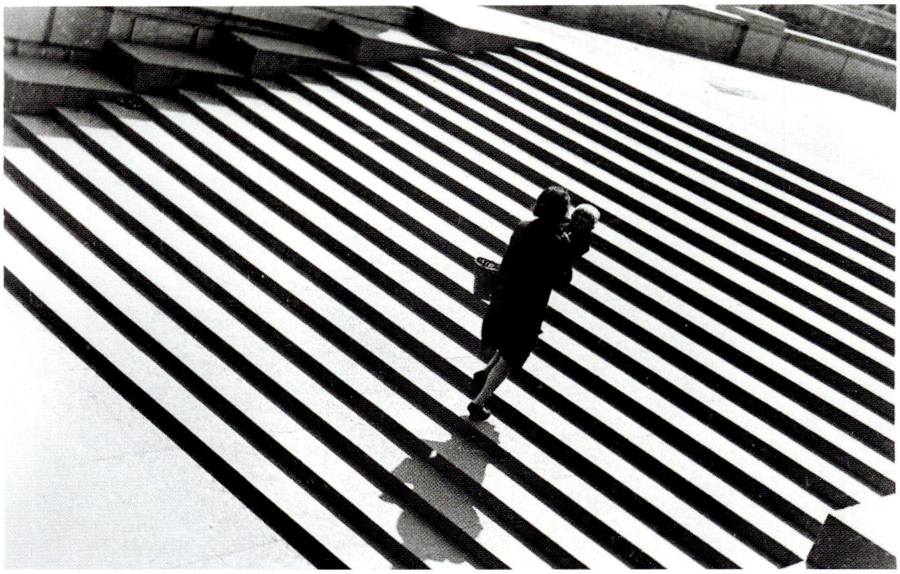

Alexandre Rodtchenko

1891, St. Petersburg (Russia)
1956, Moscow (USSR) †

[Alexander Rodchenko] Having proclaimed the death of easel painting, Alexander Rodchenko threw himself wholeheartedly into the Constructivist adventure. Initially, he concentrated his photographic research on photomontage but from 1924 he started taking his own photographs.
In *Stairs*, the Soviet artist has come up with a composition which succeeds in harmonising the dynamics of the diagonal with a high-angle shot to show a woman passer-by climbing the stairs with a child in her arms. The radical interplay between the starkly outlined steps and orthogonal overall composition are in sharp contrast with the irregular silhouette crossing the picture. The geometric immobility of the mineral setting and the living movement serve to accentuate one another. The photographs of stairs and high- and low-angled shots of streets were a common manifestation of the modern visual lexicon at the time. Following the guidelines of Constructivism, these images are an attempt to transform architectural landscapes into abstract compositions and, as in this case, enable the geometric form underpinning particular subjects to exist independently •

Paul Klee

1879, Münchenbuchsee (Switzerland)
1940, Locarno (Switzerland) †

In 1911, Paul Klee joined forces with the *Blaue Reiter* painters, Franz Marc, August Macke and Kandinsky in particular, and took part in the movement's second exhibition. The following year saw him in Paris, where he met Robert Delaunay and translated his text entitled "La Lumière" [Light]. Klee did not wish to belong to any group, however, and it was really the physical discovery of the Mediterranean landscape, during a visit to Tunisia in 1914, that revealed the power of colour to him. Keen to link poetry, painting and music, the artist blended precision and the imaginary to construct a universe in which botany, architecture and geology could be intertwined.
At the invitation of Walter Gropius, Klee then joined the Bauhaus School. From 1921 to 1931, while continuing to teach, he experimented with the foundations of painting, as illustrated by the "magic squares" in *Rhythmisches*. Klee reduced his pictorial range and found inspiration in the chequerboard in his research into the tensions between the three values: white, black and grey. In order to gauge their respective qualities, he varied the size of the squares and analysed their potential in creating a rhythm. After the fourth line, the layout progresses more haphazardly, as though life was insinuating itself into the heart of the geometric strictures. Similarly the irregularities created by applying the paint with a knife created a vibration, accentuated by the ochre background. The painting thus produced an effect of optical mobility, which was taken up by a whole generation of artists •

1930

Rhythmisches
[In Rhythm]
Oil on hessian canvas
69.6 × 50.5 cm
Purchased 1984 - AM 1984-356

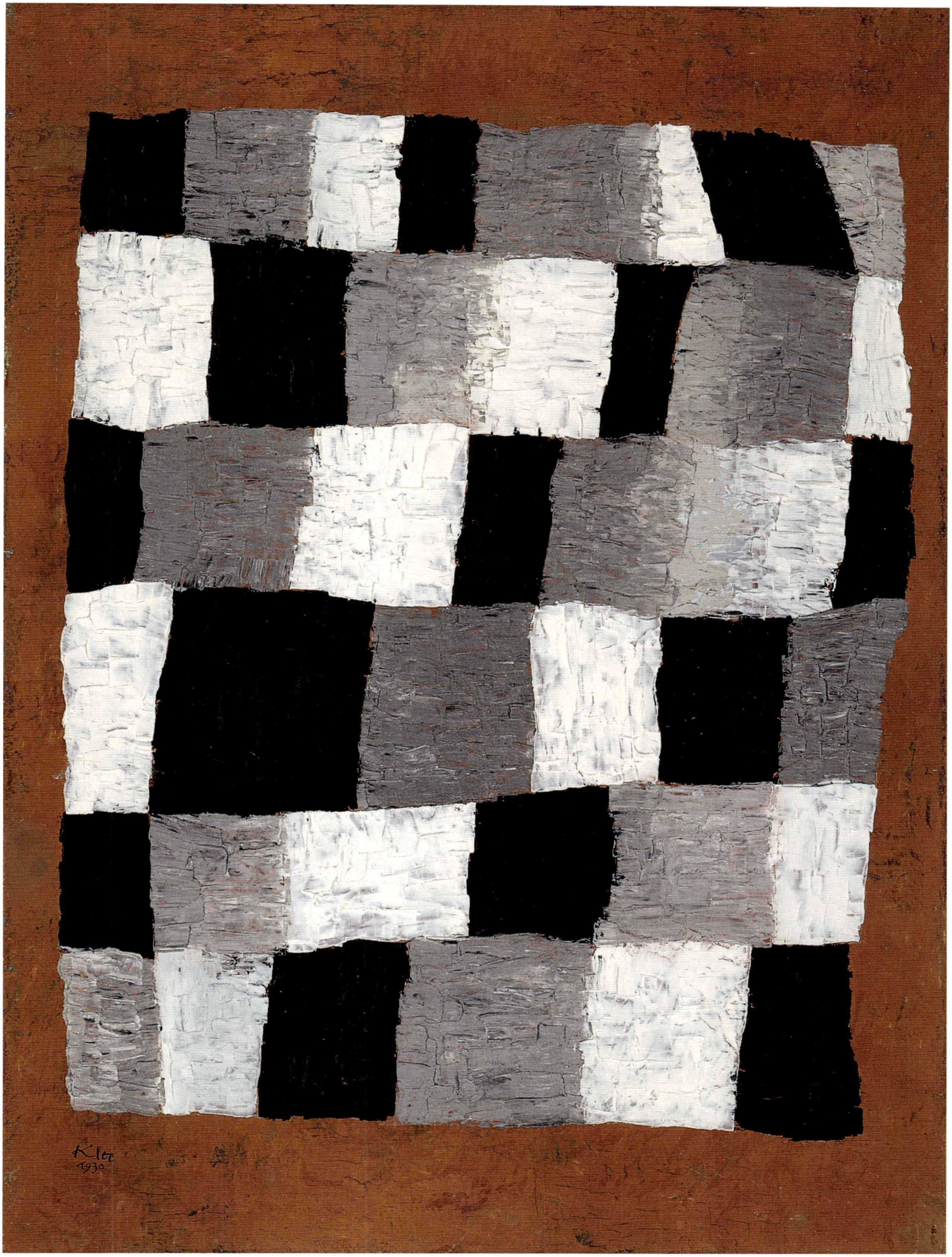
Klee
1930

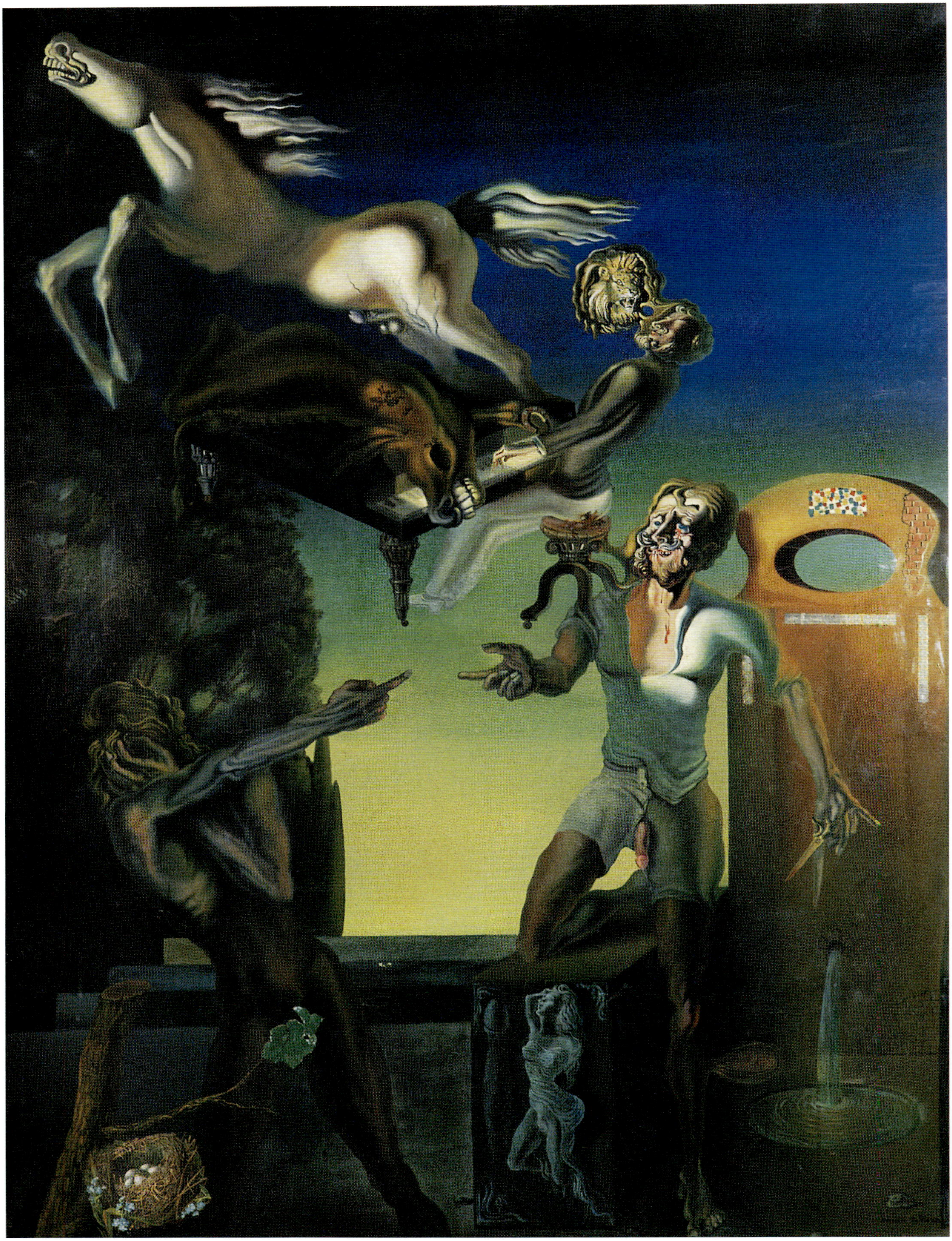

1930

Guillaume Tell
[William Tell]
Oil and collage on canvas
113 × 87 cm
Purchased with the contribution of the Fonds du Patrimoine, 2002 - AM 2002-287

Salvador Dalí

1904, Figueras (Spain)
1989, Cadaquès (Spain) †

Sent down from the Madrid School of Fine Arts for insubordination, his artistic training nevertheless left the Catalan artist Salvador Dalí with a love of classical painting, which he was to complement by his discovery of avant-garde trends. He rapidly came to epitomise the canons of Surrealism at their most absolute. The spectacular flaunting, or distortion, of his personal obsessions took the form of hallucinatory or illusionist visions betraying remarkable formal acuity. Dalí was one of the first to link Surrealism with a quest for new mythologies, turning the legend of William Tell into a seminal narrative.

"William Tell is my father", declared Dalí in 1974. This autobiographical canvas stemmed from the banishment of the painter from the family home. His father resented him for painting *Parfois je crache par plaisir sur le portrait de ma mere* [Sometimes I spit with pleasure on the portrait of my mother] and for his ongoing affair with a married woman (Gala Éluard). The Swiss hero aiming his bow and arrow at an apple on his son's head personified crushing paternal domination. His penis, the symbol of his authority, is exposed and he is holding a pair of castratory scissors, his knee leaning on a plinth adorned with a female figure. Crushed by this surfeit of power, the son can only turn his head away. This critical view of authority was later transposed to the political and artistic arena, William Tell being elided with Lenin (*L'Énigme de Guillaume Tell*, 1933) and with the "father of Surrealism", André Breton – who ended up excluding Dalí from the movement •

Luis Buñuel

1900, Calenda (Spain)
1983, Mexico City (Mexico) †

Following the success of *Un chien andalou* in 1929, Charles de Noailles, a wealthy patron of the arts, offered to provide the financial backing for Buñuel's next film, while giving him an entirely free hand. Whereas *Un chien andalou* was conceived on the lines of automatic writing – the film-maker and Salvador Dalí had brought to the screen their own dreams and obsessions, dismissing those that appeared too logical – *L'Âge d'or* was created as an ode to unfettered desire. Deliberately subversive and violently anti-clerical, the film set out to declare war on bourgeois society and middle-class morality, triggering one of the most memorable Surrealist scandals ever, when it was first screened at Studio 28 on 28 November 1930. On 3 December, Fascist and anti-Semitic leagues descended on the cinema and lacerated the Surrealist canvases on display in the lobby. The screenings continued for a few more days, under police protection, before the film was finally banned on 11 December. Buñuel wrote in 1930 that he would have expected such a scandal to affect *Un chien andalou* rather than *L'Âge d'or*, given its disquieting scenes such as an eye slashed with a razor and a hand crawling with ants. It was only in 1981 that this period Surrealist testimonial was finally rediscovered, when the Museum was able to accept it in lieu of tax and restore the original negative •

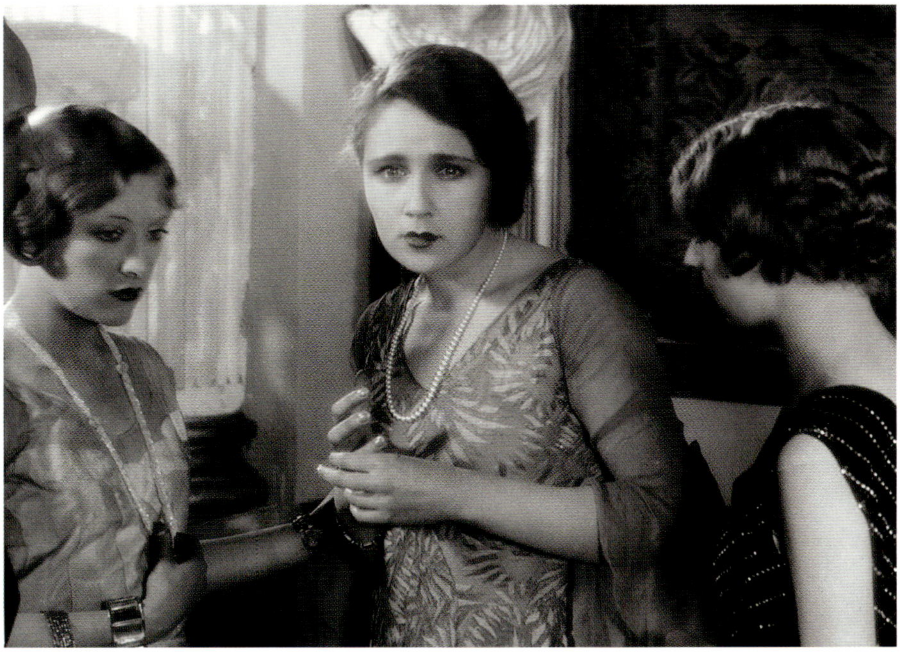

1930

L'Âge d'or
[The Golden Age]
35 mm black and white sound film, 63'
Accepted in lieu of tax, 1989 - AM 1989-F1128

Julio González

1876, Barcelona (Spain)
1942, Arcueil (France) †

Born to a family of Catalan goldsmiths, Julio González early mastered metalwork, though for a long time he practised it as a craftsman rather than an artist. It was in Paris, where they moved in 1900, that he embarked twenty-eight years later, in collaboration with his friend Picasso, on the exploration of the possibilities of welded-iron sculpture.
Now over fifty, and having practised in the meantime as a painter and draughtsman, González went on to develop his own sculptural language, producing in 1930 a series of abstract heads in forged iron, cut and welded in accordance with a new principle, constructing volume through a succession of independent planes, assembling flat or curved metal plates in such a way as to create a sense of depth. The features here are schematically rendered by a curved, projecting strip that confers its forceful expression on the face, echoing in its economy the noses of the two central figures of Picasso's *Demoiselles d'Avignon*. Now linear, sculpture also loses any frontality, its forms shifting with the movement of the viewer.
It was to these discoveries that González owed his artistic reputation, showing with Giacometti, Arp and Miró. Considered the founder of modern iron sculpture, linked to both Cubism and Surrealism, he was an important influence on Eduardo Chillida, David Smith and the early César •

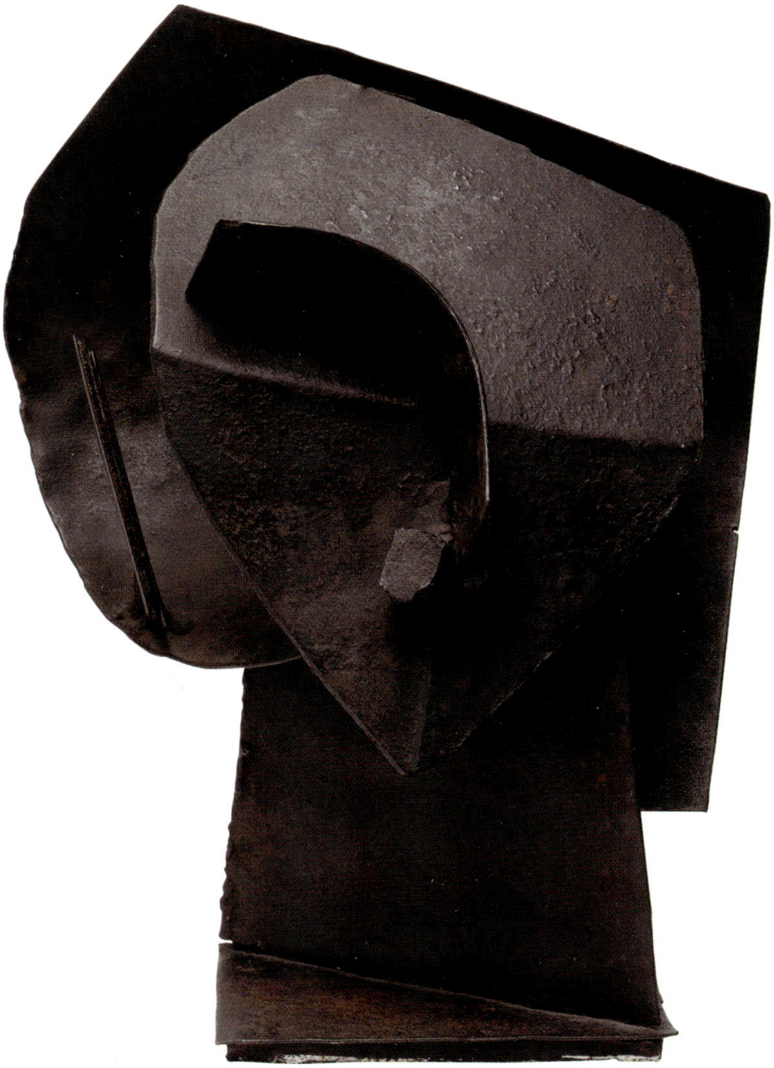

1930

Tête en profondeur
[Head in Depth]
Welded, patinated, wrought iron
26 × 20 × 17 cm
National treasure, acquired through the patronage of Pernod Ricard, 2003 -
AM 2003-408

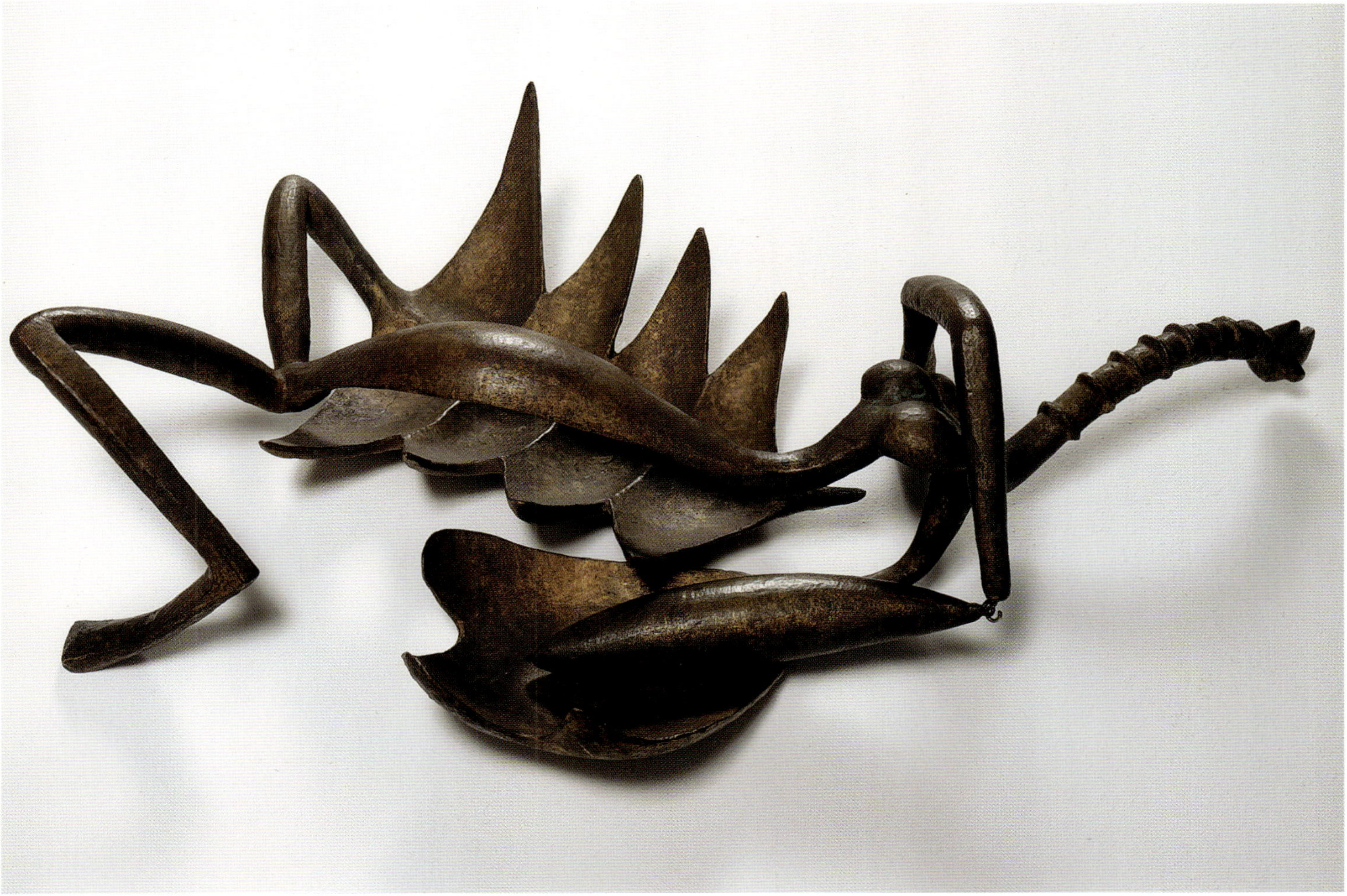

Alberto Giacometti

1901, Stampa (Switzerland)
1966, Coire (Switzerland) †

Alberto Giacometti, the son of painter Giovanni Giacometti, came from a background conducive to an artistic career. Influenced by Cycladic art, the primitive arts and Cubism, he joined the ranks of the Surrealists in the early 1930s.
He turned away from his classic, Cubist legacy to delve into the "primitive" and concentrate on the myth of origins and a form of sexuality nourished by the repressed urges of the subconscious. *Femme égorgée* is perhaps the most enigmatic and complex work of the artist's Surrealist period. Almost headless, its body with its parted legs and splayed, gaunt ribs strains is arched with powerful tension, this ultimate spasm and final moan akin as much to agony as to ecstasy. The work, with its acute, violent forms, seems to express the lethal undercurrent of desire.
It illustrates, as Giacometti himself put it when describing his Surrealist works, all the characteristics of an "unpleasant, disposable object". This ambivalent creature, drawing on the female form (breasts, legs), the animal kingdom (scorpion, praying mantis, spider) and the world of plants (leaf, stem, pod), is an unequivocally concrete interpretation of the subconscious and of the "disquieting strangeness" the Surrealists held so dear •

1932 - 1933 /1940

Femme égorgée
[Woman with her Throat Cut]
1932–1933/1940
Bronze, gilt patina
Copy: 2/5; cast: Rudier
21.5 × 82.5 × 55 cm
Purchased with the participation of the Fonds du Patrimoine, 1992 -
AM 1992-359

1932

Le Clown blessé
[The Wounded Clown]
Oil on paper mounted on canvas
199 × 119.5 cm
Gift of Isabelle Rouault, 1987 -
AM 1987-564

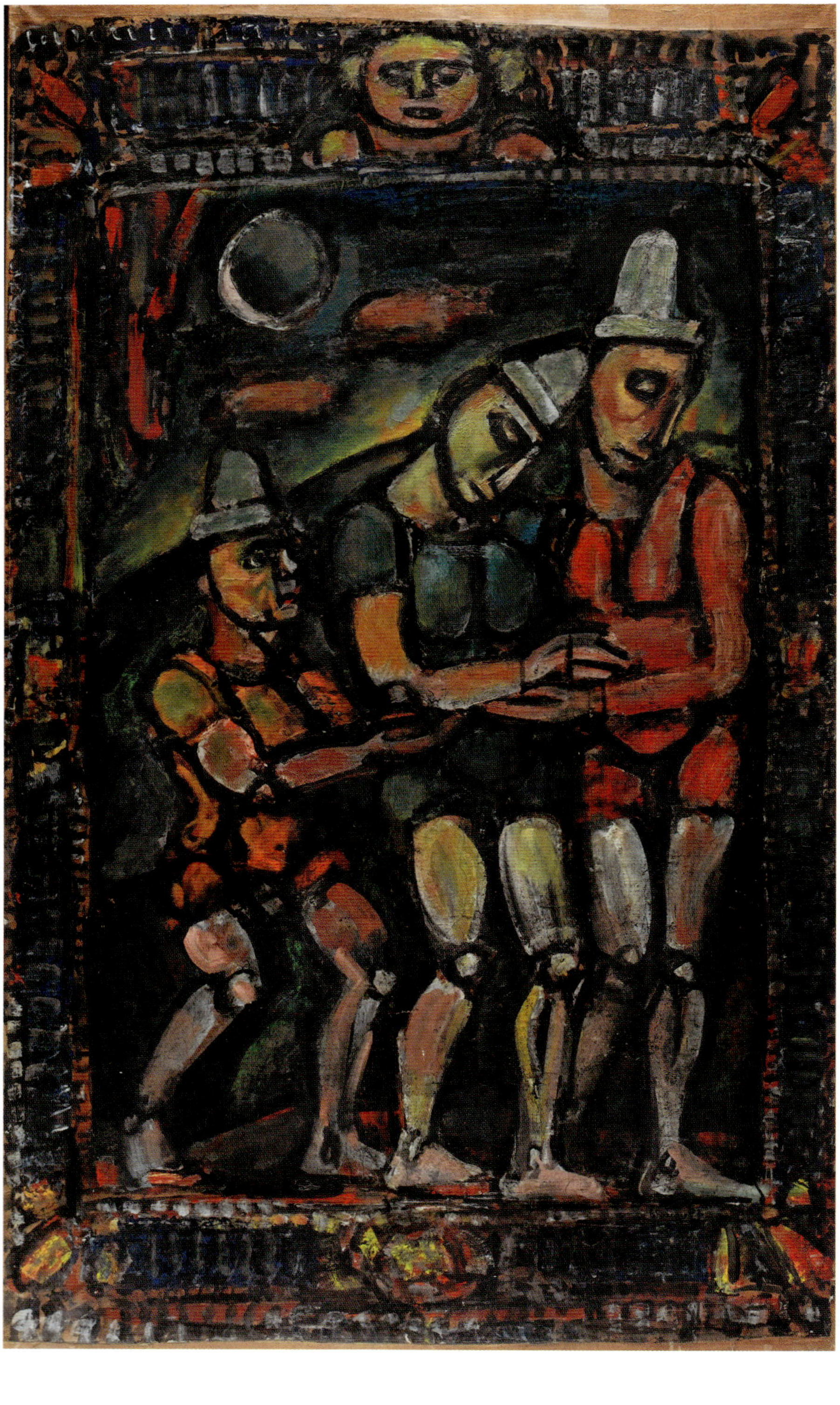

Georges Rouault

1871, Paris (France)
1958, Paris (France) †

Georges Rouault was brought up among Christian craftsmen. His brushstroke, characterised by bold *chiaroscuro*, together with his predilection for precious materials, stem from the training he received in a firm of stained-glass restorers and his time at the École des Beaux-Arts in Paris, in Gustave Moreau's studio. Alongside his religious subject-matter, a vital component in his work from the outset, the painter tackled the sphere of human destitution, denouncing the hypocrisy of society. Prostitutes, entertainers and the poor are often depicted in reflective poses, with solemn, sad expressions. *Le Clown blessé* is emblematic of his 1930s paintings, in which colour, often applied layer by layer, juxtaposed its rich enamel with contrasting black contours, introduced to lend structure to the forms. This work corresponds to a project for a tapestry, which explains its atypical size and decorative border. The artist has managed to step inside the three characters leaving the circus ring, capturing them and revealing their innermost vulnerability. In the centre, the wounded clown is being helped along by his supportive companions. The tallest of the three is leading them through the darkness while the smallest is looking with commiseration at his suffering friend. The subject is not purely anecdotal – here Rouault is highlighting the themes of trust and solidarity. After all, as he was to remark in 1948: "The wounded clown is perhaps just as religious a topic as some of my Biblically-titled compositions." •

Pierre Bonnard

1867, Fontenay-aux-Roses (France)
1947, Le Cannet (France) †

In 1888, Bonnard decided to study painting as well as law and enrolled at the Académie Julian. It was there that he met the painters with whom he was to launch the Nabi movement. He soon broke away from them, however, and traditional Japanese art remained the only lasting influence on his work. This is illustrated by his choice of themes but more specifically by his treatment of perspective. The horizontal foreground is normally seen from above, the horizon line is either high or non-existent and the vanishing point has disappeared all together. Bonnard's painting reaches beyond the immediate appeal of colours and themes to reveal to the attentive eye a complexity redolent with nuance and contradiction.
This *Nu à la baignoire* is a case in point. It depicts Marthe, who appears in most of the painter's canvases. The firm, voluptuous body of Bonnard's companion, captured just after her bath, recalls the theme of Venus. The white of the enamel is conveyed by a pearly surface reminiscent of foam. Only the contours of the white conch and the model are defined with precision. Elsewhere, the elements pave the way for a pictorial process involving vibrant, fluid strokes. The tiles on the floor and clothes scattered over a chair, with their fluid boundaries, form abstract patterns, sublimating this scene from everyday life •

➔ 1931

Nu à la baignoire
[Nude with bathtub]
Oil on canvas
120 × 110 cm
Purchased through contributions from an anonymous donor in memory of Emery Reves, J.P. Morgan, the Fonds du Patrimoine and public contributions, 1984 - AM 1984-351

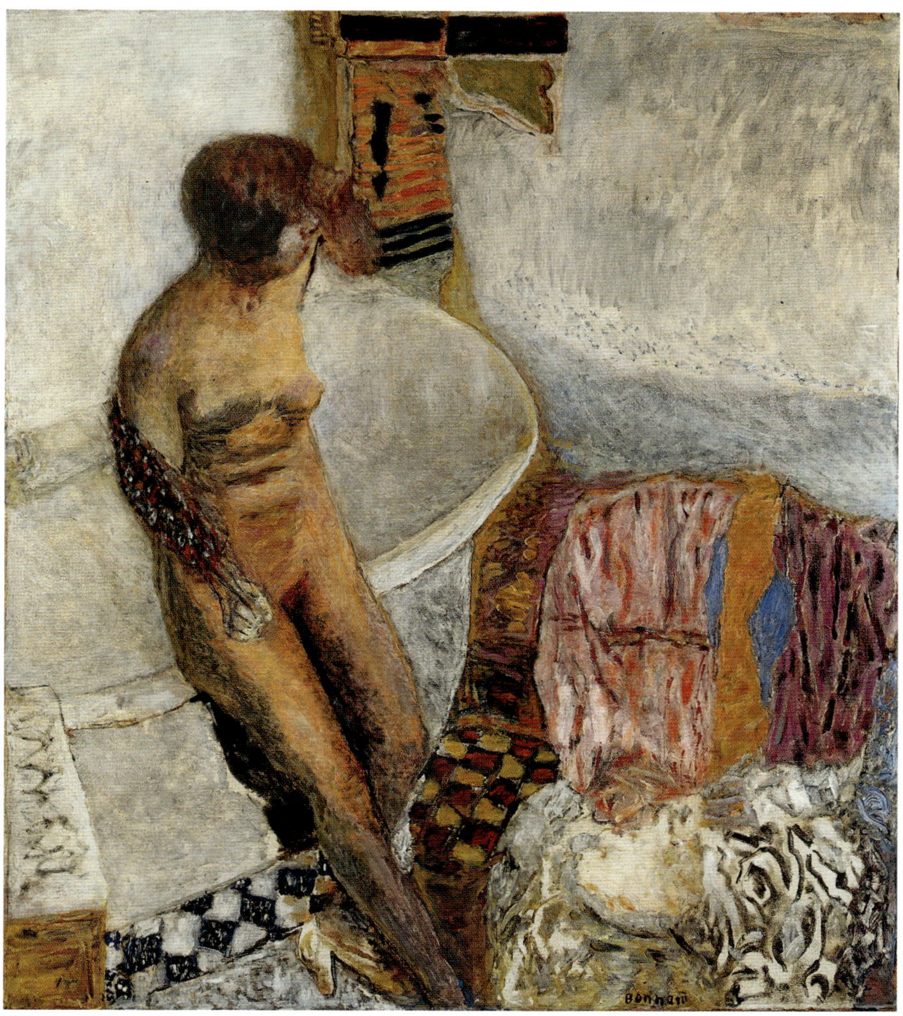

1933

Alice

Oil on canvas
162.3 × 112 cm
Purchased with the help
of the Fonds du Patrimoine, 1995 -
AM 1995-205

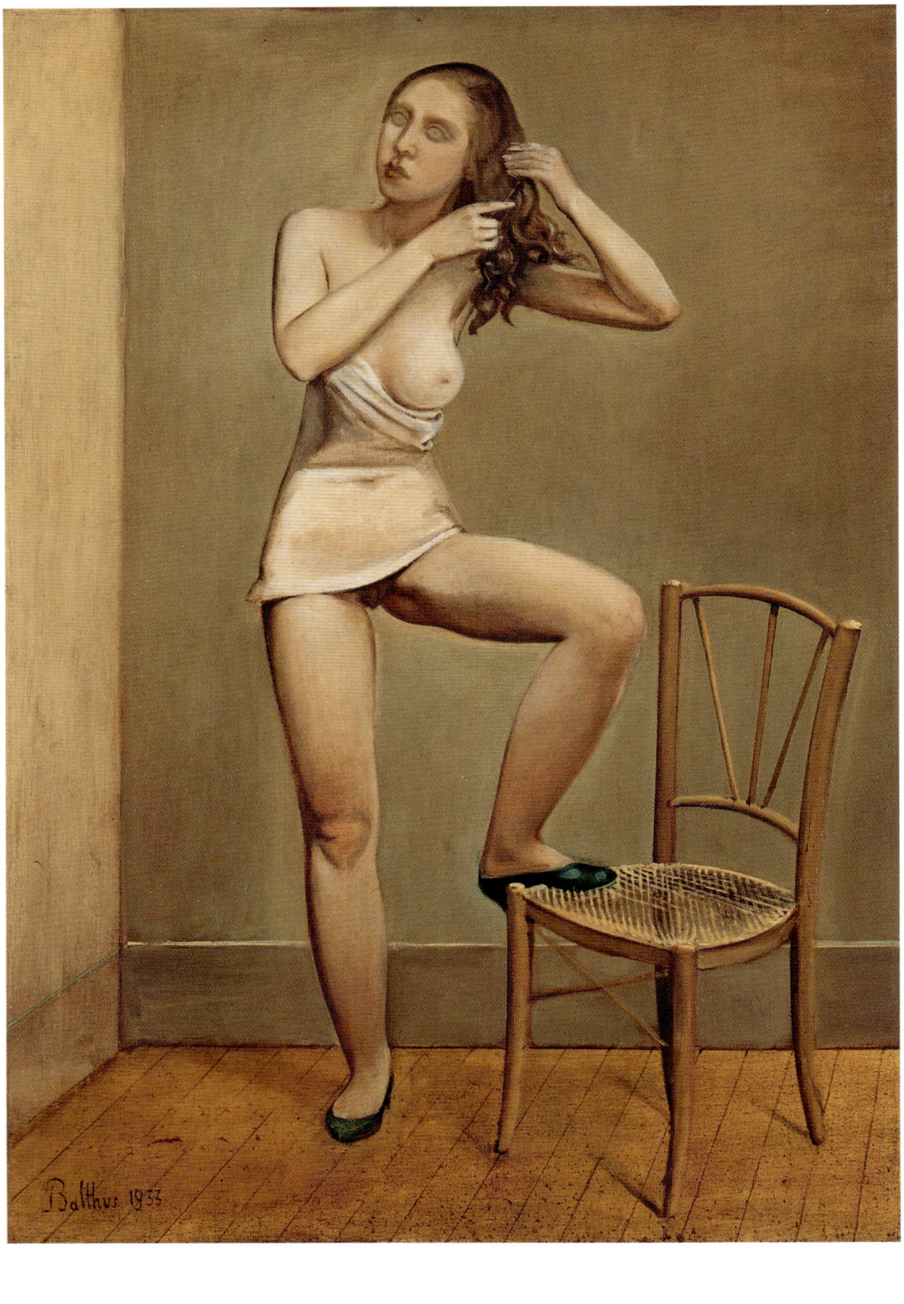

Balthus

(born Balthazar Klossowski de Rola)

1908, Paris (France)
2001, Rossinière (Switzerland) †

Balthus is one of the great loners in twentieth century art. This does not mean that he was indifferent to the achievements of modern art – his parents moved in international, particularly literary, artistic circles. But his fascination with the Italian Primitives, such as Piero della Francesca, as well as Courbet and Poussin, and his attachment to strange, fantastic tales, led him to create paintings with a mysterious and dreamlike atmosphere.
Alice, shown in April 1934 at the artist's first solo exhibition, is one such example. In the artificial brightness of an amber light, in a warm yet acrid glow, the artist has captured *Alice* at her ablutions, her nudity offered up to the viewer. The fact that the nude has been drawn from a recognisable model is all the more disturbing. This is a friend of the painter's, Betty Holland, whose charming features are disquietingly portrayed through washed-out, almost blind eyes. The unease is compounded by the heavy breasts, which seem to be curbing the body with its overly slender waist, hefty legs and small childlike feet. Disturbingly, the hair, like someone drowning, conjures up a figure removed from everyday time and space. Antonin Artaud was the first to comment on this canvas with its hallucinatory reality: "featuring coarse, excrescent genitals", this nude "has an element of something dry, hard [...] and even cruel []. It incites love, but does not conceal its dangers." •

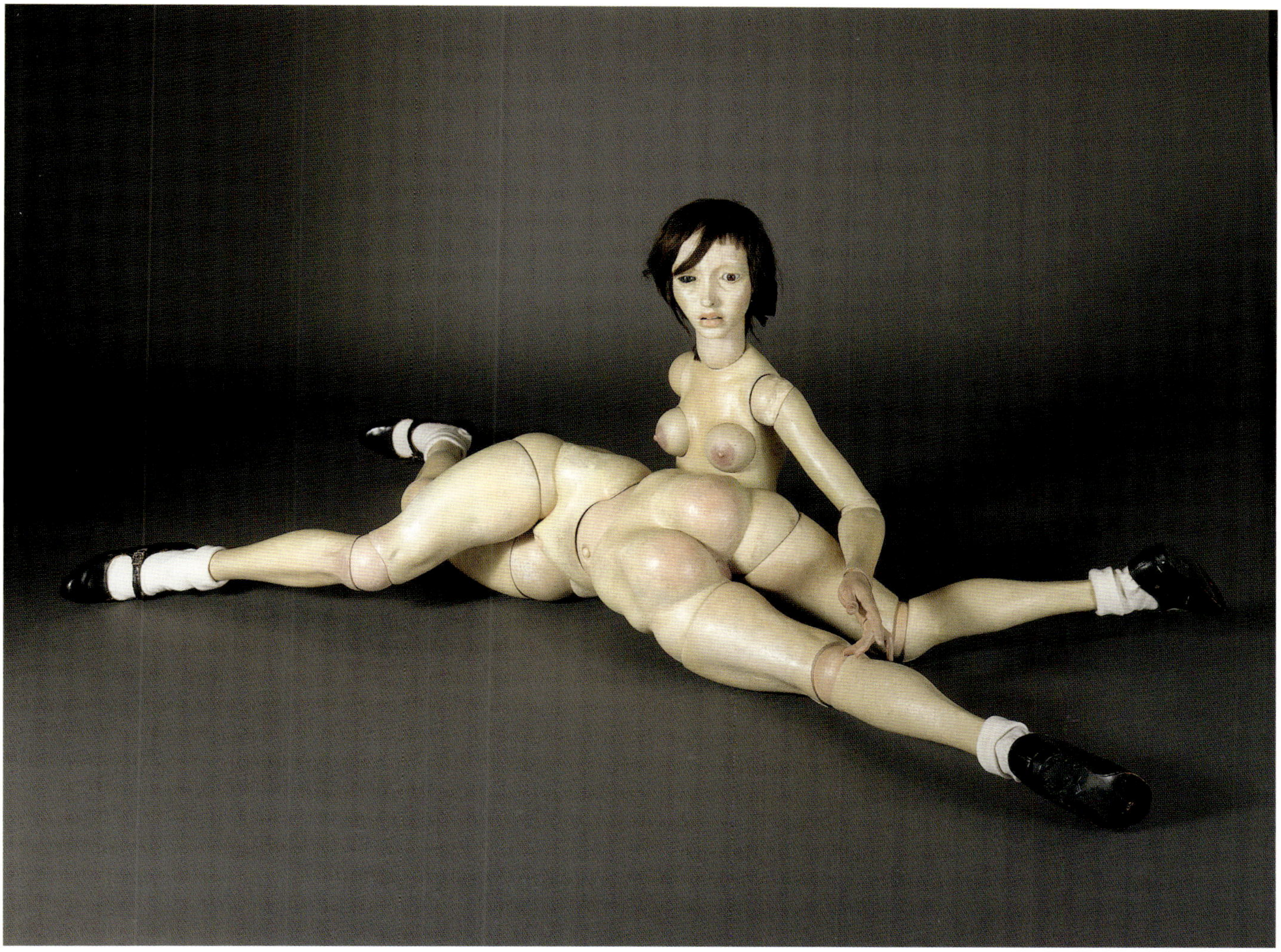

Hans Bellmer

1902, Katowice (German Silesia)
1975, Paris (France) †

Bellmer, who was born in Silesia, began an engineering course in Berlin but gave it up in 1924, when he discovered Dada. In 1933 he was earning a living in advertising as a graphic designer but in reaction to Hitler's accession to power he decided to cease "any socially useful activity". He applied his mind to producing an articulated human-sized wooden puppet with a lifelike expression, a project he had begun in 1932 with his brother, an engineer. Dismembered and then reassembled in an erotic sublimation, *La Poupée* lies at the heart of Bellmer's work and was portrayed in the artist's drawings, photographs and writings. Disjointed and an object of fantasy, she represents a variation on the theme of the mannequin, a tradition spanning the Dadaist automatons from George Grosz to De Chirico. In 1935, the artist started making another doll with spherical joints. This enabled him to stage more elaborate scenes, against different backgrounds, which he then photographed. The disquieting oddity of this "provocative object", which stirred up forbidden, suppressed desires, fired the enthusiasm of the Surrealists. Bellmer coloured in the prints by hand, using a technique applied to period photographs, which accentuated their violent eroticism. These photographs inspired fourteen poems by Paul Éluard, published in 1949 under the title *Les Jeux de la poupée* [The Doll's Games] •

1935-1936

La Poupée
[The Doll]
Articulated object (with elements from 1933–1934), additions and restoration in 1945 and 1970–1971
Painted wood, painted, pasted papier mâché, hair, shoes, socks
61 × 170 × 51 cm
Donated to the State by the artist, 1972; attribution, 1976 - AM 1976-927

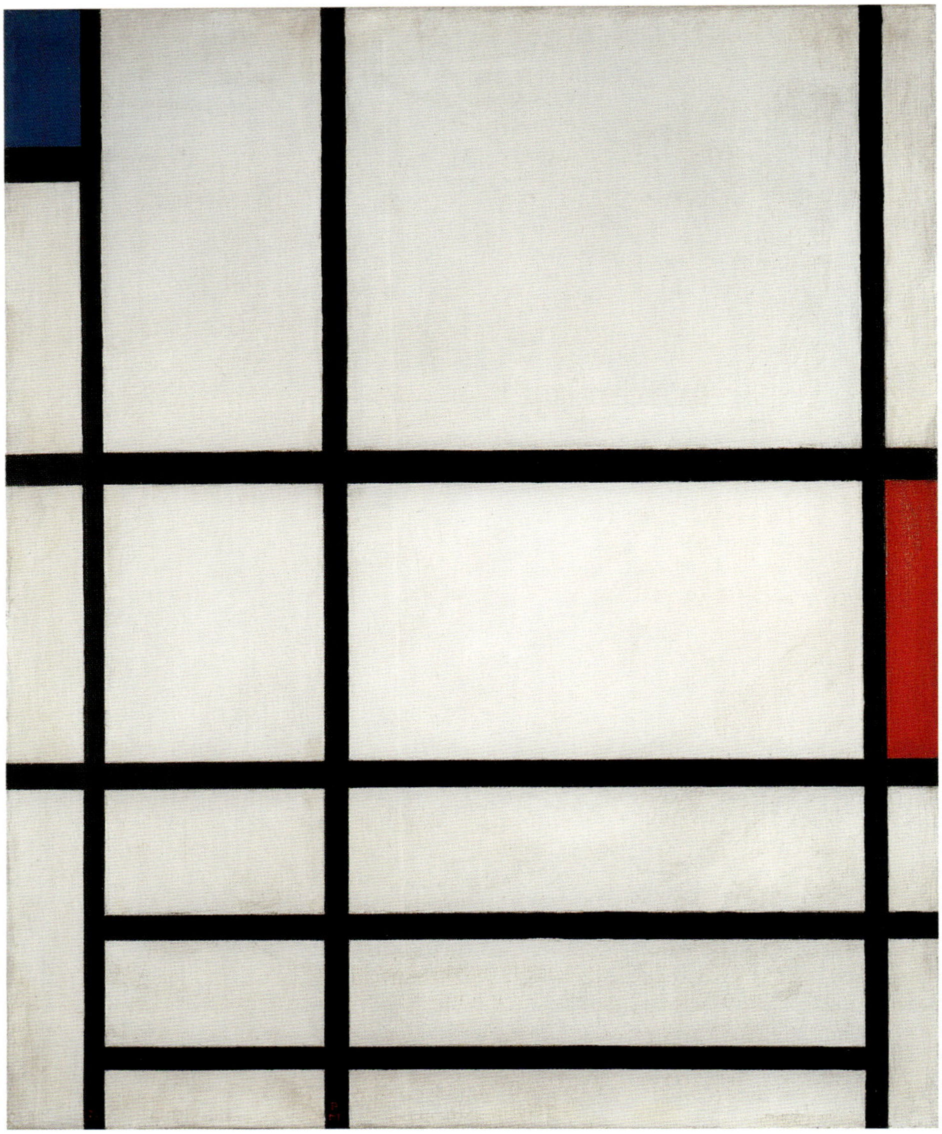

© 2010 Mondrian/Holtzman Trust c/o HCR International, Virginia

1937

Composition, rouge, bleu et blanc: II

Oil on canvas
75 × 60.5 cm
Purchased 1975 - AM 1975-53

Piet Mondrian

(born Pieter Cornelius Mondriaan)

1872, Amersfoort (Netherlands)
1944, New York (NY, United States) †

Together with Malevich and Kandinsky, Piet Mondrian was one of the great pioneers of abstraction. At first a figurative painter in the manner of Jondking, he came under the influence of Cubism when he moved to Paris in 1912. He later distanced himself from the movement, claiming that it "did not accept the logical consequences of its discoveries". In 1917, the year he joined Theo Van Doesburg in founding the journal *De Stijl*, Mondrian committed himself to a radical abstraction without reference to any natural reality. The definitive vocabulary of Neo-Plasticism was now in place, with its tension between the invariable – the constant of the right angle – and the variable – the position, size and colour of the coloured planes.
Privileging black line over coloured plane, *Composition en rouge, bleu et blanc: II* is typical of Mondrian's compositions after 1934. The optical dynamism of the grid that structures the work is reinforced by the presence of the narrow rectangles of colour at the edges. These areas, like the intersection of the lines, emphasise the flatness of the canvas, and bring out the individuality of the white rectangles. Horizontality and verticality are in balance while symmetry is excluded, leaving the field open to the dominance of rhythm. According to Mondrian, "the rectangular planes, formed by the plurality of straight lines in rectangular opposition [...] are dissolved by their homogeneity, and rhythm alone emerges, leaving the planes as 'nothing'" ("De l'art abstrait," 1931) •

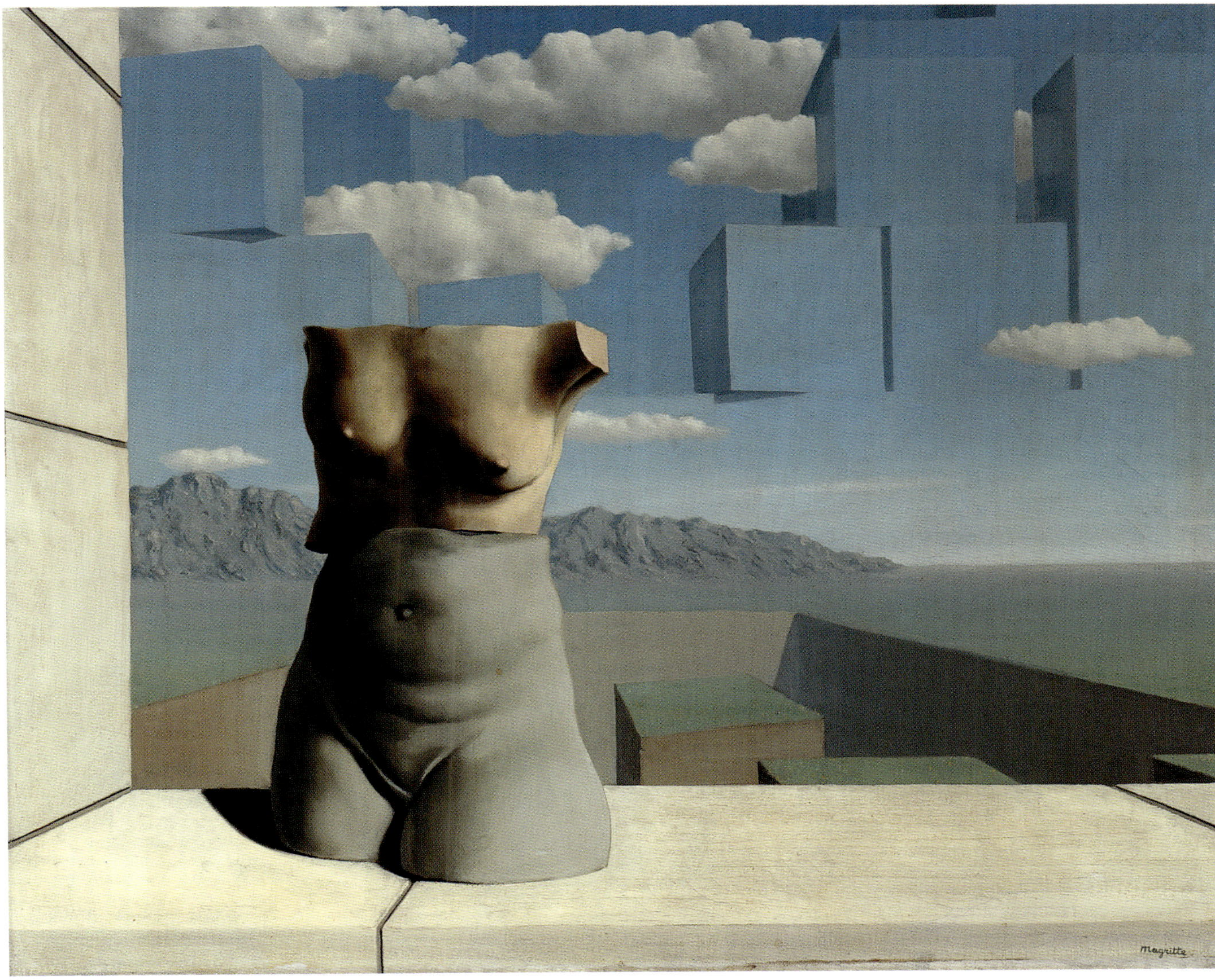

1938

Les Marches de l'été
[Steps of Summer]
Oil on canvas
60 × 73 cm
Purchased 1991 - AM 1991-138

René Magritte

1898, Lessines (Belgium)
1967, Brussels (Belgium) †

A subversive character, deliberately concealed beneath a veneer of modesty and banality, René Magritte soon emerged as the figurehead of Belgian Surrealism. His discovery of the work of De Chirico encouraged him to turn away from the formal abstraction of his early canvases and follow a path that challenged the real world, "the visible being sufficiently rich in itself to form a poetic language redolent with mystery". His realist stroke, here reduced to a simple technical process, allowed the painter to explore the actual workings of the mental image. In order to depict thought, he had frequent recourse to ordinary, everyday objects, either reappropriating them or juxtaposing them in a totally eccentric manner. Subject to the strangest metamorphoses, the bodies overstep the boundaries between the outer and inner world, relating back to the subconscious, to dreams and to free association between different realities.
Here the female body, which haunted the Surrealist imagination, lends itself to a subtle transformation from inanimate stone to human being. The "transubstantiation" of the statue into woman rises up against the azure landscape while, in the summer sky, clouds pervade the air, petrified into cubes. Inanimate and animate intermingle on several levels in this picture, in which art and life astutely interact with one another, and all is but transition and transformation •

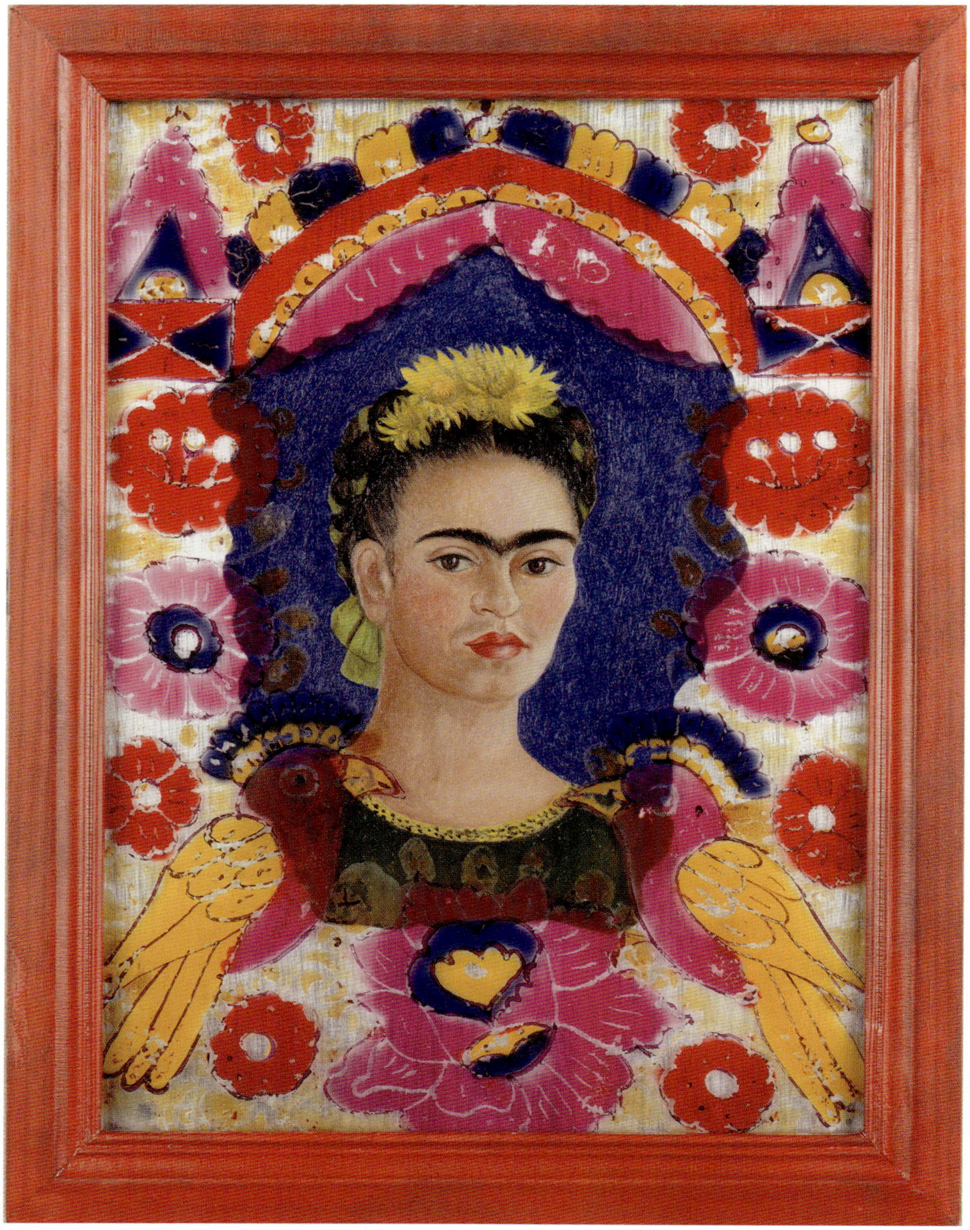

[1938]

The Frame

Oil on aluminium, under-glass and painted wooden frame
32.2 × 24.4 cm (incl. frame)
Purchased by the State, 1939; attribution, 1939 - JP 929 P

Frida Kahlo

(aka Frieda Kahlo Calderón)

1907, Coyoacan (Mexico)
1954, Mexico (Mexico) †

When André Breton visited Mexico in 1938, he not only met Leon Trotsky and Diego Rivera but discovered the paintings of Frida Kahlo. The father of Surrealism was attracted to this art, which drew on far more than the autobiographical to create a sensual blend of dreams and reality, projecting the emotions and desires of a young woman curbed by physical handicap. Indeed it was Breton who wrote the introduction to the catalogue of the artist's first solo exhibition, to be held in New York that same year.
Among the works on show was *The Frame*, which had been produced in an original fashion. Only the self-portrait itself and the blue uniform block of colour that surrounds it were actually painted on to the aluminium, its surface scored in order to ensure that the paint would adhere effectively. The shimmering floral composition framing this central area was not the artist's own work but a handcrafted adornment, created by translucent varnishes applied directly on to the glass. Frida Kahlo astutely readapted this element, probably designed to frame a mirror, photographic portrait or religious effigy, so that her face could be set back. The under-glass takes on an important role here, as a substitute for the accessories and ornaments with which the artist liked to frame her image – hence its title •

Marc Chagall

1887, Vitebsk (Russia)
1985, Saint-Paul (France) †

Chagall had been living in Paris for about fifteen years when he painted *Les Mariés de la Tour Eiffel* and his talent was already established. Paris had become *his* city and like his friends the Delaunays the most modern and emblematic monument of the City of Light became a popular feature in his works. The Eiffel Tower is indeed a fitting backdrop for this depiction of a bride and groom – Chagall and his wife Bella – characterised by a joyful, luminous atmosphere. The solid reality of the monument strikes a contrast with the soaring happiness of the couple and the supernatural aspect of the hybrid (man/goat/violin) creature above their heads. The couple appear indissolubly attached to an oversized rooster. This bird frequently recurs in the painter's works but here it has transcended the merely realist or picturesque motif. Over time, it has acquired a more symbolic dimension – a reference in particular to the role played by the animal in the ritual of Yom Kippur – and has been imbued with a positive spiritual force. Chagall lends the rooster a luminous, singular power, which often rhymes with joy. These dreamlike creatures in which imagination and reality overlap and a composition governed by colour are both characteristic elements in the rich metaphorical world of Chagall's art •

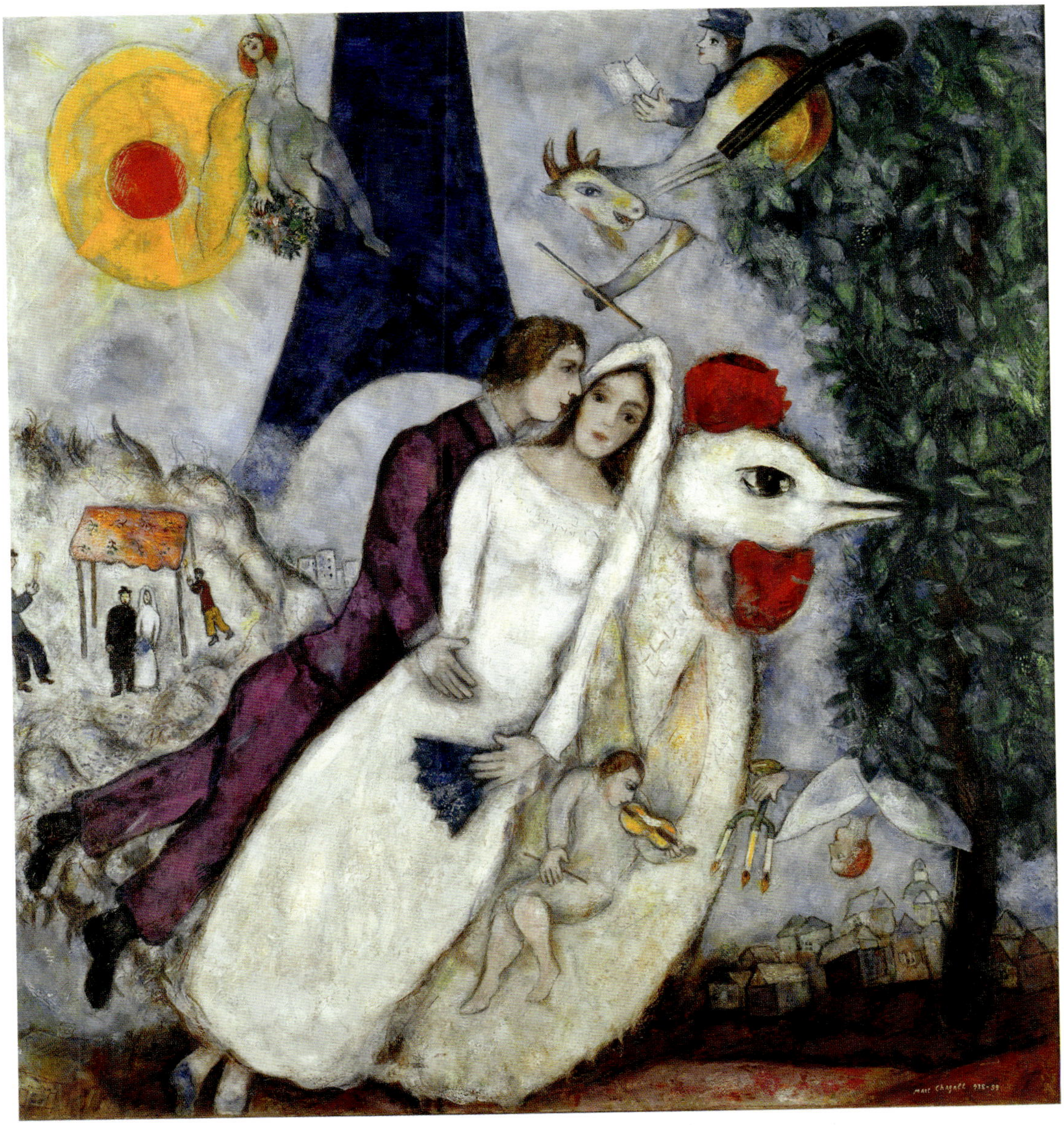

← 1938-1939

Les Mariés de la tour Eiffel
[The Bride and Groom of the Eiffel Tower]
Oil on linen canvas
150 × 136.5 cm
Accepted in lieu of tax, 1988 - AM 1988-67

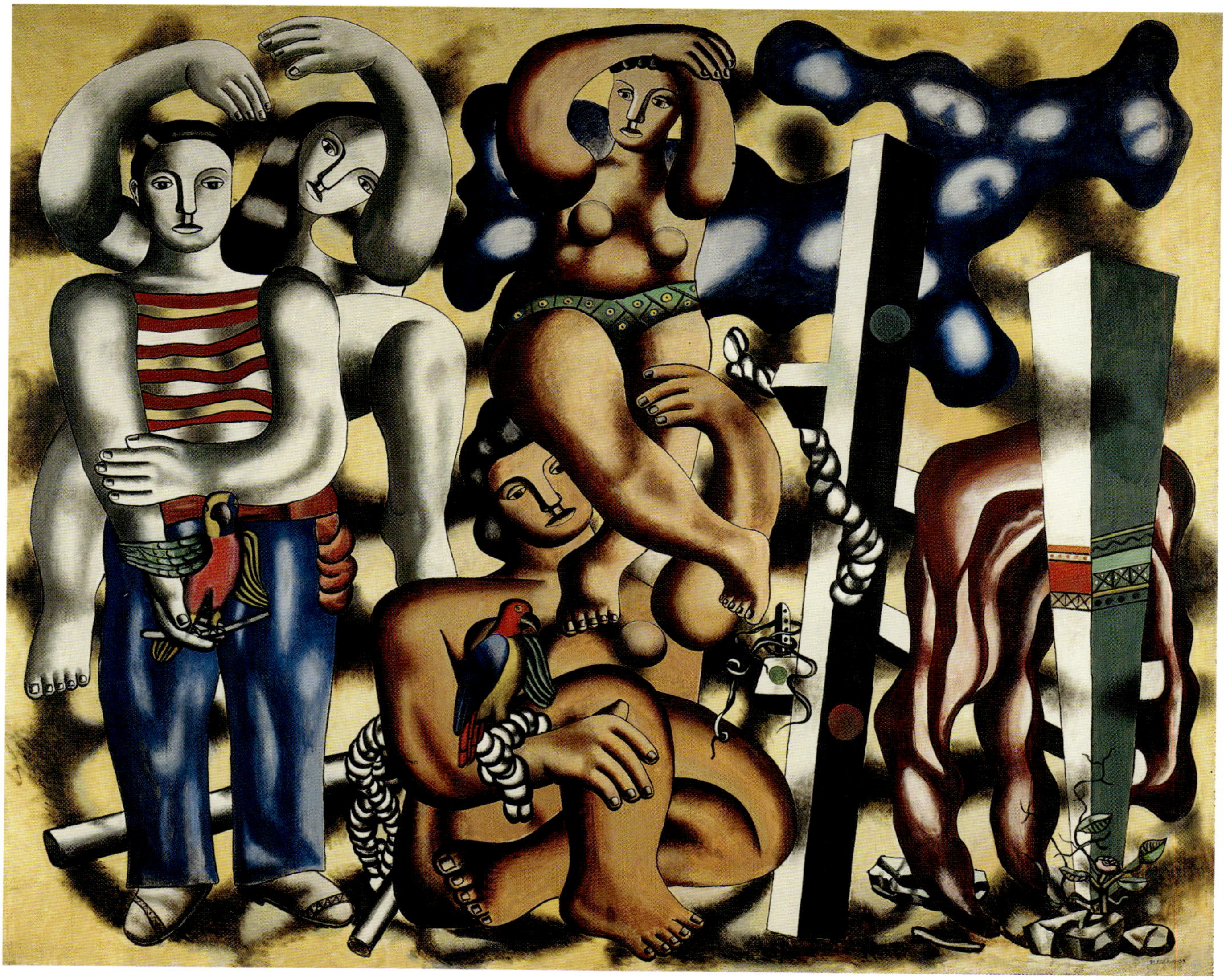

1935-1939

Composition aux deux perroquets
[Composition with Two Parrots]
Oil on canvas
400 × 480 cm
Gift of the artist, 1953 -
AM 3026 P

Fernand Léger

1881, Argentan (France)
1955, Gif-sur-Yvette (France) †

Before choosing painting, Fernand Léger was apprenticed to an architect, and it was perhaps this early experience that inspired his interest in murals. In the 1930s, freed from the standard formats imposed by dealers, he produced the large-scale works he dreamed of: "I am happy when in an apartment my painting dominates the room, imposing itself on everything, people and furnishings.
It has to be the most important character. I can't stand discreet paintings."
Composition aux deux perroquets is one such painting, four metres by almost five. Preceded by numerous preliminary studies, it features the acrobats that had appeared in Léger's work since the 1920s, the artist seeing in the circus, as a popular entertainment, a modern expression of the bond that unites humanity. The paired acrobats in the centre and on the left of the painting illustrate this idea, with their linked arms and legs. On the right is a rope and ladder combination already seen in *Composition aux trois figures* (1932). As in that painting, irregular, somewhat nebulous forms help draw the elements together. The figures are massive, the composition dense, yet there is also a sense of lightness and movement. The full force of the work is also modulated by the presence of the two parrots, which despite their modest scale introduce a significant sense of contrast and surprise.
Léger would continue to produce works on similar themes in the 1940s and 1950s, with the "Plongeurs" and "La Grande Parade" series •

1940

La Blouse roumaine
[Romanian Blouse]
Oil on canvas
92 × 73 cm
Donated to the State by the artist, 1953; attribution, 1953 - AM 3245 P

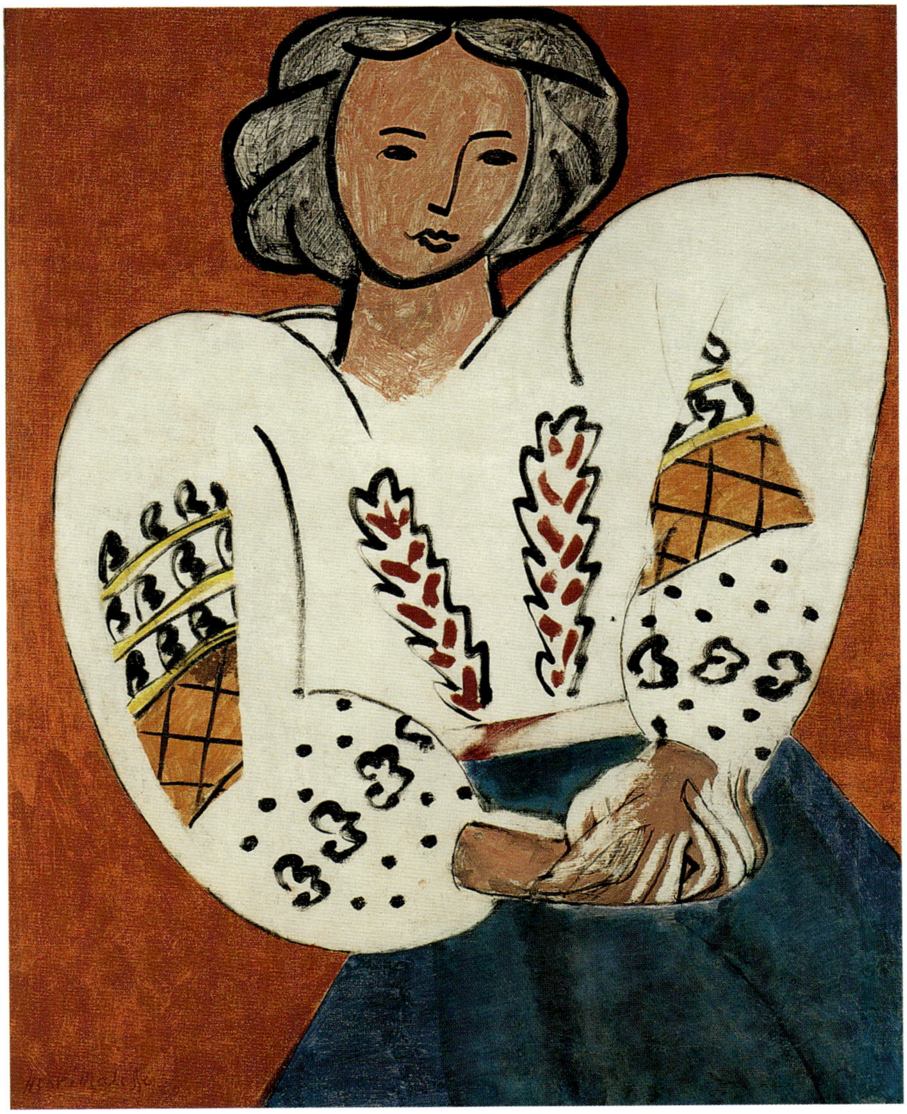

Henri Matisse

1869, Le Cateau-Cambrésis (France)
1954, Nice (France) †

The motif of the embroidered blouse with billowing sleeves appeared as early as 1936, in several pen drawings and studies. Matisse's treatment of the lavishly decorated garment (worn here by Lydia Delectorskaia) showed consummate plastic skill but it also gave the painter an opportunity to demonstrate his artistic technique: such simplification of forms could only be achieved by means of a lengthy period of decantation. This way of synthesising elements is far more complex than it appears and involves a meticulous process of paring down and eliminating details. This no doubt explains why in 1945 Matisse juxtaposed eleven photographic prints around the canvas, which were taken in order to record some of the landmarks in the painting's creation, which took six months to complete. The photographs document the elimination of a number of adornments, by scraping or covering them over: the flowery background, the floral pattern of the skirt, the check upholstery of the chair... This simplification of contours and motifs, combined with the unfurling of the wide sleeves, evoking wings, lends remarkable vitality and momentum to the entire composition •

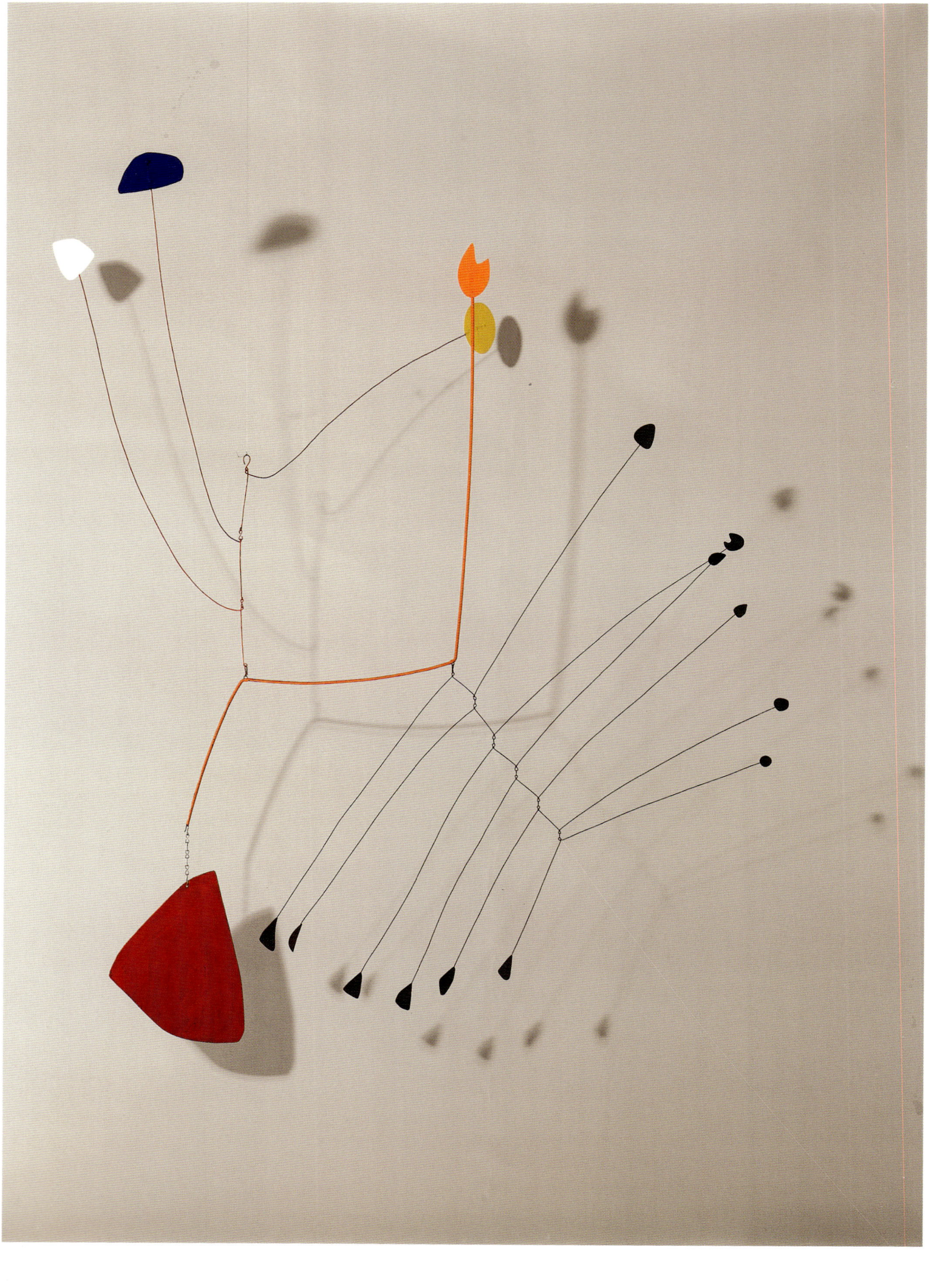

Alexander Calder

1898, Lawnton, PA (United States)
1976, New York, NY (United States) †

Until 1930–1931, "drawing in space" continued to form the crux of Calder's artistic reflection. It underpinned his sculpted work through a variety of themes, ranging from his *Cirque* entertainers (animals, acrobats, jugglers and trapeze artists) to portraits (*Joséphine Baker*) and mythological subjects (*Romulus et Rémus*). The success of Calder's miniature circus performances, which he animated himself, featuring articulated wire subjects enlivened by scrap material, soon led him to Miró, Léger, Arp and Duchamp.

It was his visit to Mondrian's studio in 1930, however, which was to prove seminal in the sculptor's move towards abstraction. It triggered his idea of using coloured sheet metal plates, articulated by metal rods, and making them move in space, each element swaying at the slightest breath of air. In order to become fully-fledged "compositions in movement", these constructions, precariously balanced through a play on weights and counterweights, could be activated either by hand or by engines. In 1932, Marcel Duchamp coined the word "mobiles" to describe them.
Fish Bones belongs to this group and is totally in keeping with Calder's unique poetry of space. It conveys the harmony of a fragmented yet dynamic composition of weightless forms, which appear to be breathing in space •

1939

Fish Bones
Suspended mobile: sheet metal, painted metal rods and wires
207.2 × 192 × 137.1 cm
Accepted in lieu of tax, 1983 - AM 1983-57

Kurt Schwitters

1887, Hanover (Germany)
1948, Ambleide (United Kingdom) †

Kurt Schwitters played a major role in the Dada movement. In a country decimated by war, he salvaged odds and ends of all kinds and assembled them, going so far as to erect a total work of art in his home in Hanover: the *Merzbau*. This tentacular installation, which he constructed with no compunction about opening up the storeys, became the ideal venue for hosting Dadaist get-togethers. In order to avoid falling into the stylistic categorisations of traditional art criticism, in 1919 Schwitters began calling all his creations "Merz". This meaningless syllable, taken from a word he had cut out of a newspaper (Kommerzbank), signifies the repudiation of "isms", which, according to the artist, reflected disdain tainted with lack of understanding.
In 1933 Schwitters found himself obliged to move to Norway, where he continued to produce a number of collages out of disparate elements (photos from magazines, newspapers or scrap materials). *Prikken paa 1 en* features two leaves of a calendar, dated 15 and 16 November. They represent a direct reference to the outbreak of the Second World War. A photograph of a Luftwaffe commander and the split emblem of the Nazi eagle (bottom centre) conjure up the shadow of the drama unfolding. In the middle one can see Schwitter's Hanover address, which he had been forced to leave. This complex collage therefore encourages the eye to rove around, deciphering the elements that underpin the artist's visual testimonial •

1939

Prikken paa I en
[The Dot on the I]
Collage: graphite pencil, Conté pencil, gouache and paper cut-outs on painted plywood, pasted on to chipboard
75.5 × 91.8 cm
Accepted in lieu of tax, 1988 - AM 1988-653

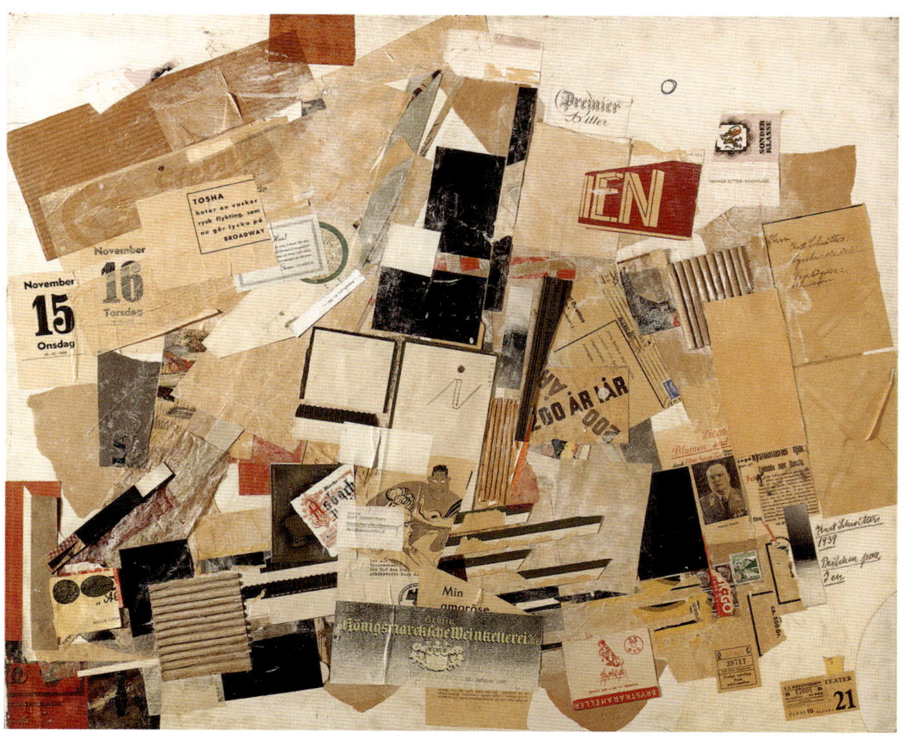

Pablo Picasso

1881, Málaga (Spain)
1973, Mougins (France) †

As the Second World War approached its mid-point, Picasso found refuge in his Paris studio in the rue des Grands Augustins, where he worked on *L'Aubade*. This complex and monumental composition, typical of his production under the Occupation, is profoundly marked by the historical circumstances: if he did not paint the war – "I am not the kind of painter who goes out, like a photographer, in search of a subject" – Picasso nonetheless gives expression in this work to danger, curfew, lack of freedom, the torture of those dark days. Initially, in May 1941, *L'Aubade* was another essay at the classic theme of the odalisque, a nude reclining in a bedroom, as painted by Titian, Ingres or Matisse. The preparatory drawings show that in August a second figure made its appearance, standing beside the bed. Then in May 1942, as Picasso moves the image on to the canvas, the anecdotal details disappear: lamp, carpet and mouldings are all gone, and the mood is radically transformed. The reclining odalisque is no more than a naked body, bloated and disjointed, lying as if dead on a hard bed. The contrast with the seated but upright woman playing the mandolin is striking: the sharp-featured musician has become a frightening jailer. The room is dark and enclosed, and everything contributes to a sense of confinement, violence and cruelty. Picasso would later offer this work to the Museum as an expression of his opposition to war •

1942

L'Aubade
[Dawn Serenade]
Oil on canvas
195 × 265 cm
Gift of the artist, 1947 - AM 2730 P

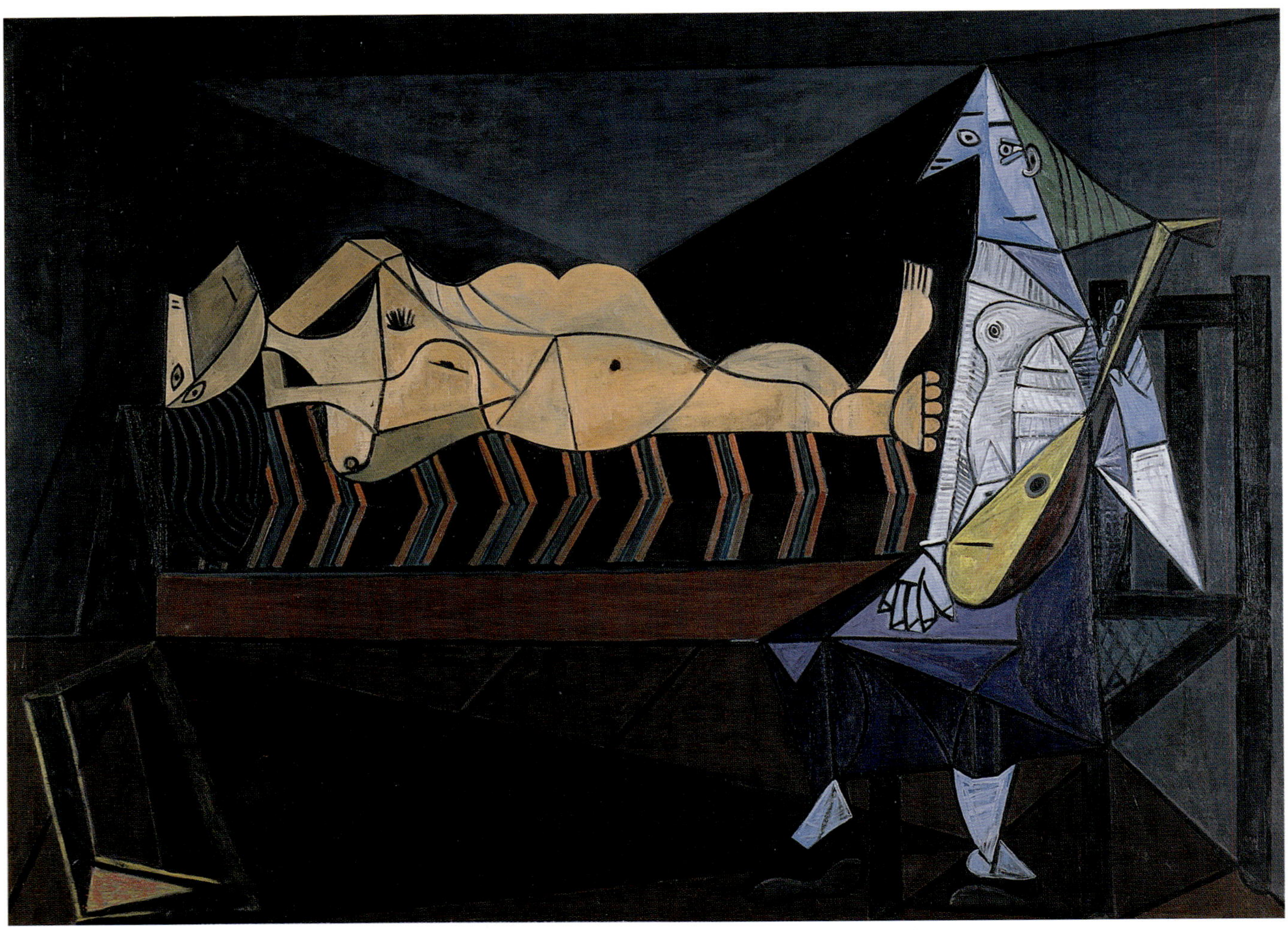

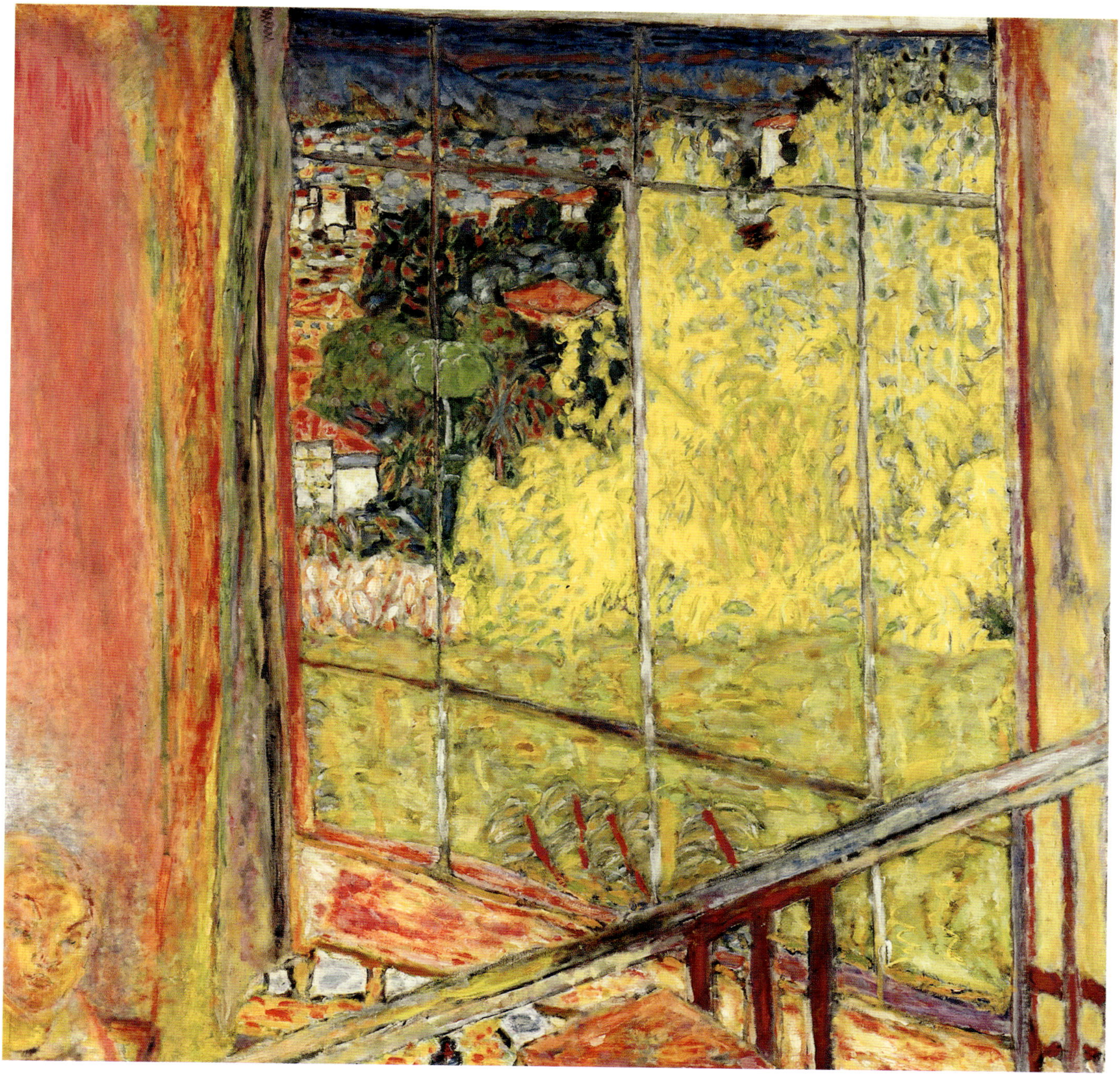

Pierre Bonnard

1867, Fontenay-aux-Roses (France)
1947, Le Cannet (France) †

L'Atelier au mimosa is one of the last of Bonnard's great works. Begun during the war and touched up in 1946, the painting depicts the heights of Cannes, which the artist could see from his modest studio in Le Cannet, where he settled in 1939. The high angle view and intersecting diagonals of the balustrade and window provide depth and create a dizzying effect, which the painter rectifies by introducing the face of his companion Marthe, who had died in 1942. The appearance of the mimosa is transformed into an abstract swathe of bright yellow, contrasting with the background, which features houses and hills, treated more precisely, in cold colours. Although reality seems easier to grasp and describe from a distance, here Bonnard wants to express his wonder at the proximity of nature and the immediate light of this intimate yet open space •

1939/1946

L'Atelier au mimosa
[Studio with Mimosa]
Oil on canvas
127.5 × 127.5 cm
Purchased 1979 - AM 1978-732

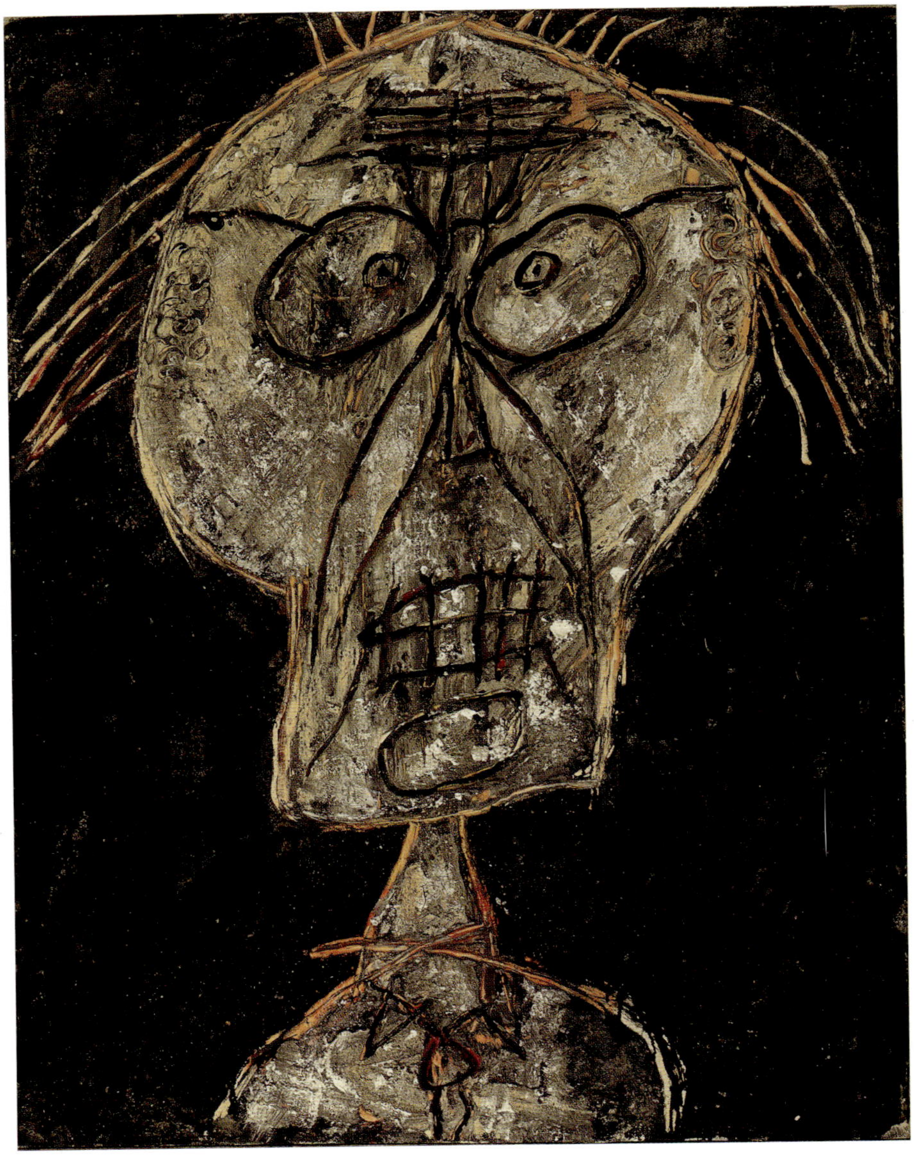

1947

Dhôtel nuancé d'abricot
[Dhôtel with a Tinge of Apricot]
Oil on canvas
116 × 89 cm
Purchased with the participation of the Scaler Foundation, 1981 - AM 1981-501

Jean Dubuffet

1901, Le Havre (France)
1985, Paris (France) †

Between 1917, when he enrolled in the École des Beaux Arts' evening classes in Le Havre, and 1942, when he decided to devote himself irrevocably to art, Dubuffet gave up painting and sculpture on two occasions, in order to earn a living, mainly by taking over his father's wine business. Shortly after his first solo exhibition, in October 1944, he began building up a collection of "art brut", devoted to works by people outside the professional artistic circuit, such as self-made men, people with a mental deviance and mediumnic painters. During this period, he also developed a lexicon which broke away from traditional pictorial conventions: elimination of perspective, succinct, almost childlike drawings, gouged into thick, earthy matters, reflecting "the urges and age-old spontaneity of the human hand when tracing signs". Between 1946 and 1947, Dubuffet thus portrayed his fellow-artists and writers. The portrait of André Dhôtel is one of the most striking. From beneath the traits, passionately incised into oil thickened with sand and gravel, a mesmerising, tender and ferocious effigy emerges. The portrait is devoid of any naturalist or psychological accuracy – to Dubuffet, a work had to stem from material and tool and render the individual's basic need for artistic expression •

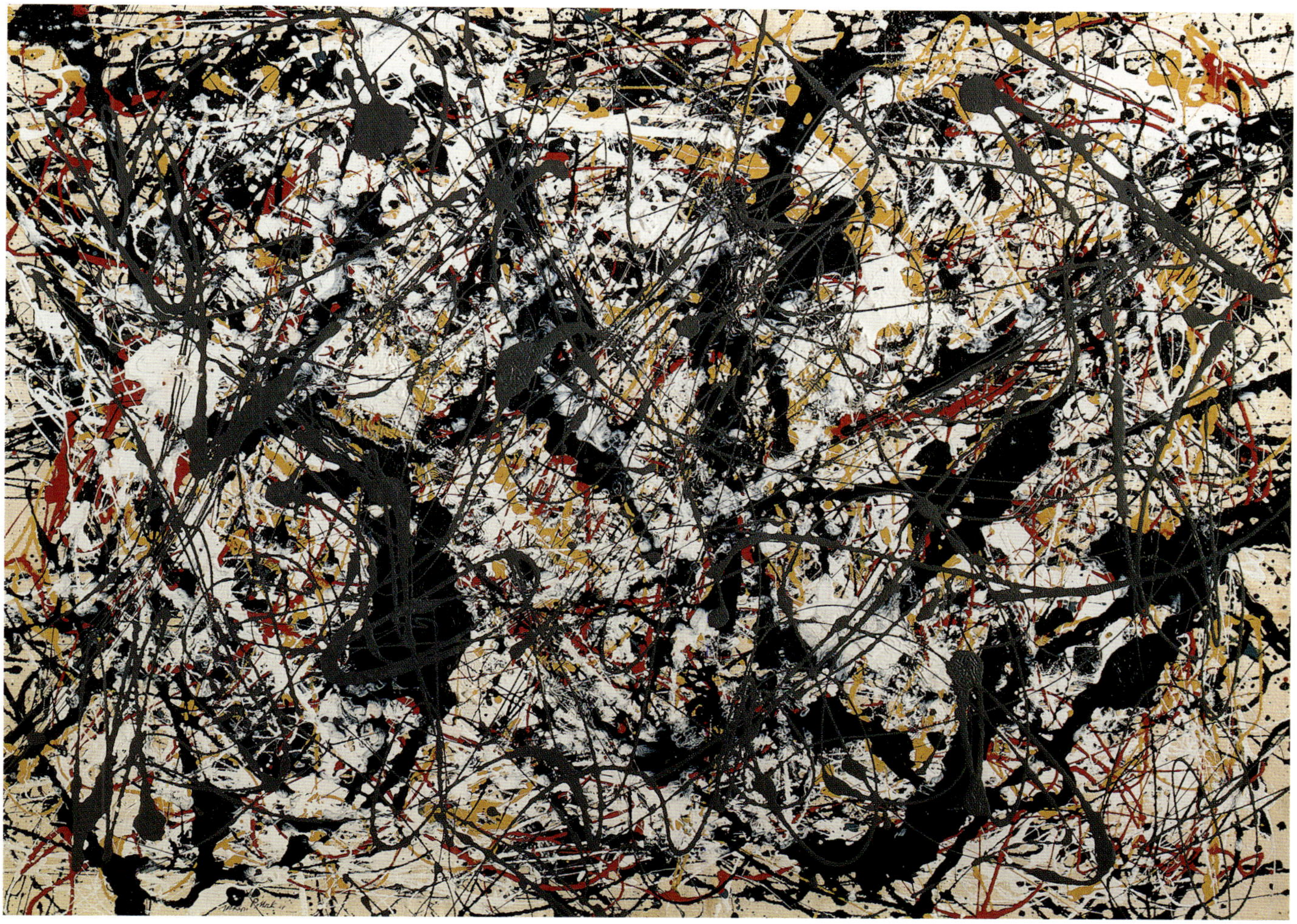

Jackson Pollock

1912, Cody, WY (United States)
1956, East Hampton, NY (United States) †

At first, Pollock developed an Expressionist art form, in which the subject-matter was often mythological. His signature European references at that time were Picasso, Miró and Masson. In the late 1940s, by combining their influence with those of the ground sand paintings made by the Navajo Indians, Pollock came up with his "dripping" technique. The painter would stand over a canvas stretched out across the floor and then throw paint as he moved quickly around it. The medium itself therefore bore the traces of this swift execution and violent gesture, in which matter was projected according to the inspiration of the moment. The entire surface was covered in a tracery of lines of varying thickness, in which form and content cancelled one another out. In each part of the picture a composition was therefore repeated, endlessly spilling out from the edges of the canvas.
This process, also known as Action Painting, does away with the need for depiction of any kind. It is the physical movement that triggers its own depiction, with the picture recording the trace of energy in progress. In these curious lines, from which the image has disappeared, a body of painting emerges, that of the painter at work. By applying his dripping technique, Pollock turns the canvas into an arena. It is no longer merely an image which is imprinted upon it, but an event, a moment in time •

1948

Painting (Silver over Black, White, Yellow and Red)

Paint on paper mounted on canvas
61 × 80 cm
Purchased 1972 - AM 1972-29

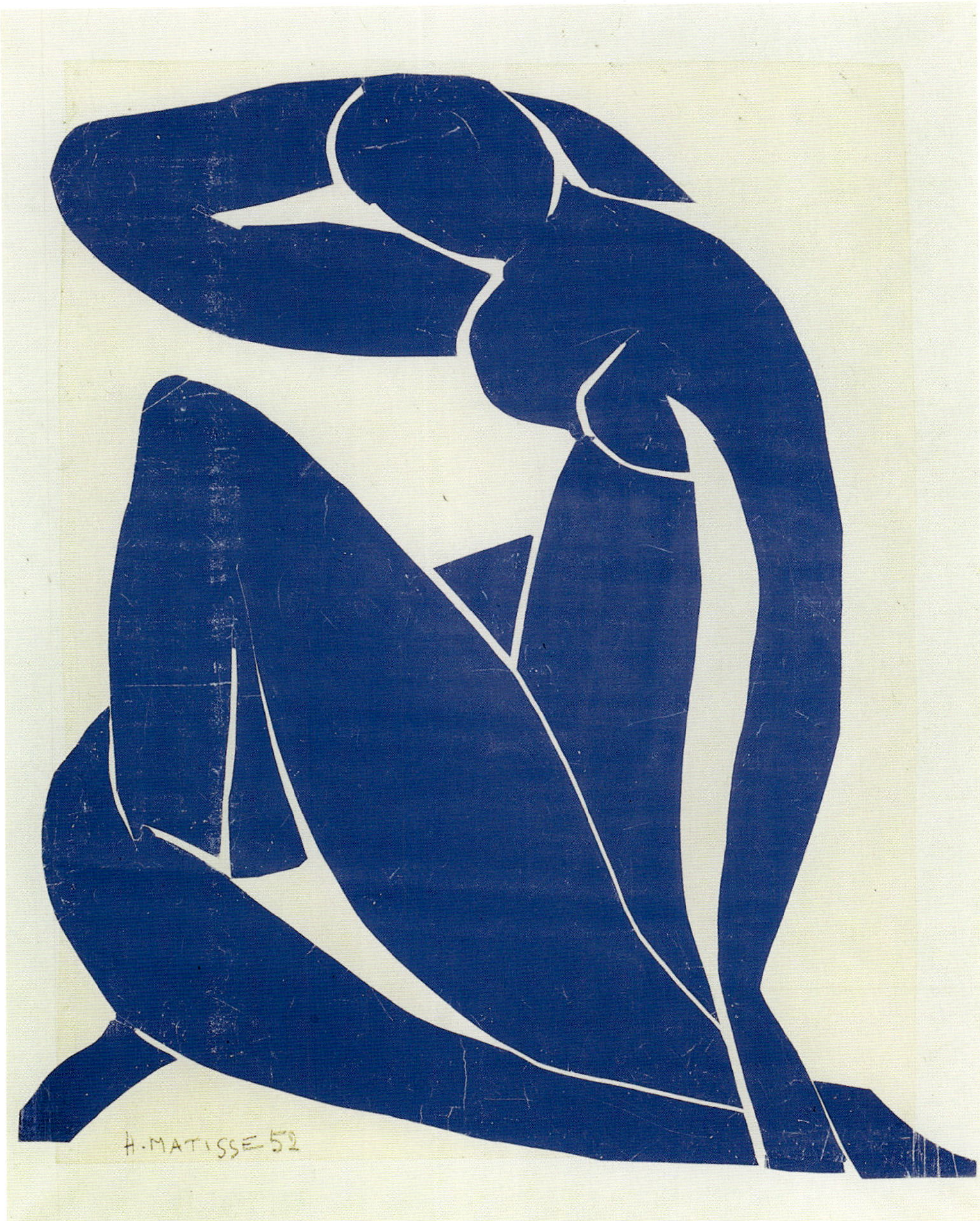

1952

Nu bleu II

[Blue Nude II]

Gouache on paper cut-outs, pasted and mounted on canvas
116.2 × 88.9 cm
Purchased 1984 – AM 1984-276

Henri Matisse

1869, Le Cateau-Cambrésis (France)
1954, Nice (France) †

At the beginning of the Second World War, Matisse sought refuge in the heights of Nice, before moving into his villa in Vence in 1943. Following his operation in 1941, which forced him to work lying down, he developed a new process. He would take the shapes he required to develop his compositions by "slicing into colour", cutting them out directly from large gouache-painted sheets of paper. This technique, used to produce his book *Jazz* (1943–1947), was also the basis for his stained-glass, ceramic tiles, furniture and liturgical garments in Vence Chapel, a project that is considered to be his pictorial and spiritual testament. This experience brought him closer to Biblical themes, as *La Tristesse du Roi* illustrates. The work combined a number of inspirational sources, such as *The Song of Songs* or the scene featuring Salome dancing

1952

La Tristesse du roi
[The King's Sadness]
Gouache on paper cut-outs, pasted and mounted on canvas
292 × 386 cm; Purchased by the State, 1954; attribution, 1954 - AM 3279 P

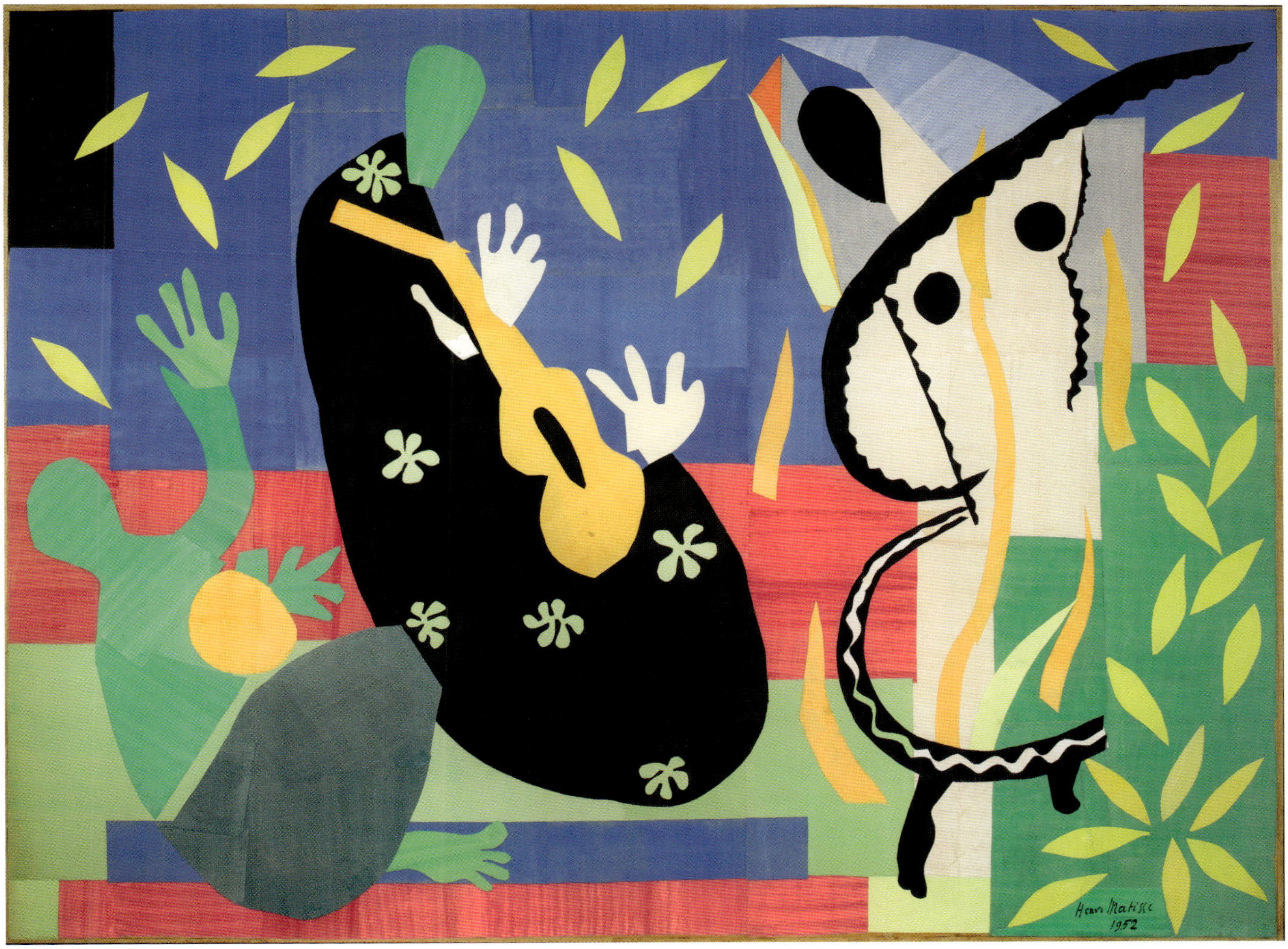

before Herod. Its main reference, however, was to Rembrandt's *David Playing the Harp before Saul*, with Matisse taking up the theme of the young Biblical hero trying to distract the king from his misery through music. Behind its jubilatory appearance, this monumental composition really stems from a reflection on age and memory, a final portrait in which the painter seems to be depicted within the black form, surrounded by the pleasures that enriched his life: music, the great soother, dance, the female body and the Orient •

It was also in 1952 that Matisse cut out his four seated nudes, including this *Nu bleu II*. Preceded in 1951 by pencil and ink drawings, here the silhouettes were cut out in a single scissor movement, each on a different day, from blue gouached paper – blue epitomising for Matisse the colour of volume and distance. The four figures adopt the same pose, arms draped behind the neck and legs drawn up, a position the artist had already depicted on several occasions. The gaps indicating the joints of the body, whilst unifying the fragmented parts with their contours, allow slivers of air and light to filter through. These give *Nu bleu II* the effect of being in the round, enabling the figure to meld with its background on one and the same plane. By filling the whole sheet, which is only just big enough to contain it, the nude also takes on a monumental dimension •

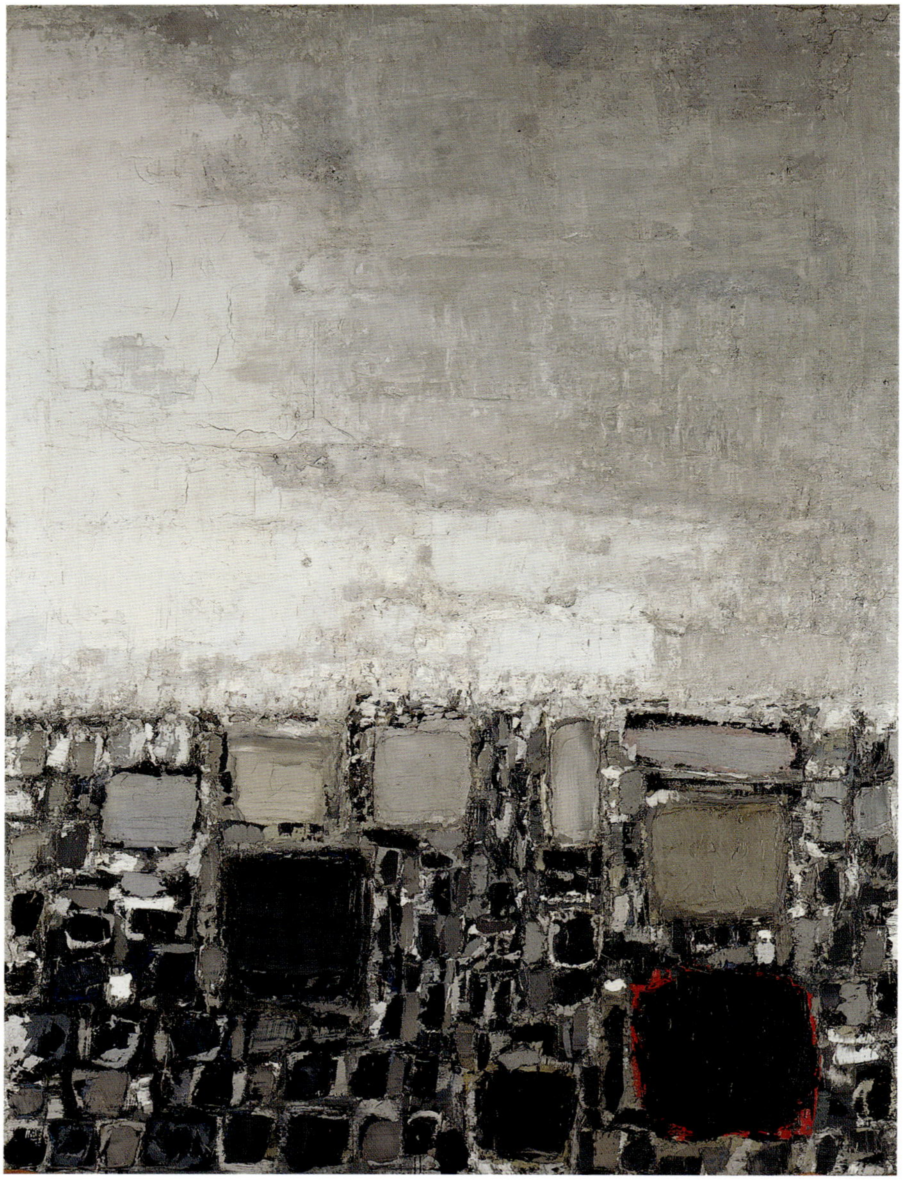

1952

Les Toits
[The Roofs]
Oil on Isorel
200 × 150 cm
Donated to the State by the artist, 1952; attribution, 1952 - AM 3159 P

Nicolas de Staël

(born Nikolai Vladimirovich Staël von Holstein)

1914, St. Petersburg (Russia)
1955, Antibes (France) †

Nicolas de Staël was exiled from Russia with his family in 1919 but orphaned soon afterwards. He was brought up by friends in Brussels, where he went on to study art. His trip to Morocco in 1936, which inspired him to paint from life, was a seminal experience. He spent part of the war living in Nice and it was there that his art gravitated towards abstraction. De Staël then moved to Paris, where he held his first solo exhibition in 1944. Following the death of his companion in 1946, he sought refuge in painting. In 1952, however, at the peak of his abstract period (1949–1951), *Les Toits* saw him veering towards a form of figurative art. The other titles given to this work (*Le Ciel de Dieppe* and *Les Toits de Paris*) pay specific reference to the skies of Northern France and the roofs the painter could see from his studio. As always, the artist brought his imagination into play and rewrote the motif in his own way. Within this unremittingly frontal composition, he opposed a great, significantly nuanced field with a "wall" made up of simple rectangles of varying sizes, like solid masonry tiles trowelled in the thick impasto. The duality between the two surfaces underscores the verticality of the medium. Below the upper section of the painting, which illustrates the painter's predilection for vast horizons and vanishing spaces, the roofs with their subtle, contained hues vibrate with a thudding, melancholic energy •

1953

Le Peintre de la tour Eiffel
[The Eiffel Tower Painter]
Gelatin silver print
30.3 × 20.4 cm (excl. margins)
Purchased 1981 - AM 1981-872

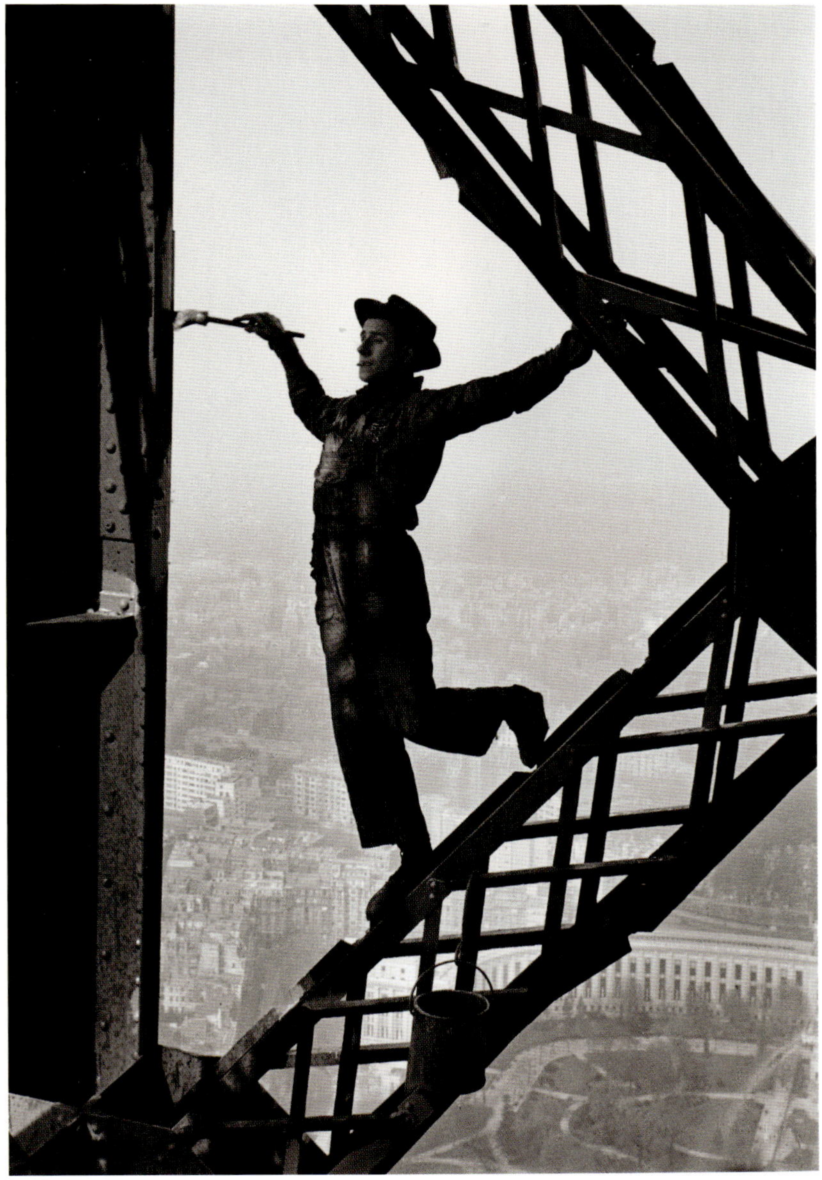

Marc Riboud

1923, Lyon (France)

In 1937, the young Marc Riboud took his first photographs at the Universal Exhibition in Paris, using the Vest-Pocket he had received as a fourteenth birthday present. In 1944 he took part in the Resistance battles of the Vercors and the following year was admitted to the École centrale de Lyon. In 1951, having taken a week off to photograph the Lyon Festival, the young engineer decided to change career and devote himself to photography.

Le Peintre de la Tour Eiffel is one of his most emblematic pictures. This is not really a portrait – he has captured an unexpected moment of grace. At dizzying altitude, brush in hand, the craftsman (known as Zazou) appears to be dancing between the bolted beams of the sturdy metal structure. The poetry of this instant forms a delightful contrast with the geometric forms of the armature. The incongruous seems somehow to be wrong-footing this symbol of the modern age. To Riboud, "Beauty is everywhere. As is strangeness..." One just needs to "watch for the surprise element, the right, quirky or moving note."

In 1953, the photographer joined Magnum, becoming a "committed" photojournalist, tirelessly scouring the world (India, China, Vietnam, the United States, the Middle East) and recording events such as the Cultural Revolution and the anti-Nixon and anti-Vietnam demonstrations, as he waited for inner truth to rise to "the surface of things" •

[1950-1952]

Woman

Graphite pencil and pastel on paper
37.3 × 29.3 cm
Accepted in lieu of tax, 1995 - AM 1995-176

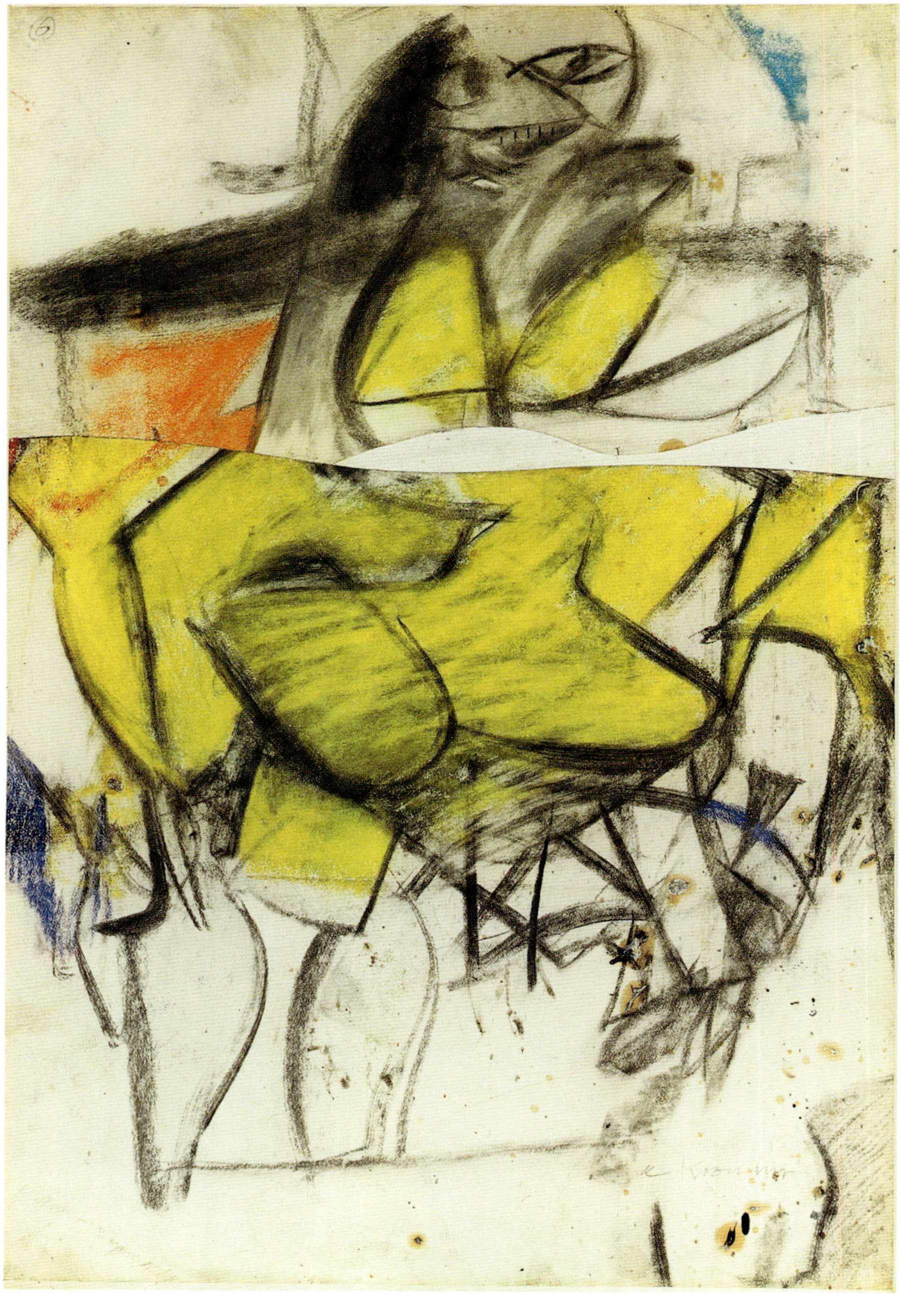

Willem De Kooning

1904, Rotterdam (Netherlands)
1997, East Hampton, NY (United States)) †

De Kooning studied art in Rotterdam before emigrating to the United States in 1926. He worked as a house painter and window display designer for over ten years before taking up painting full-time. Influenced by Picasso, as well as the Surrealists Gorky and Matta – who had also moved to New York – the artist developed a form of non-figurative action painting that was emblematic of post-war American art. People were taken aback, therefore, not to say scandalised, when De Kooning returned to figurative art in 1952, with his series entitled "Women".

This drawing belongs to the first series of women, structured by vigorous strokes which sweep across the surface of the paper. By implying the figures with broad charcoal lines and then blurring them by covering, cut-outs or transfer, the painter introduced destruction into the creative process. This explains the dislocated figure split in two, with the parts re-assembled, leaving an ostensibly visible piece missing.

In his relentless excavation of the material body, De Kooning refused to differentiate between drawing and painting: "I draw as I paint and I don't know the difference between painting and drawing." The force of the gesture and sweeps of violent colour lend a brutal air to these "vociferous, ferocious idols", soon to be succeeded by vast "composition-landscapes" •

1954

Sculpture méta-mécanique automobile

Iron, painted sheet metal, winder
134 × 79 × 56
Purchased 1981 - AM 1981-507

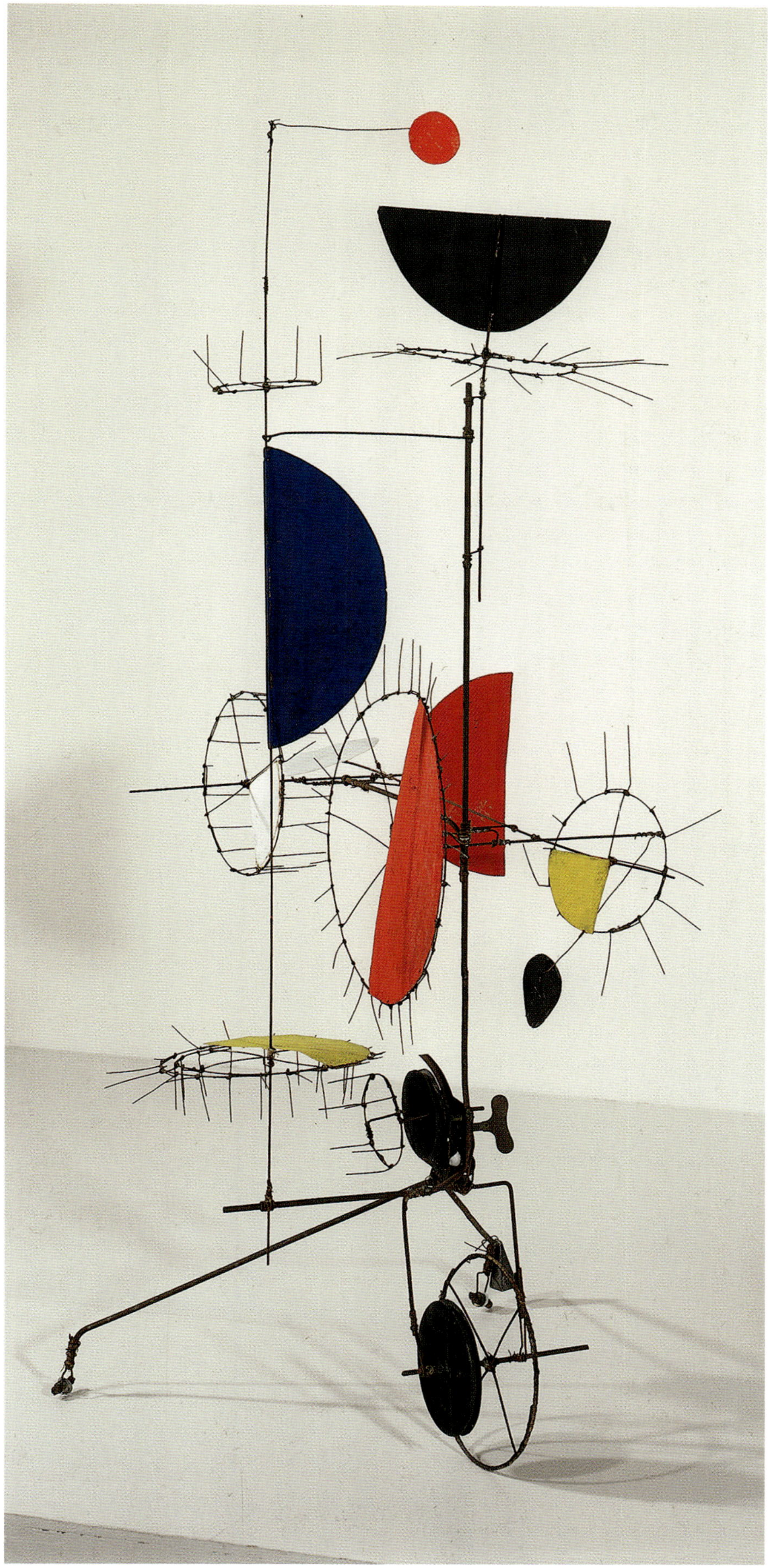

Jean Tinguely

1925, Fribourg (Switzerland)
1991, Berne (Switzerland)

Following his studies at the École des Arts Décoratifs in Basle, Jean Tinguely moved in 1953 to Paris, where he met fellow-artists equally keen to integrate movement into their works. The following year, the Swiss artist exhibited his “Reliefs”, conceived like mobile abstract pictures, and his first wire “Sculptures méta-mécaniques automobiles”, whose dentated wheels could be activated either by braces, as here, or by engines. Their ‘DIY’ aspect forms a humorous contrast with the geometric shapes in primary colours, which conjure up abstract painting. This sculpture asks no more than to spring around gleefully in space, producing random compositions in accordance with its movements. Indeed it formed part of the exhibition “Le Mouvement” at the Denise René gallery in 1955, which consecrated kinetic art.
In the wake of these machines, Tinguely presented his drawing machines, the “Méta-Matics”, at the Paris Biennial in 1959. The machines, once again parodying abstract painting, sought to prove that a work of art in itself can generate its own creations •

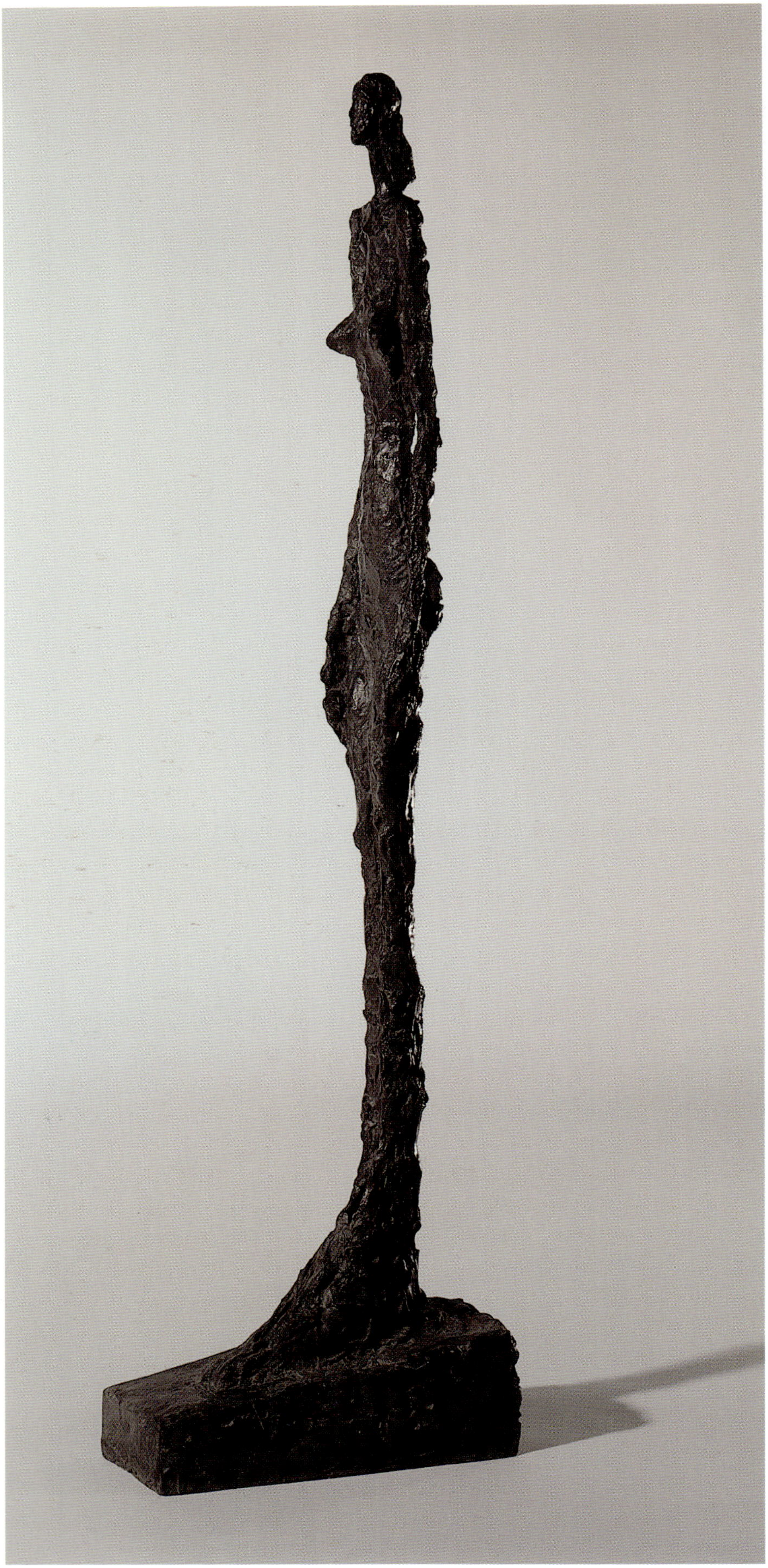

← 1956

Femme de Venise V
[Woman of Venice V]
Bronze; cast for the Venice Biennial in June 1956;
110.5 × 31.3 × 14 cm
Accepted in lieu of tax, 1991 - AM 1991-301

Alberto Giacometti

1901, Stampa (Switzerland)
1966, Coire (Switzerland) †

Giacometti, who was excluded by the Surrealists in 1935 on the grounds of his return to figurative art, went through a fairly long period of isolation and doubt, which lasted until 1947. His portrayals of occasionally fragmented human beings illustrated a recurrent obsession: to render the reality of a body both animated by life and frozen in its materiality as object. To Giacometti, every living creature was subject to a dual vision – through the breath of life or of a corpse. The excessive elongation of the body and the reduction of human form, which characterised his art from the 1950s, play on this ambivalence and appear to be throwing down the gauntlet in the face of so-called realist depictions. By its hieratic stance and nudity, this *Femme de Venise* also calls to mind a divinity, or else a being from another world. The silhouette with its oversized feet firmly embedded in the ground and exaggeratedly spindly body, as though eroded by the space surrounding it, is typical of the artist's aesthetic creed of disappearance. His residual beings, which are no less imposing for that, were to find an echo in Existentialism, achieving international recognition through the staunch support of Jean-Paul Sartre among others •

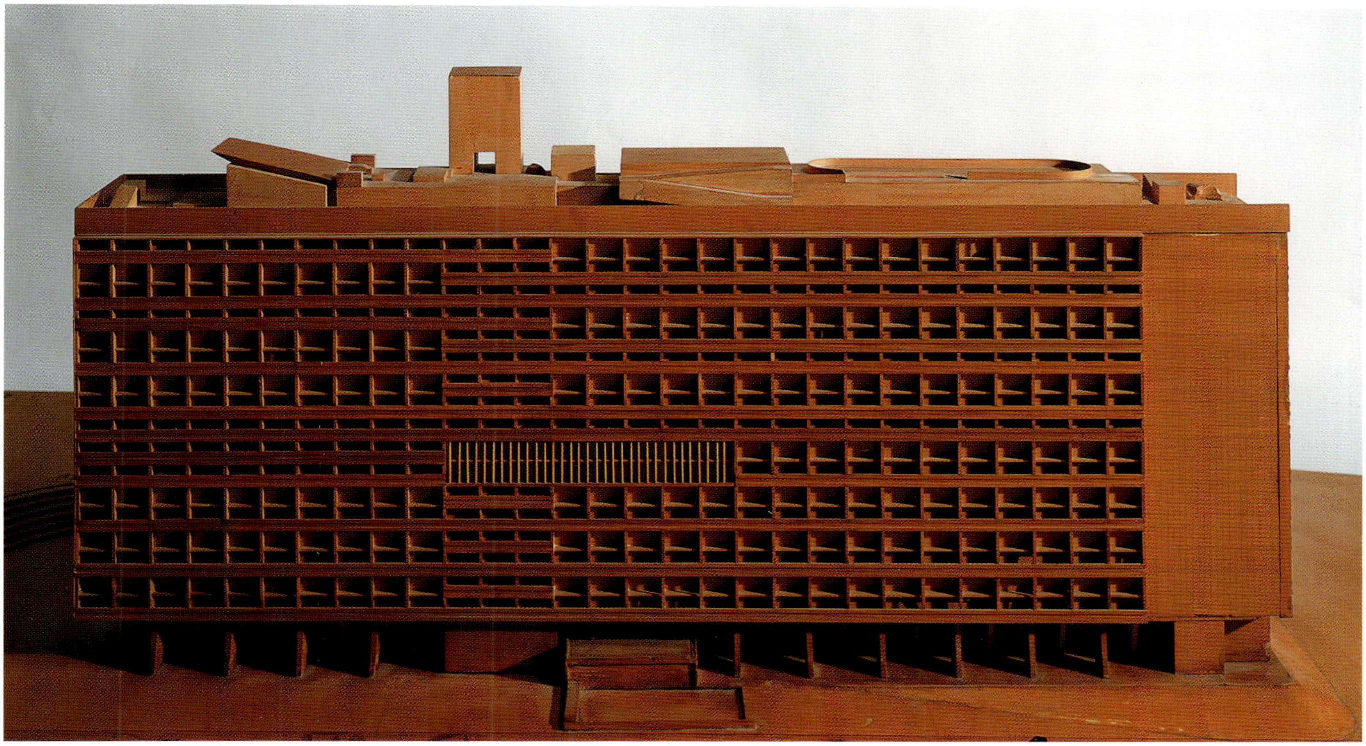

Le Corbusier

(born Charles Édouard Jeanneret)

1887, La Chaux-de-Fonds (Switzerland))
1965, Roquebrune-Cap-Martin (France) †

For the 1957 International Exhibition of Architecture in Berlin, Le Corbusier was commissioned to build a housing unit near the Tiergarten, which was intended as the cutting-edge culmination of its predecessor in Marseille (1945–1952). In order to tackle the architectural, urban and human problems of collective housing from a new angle, this unique device integrated the main functions of communal living into a single vertical unit, implementing the concepts formulated by the architect, town planner, painter and theoretician back in 1922. Erected on stilts to free up the open space at the foot of the building, the Berlin unit comprised four hundred apartments with balconies, an indoor shopping mall and community services (post office, crèche, arts centres) at roof terrace level. Despite Le Corbusier's vehement protestations, however, anarchic initiatives on the part of the property developers led to modifications in the layout, implementation and technical execution. The double height in the living-rooms of the split-level apartments was removed, the communal areas reduced to a launderette, the bas-reliefs on the wooden panels of the balconies replaced by a concrete guard and metal window, an electrical generator built between the stilts... The outraged Le Corbusier dissociated himself from the final result. The Museum's scale model represents the original version •

Ca 1955-1960

Unité d'habitation, Berlin-Tiergarten
[Housing Unit]

Berlin-Tiergarten, ca 1955–1960
Scale model; wood and miscellaneous materials
45 × 90 × 122 cm
Purchased 1994 - AM 1994-1-1

Ben

(born Benjamin Vautier)

| 1935, Naples (Italy)

A follower of Marcel Duchamp's philosophy and an advocate of Fluxus, Ben is keen to reduce the gulf between life and art, working on the premise that "all is art". In 1960 he began to "sign everything", going so far as to put himself on show in the form of a living sculpture (*Regardez-moi, cela suffit*, 1962). From then on, the ego was to become a pivotal element in his artistic approach. Slightly earlier, in 1958, the artist had opened a shop in Nice. His junk shop licence allowed him to buy and sell records, cameras and other second-hand goods. He was soon to exhibit works by artists such as Robert Filliou or La Monte Young on the mezzanine of his small shop, which became a forum for exchange, debate and publications, drawing among others proponents of the New Realism and Supports/Surfaces movements. Little by little, a juxtaposition of the most eclectic elements were placed there, transforming the venue into a sculpture, a work-in-progress, which Ben termed "N'importe quoi" [Any Old Thing]. When the shop was dismantled in 1972, the Museum purchased it, leaving the artist free to reconvert it and bring it back to life in its new environment •

1958-1973

Le Magasin de Ben
[Ben's Shop]
Miscellaneous materials
350 × 500 × 350 cm
Purchased 1975 - AM 1975-185

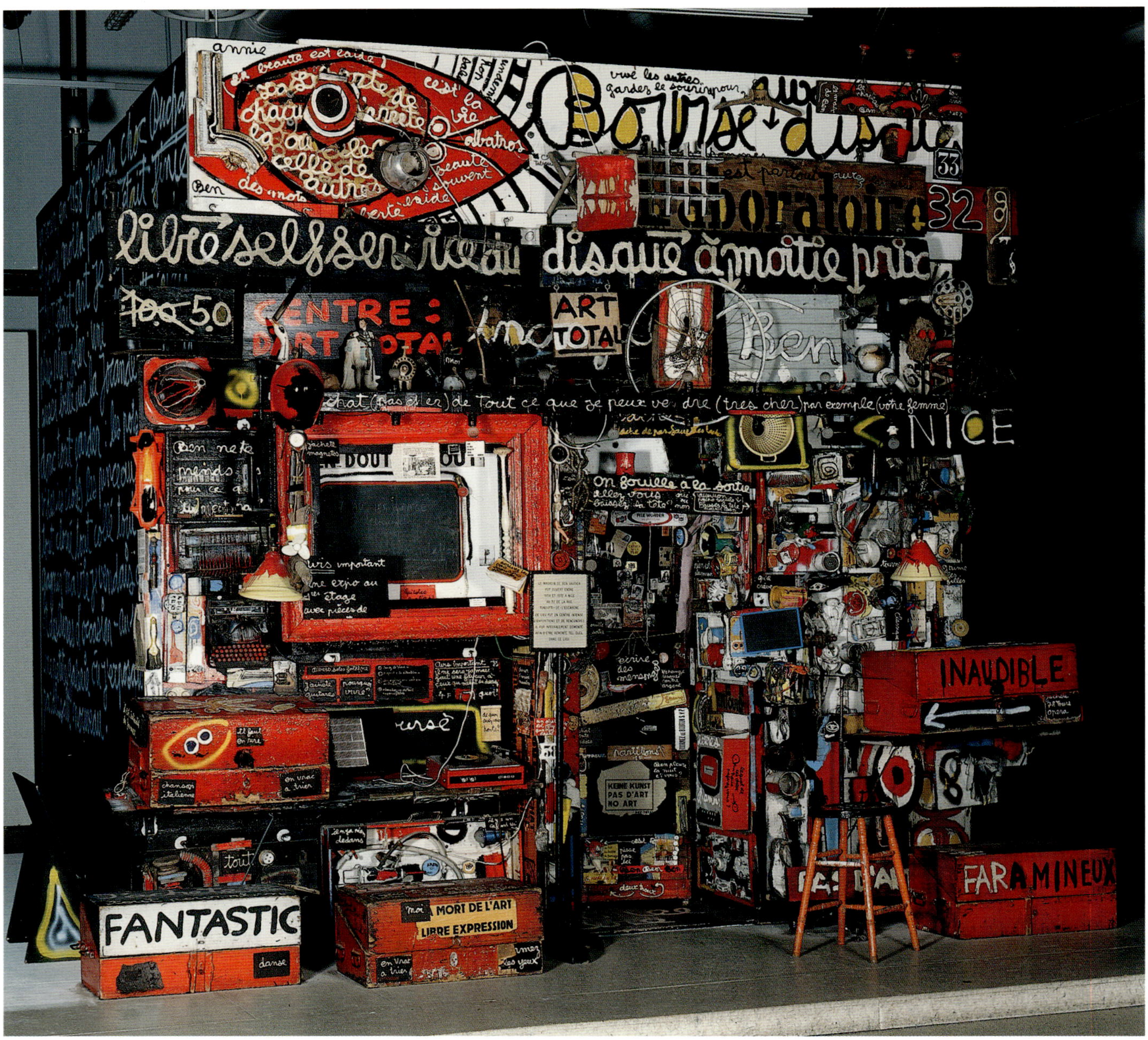

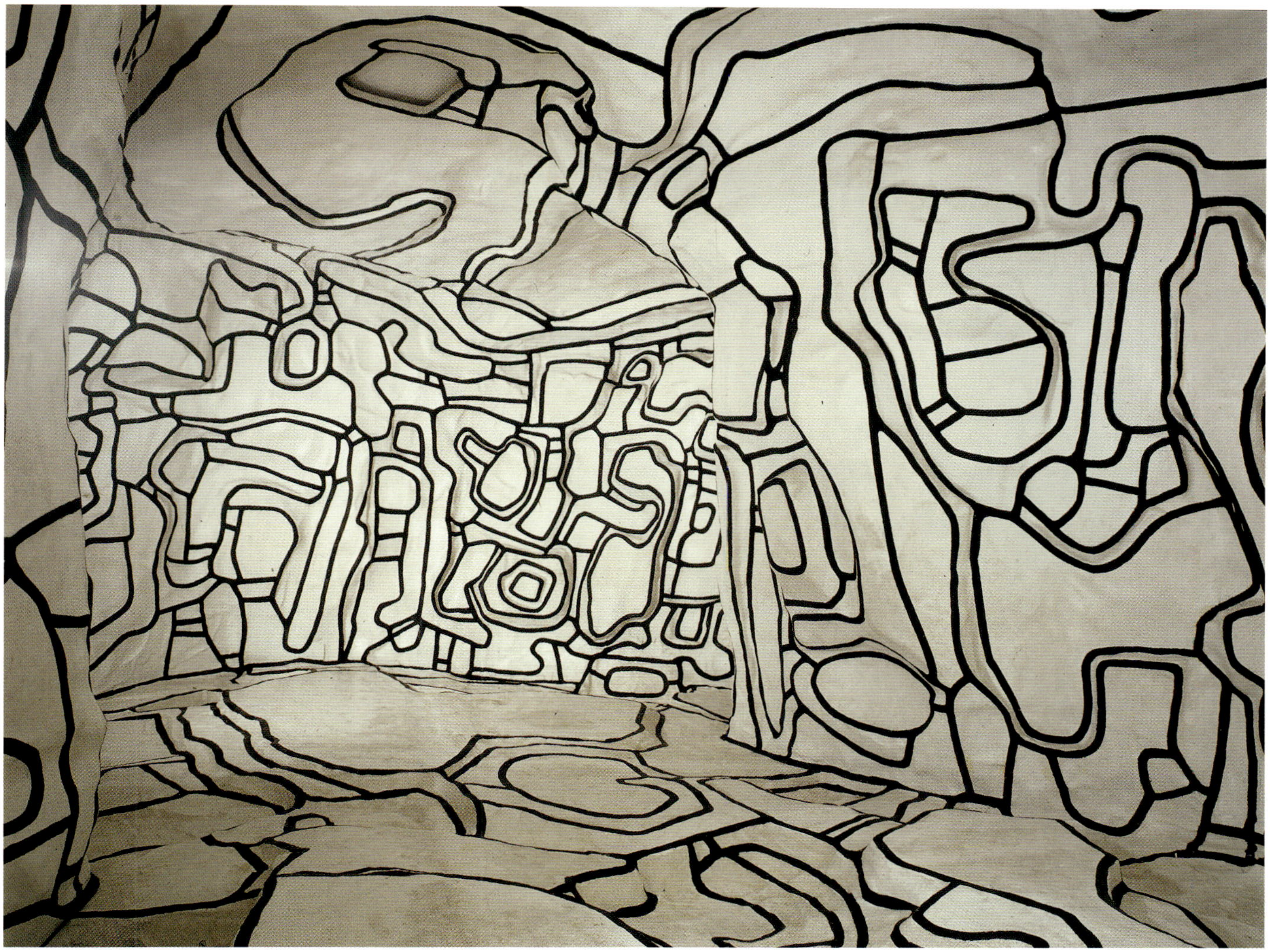

Jean Dubuffet

1901, Le Havre (France)
1985, Paris (France) †

Jardin d'hiver belongs to the "L'Hourloupe" cycle Dubuffet began in 1962, its larger-than-life characters structured like so many hatched cells. The ramifications of "L'Hourloupe" led Dubuffet to glide from painting to sculpture and on to architecture. Totally alien to the natural world evoked by its title, *Jardin d'hiver* takes the form of a curious cabin, its open door encouraging the viewer to step inside. Once there, however, getting around proves far from easy. The uneven floor and black lines, alternately accentuating and negating the reliefs, make it necessary to move with caution. It takes time, indeed, to come to terms with this new environment, where time, space and perception are called into question. It is reality itself that the artist is challenging; the viewer visiting this *Jardin d'hiver* is somehow caught up in the nets of painting. This unstable universe upturns the certainties of our physical perception and takes issue with our normal perception of the world •

1968-1970

Jardin d'hiver
[Winter Garden]
Polyurethane on epoxy
480 × 960 × 55C
Purchased by the State, 1973; attribution, 1977 - AM 1977-251

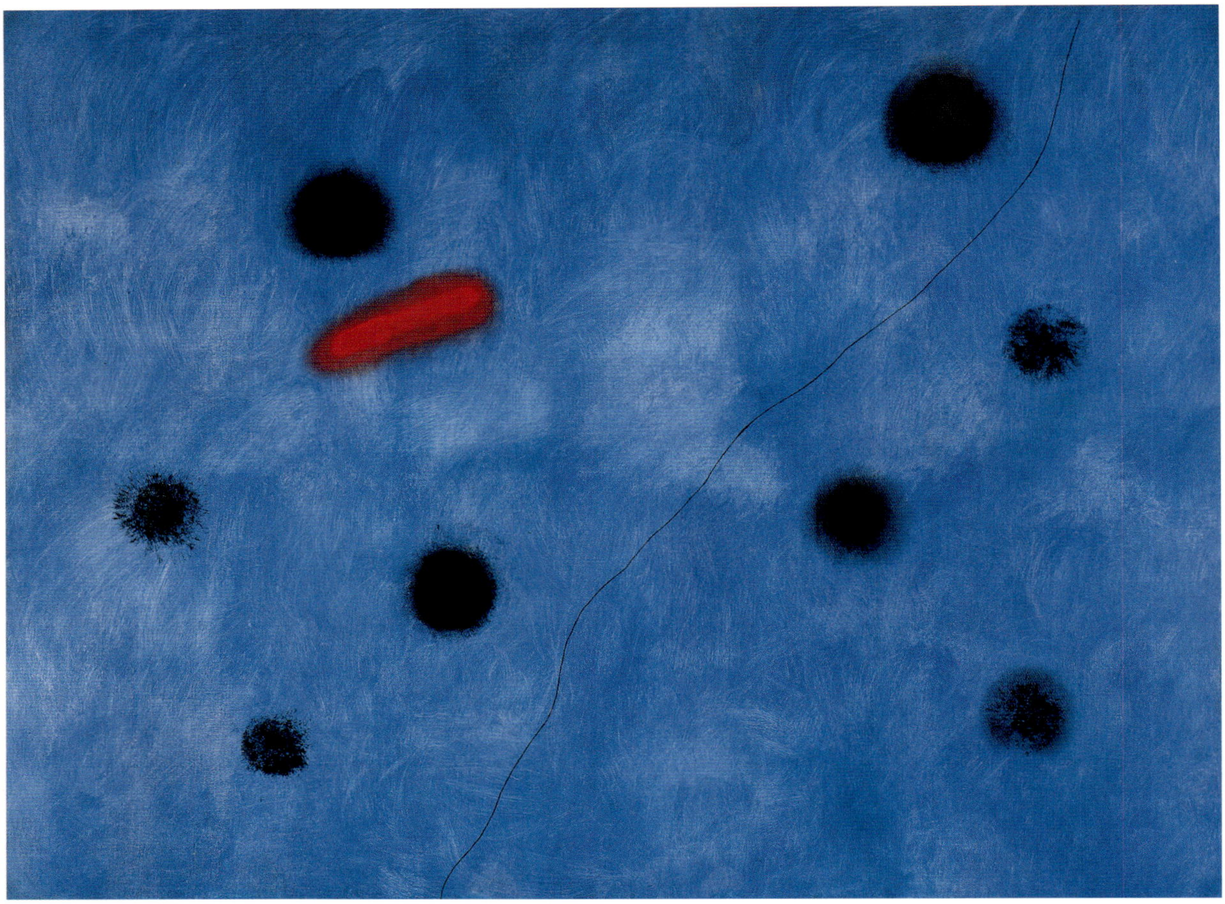

1961

Bleu I
Oil on canvas; 270 × 355 cm
Purchased in memory of Dominique Bozo, with the contribution of the Fonds du Patrimoine, the help of Sylvie and Éric Boissonas, Jacques Boissonas, Hélène and Michel David-Weill, the Société des Amis du Musée national d'art moderne, Pierre Bergé, Yves Saint Laurent, the Maison Yves Saint Laurent and the participation of numerous subscribers, 1993 - AM 1993-119

Bleu II
Oil on canvas; 270 × 355 cm
Gift of the Menil Foundation in memory of Jean de Menil, 1984 - AM 1984-357

Bleu III
Oil on canvas
268 × 355 cm
Purchased 1988 - AM 1988-569

Joan Miró

1893, Barcelona (Spain)
1983, Palma de Mallorca (Spain) †

The triptych *Bleu I, II* and *III* marked the culmination of Miró's plastic and poetic research. The artist's move to his new studio in Palma de Mallorca in 1956 enabled him to give full rein to these colourful pictograms. The more spacious premises and the probable influence of the large formats employed by American painters were conducive to this change of scale. Executed between December 1960 and March 1961, these three pictures stem from the monumental transposition on to canvas of some tiny preparatory sketches he had scrawled on bits of paper over the months. The brushed, airy, vibrant blue determines an infinite spatial field studded with signs. The dots, lines and gashes, arising from a lengthy process of mystical reflection, range from the distinct to the nebulous and capture the slightest gestural nuances. "[The great blue canvases] took a lot of time to do. Not the actual painting, the meditation. To achieve the paring-down I wanted implied [...] tremendous nervous tension. The initial stage was of a more intellectual nature [...]. I was inwardly preparing myself." These three pictures, with their free-flowing forms, acquire a universal dimension here, encouraging contemplation and exuding an intense feeling of bliss •

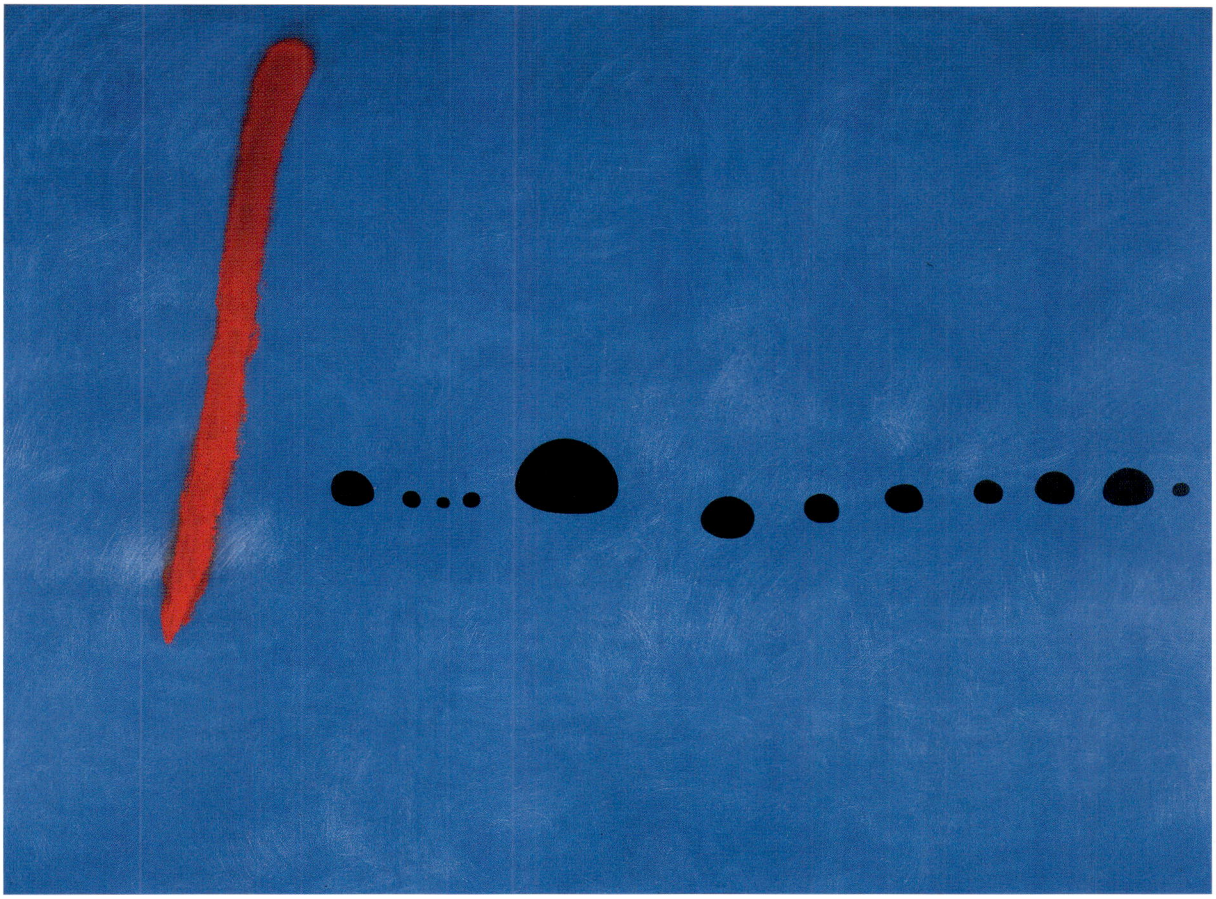

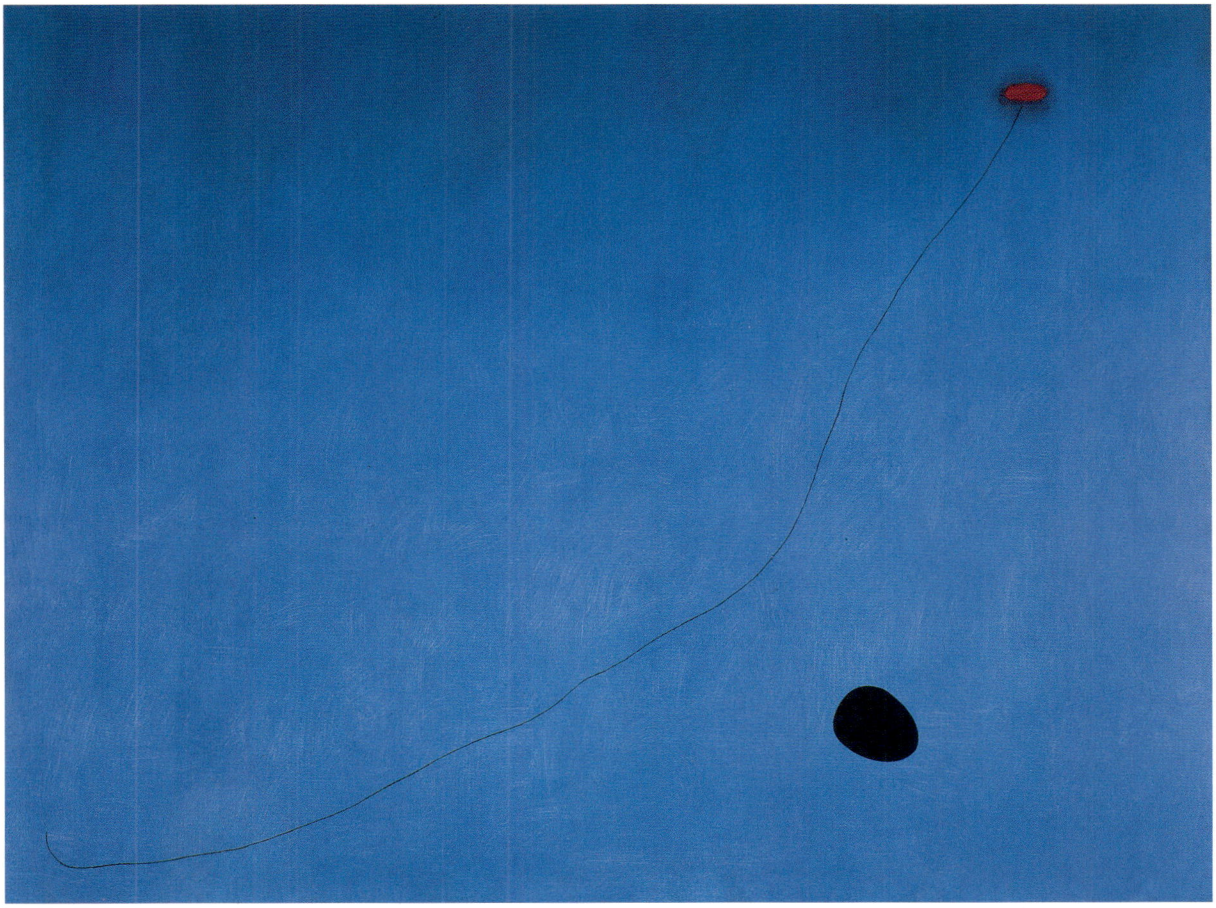

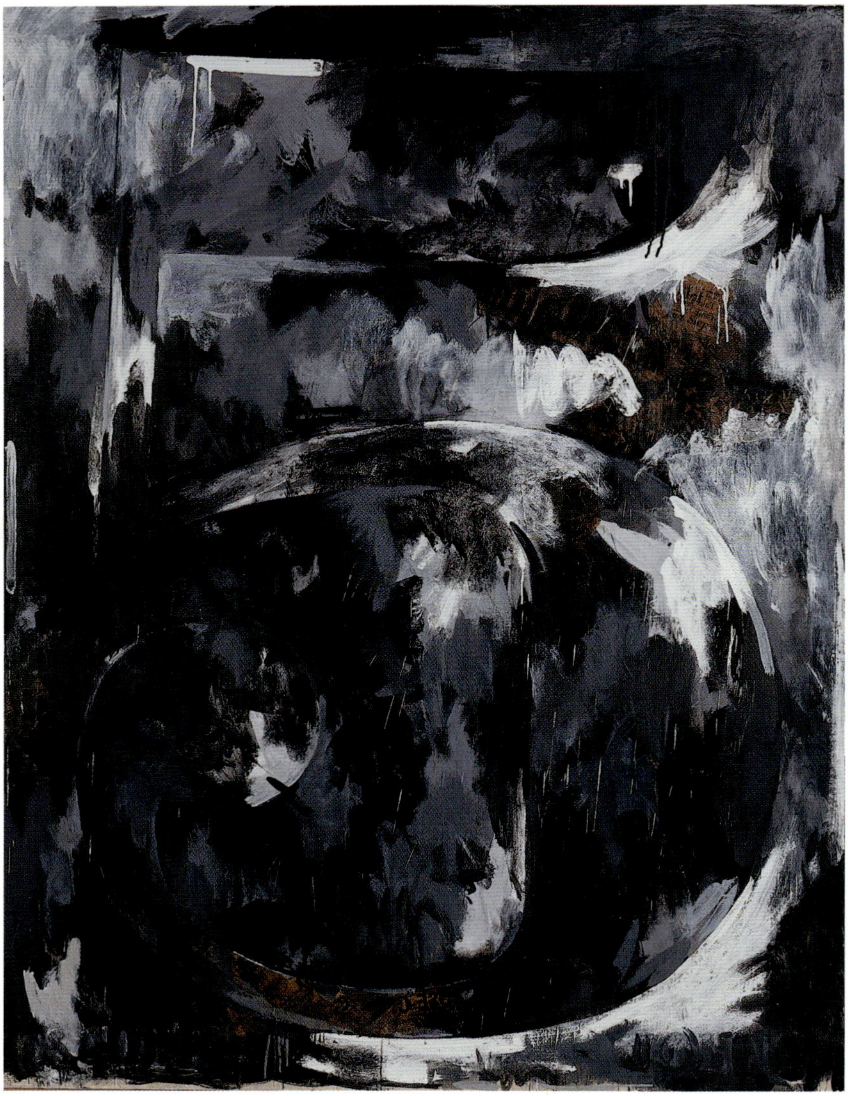

1960

Figure 5

Encaustic painting and newspaper pasted on canvas
183 × 137.5 cm
Gift of the Scaler Foundation, 1976 - AM 1976-2

Jasper Johns

1930, Augusta, GA (United States)

Jasper Johns studied Fine Arts in South Carolina before moving to New York in the late 1940s. In 1954, he got to know several artists from the Black Mountain College, notably Robert Rauschenberg. His encaustic paintings, depicting flags, targets, alphabets and numbers, date from that period. These were all bi-dimensional motifs, conventional and non-natural in origin, and shared the particularity of existing as planes before being turned into pictorial images. John's technique, which makes it easy to spot the multiple layers, lends substance to the mere planeness of the subject-matter.

The choice of familiar imagery, "things the spirit already knows", enables him to question the actual purpose of painting.
The large figure 5 is rendered in broad white, grey and black strokes, which cancel out all hierarchy between figure and background and allow glimpses of the newspaper pasted on to the canvas. As is often the case with Jasper Johns, the choice of a motif relating to a universally recognised sign does not have any hidden agenda. As a simple painting object, the number 5 seems to epitomise the transition between the Abstract Expressionist art that had developed in the United States during the post-war years and the conceptual strategies that were to dominate the Sixties •

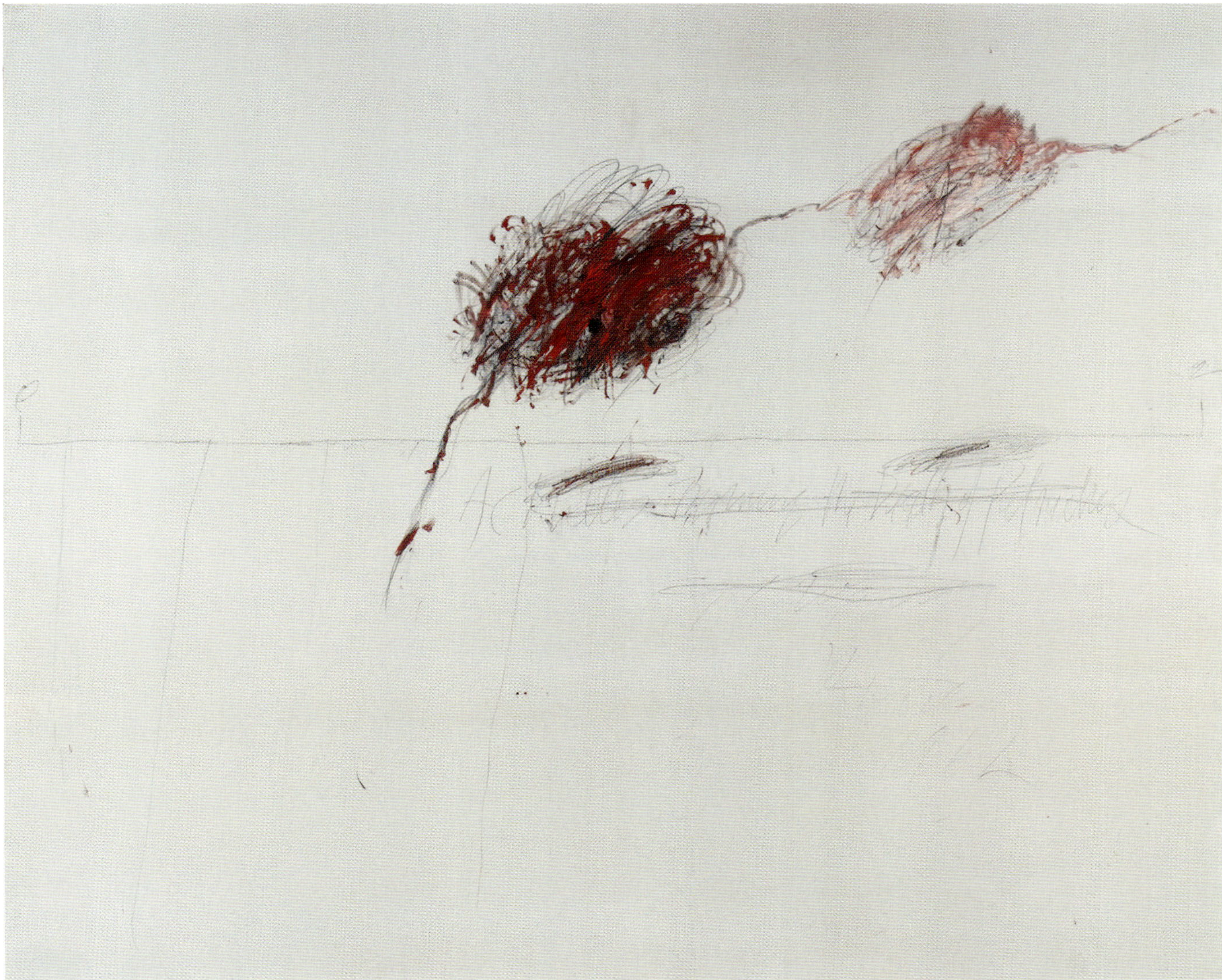

Cy Twombly

1928, Lexington, VA (United States)

Twombly's art, with its inimitable signs or lines hastily thrown on to the surface of the pictorial field, belongs to the tradition of American Abstract Expressionism that prevailed in the 1950s. Twombly stands out from his peers, however, in his contemporary yet personal dialogue with the past. His art makes abundant references to the Greek and Latin roots of Western culture and to the seminal myths of European culture, which the artist knows only too well. He started travelling around Europe in the 1950s, with Rome becoming his city of predilection.
His spirited scoring technique, as impulsive as it is vigorous, blurs the divide between drawing and painting, distinguishing itself from pure abstraction and reflecting on the visible, the legible and on writing.
In the early 1960s, the artist turned to the theme of death, with particular reference to the Homeric epic. The scene from the *Iliad* which caught Twombly's attention here is the one in which Achilles is mourning the death of his friend Patroclus, who was killed when he took Achilles' place in the Trojan war. This ghastly but emblematic example of Homeric heroism is rendered with a remarkable economy of means.
Just two red shapes – two stains of Twombly's typically sublime and bloodthirsty pictorial "dirtiness" – and the scrawled-out inscription implying the presence of a body dominate the imposing pictorial field, with a violence that is at once restrained and extreme •

1962

Achilles Mourning the Death of Patroclus

Cil, lead pencil on canvas
259 × 302 cm
Purchased with the support of the Fonds du Patrimoine and the Société des Amis du Musée national d'art moderne, 2005 - AM 2005-24

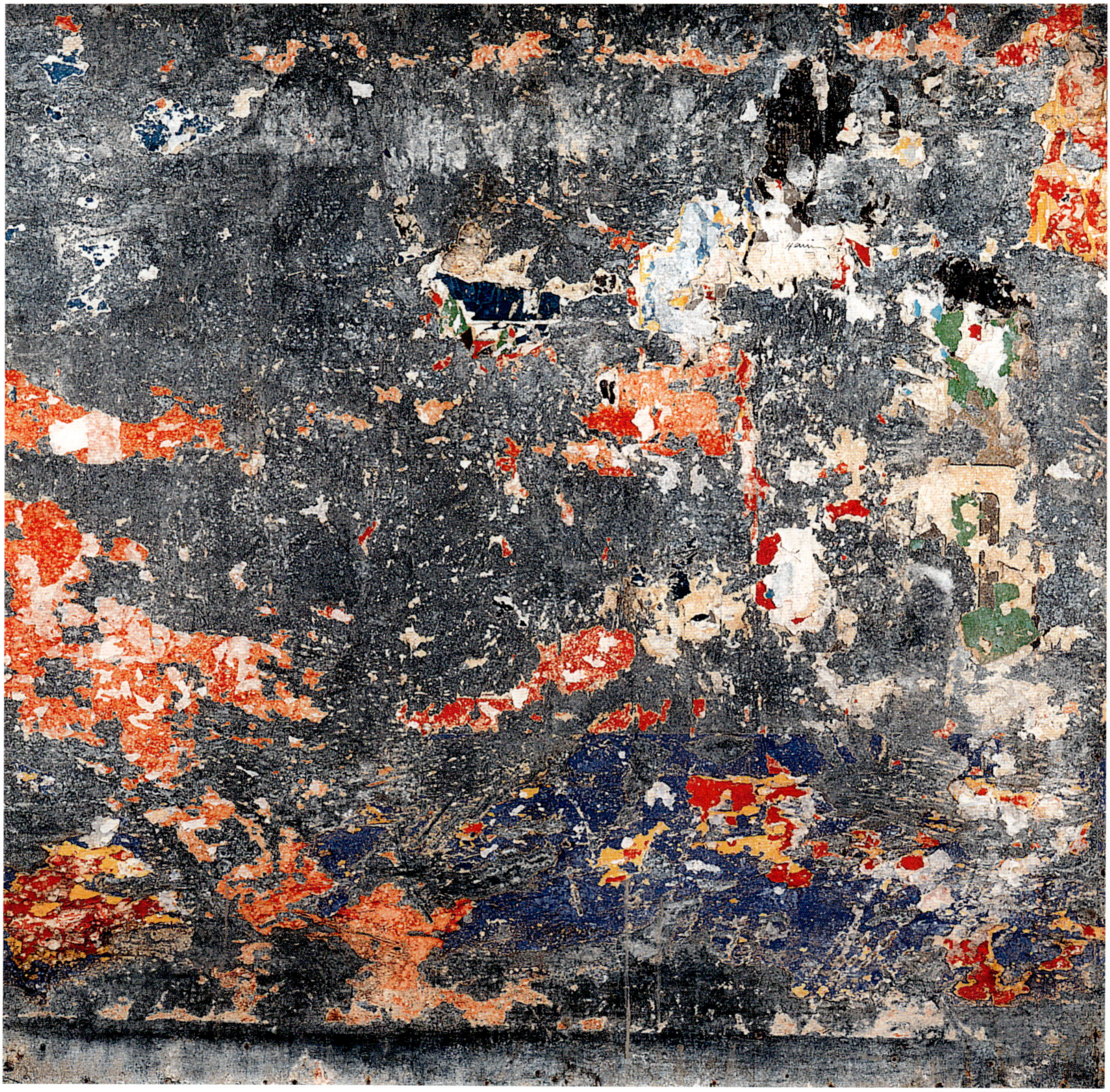

1961

Les Nymphéas
[The Water-Lilies]
Torn posters on panel
of galvanised sheet metal
100.5 × 100.5 × 0.7 cm
Purchased 1995 - AM 1995-263

Raymond Hains

1926, Saint-Brieuc (France)
2005, Paris (France) †

Following his training at the École des Beaux-Arts in Rennes, where he met Jacques Villeglé, Raymond Hains moved to Paris; between 1947 and 1951 he produced his hypnagogic photographs, using fluted glasses to give an abstract image of the subject by distorting it. In 1949, with Jacques Villeglé, Hains tore down his first poster. Viewed as an "archaeological rape", this gesture initially proclaimed a "desire to preserve samples" of advertising posters created by others, torn and ripped to pieces by anonymous hands. This gave rise to the idea of collecting them and working as an "inaction painter" from this specific material. Hains and Villeglé roamed the streets of Paris stealing these fragments from reality, much as one would pick up a pebble from the beach. Although the initial choice of elements stemmed from impulse, the process was to become more refined in accordance with the framing, like photography, or with associations and coincidences engendering new meanings. Not without humour, *Les Nymphéas* conjures up the pictures painted in Giverny by Monet in his declining years. The dissolution of the Impressionist painter's forms is countered by the vibrant shards of these scraps from the public arena, showcased by the galvanised sheet metal •

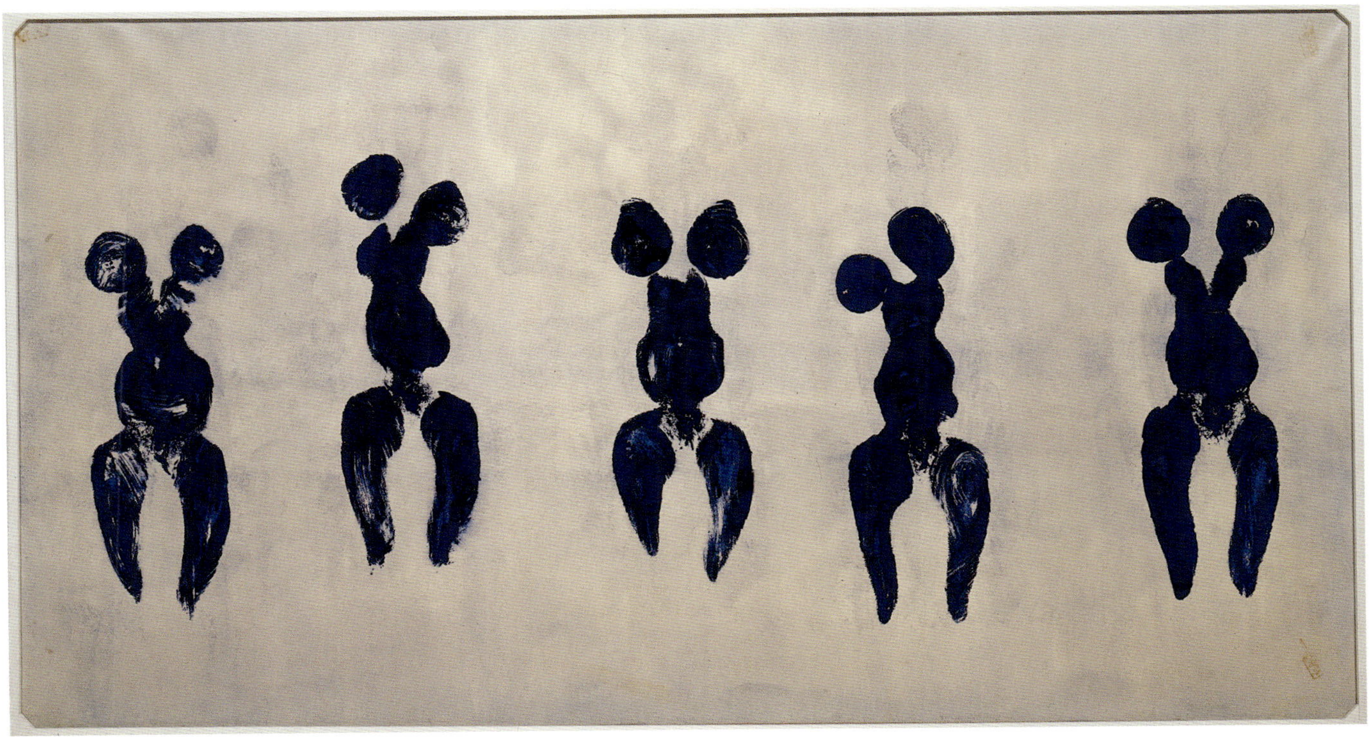

Yves Klein

1928, Nice (France)
1962, Paris (France) †

Yves Klein, whose parents were artists, found himself immersed in the painting experience from an early age. From his first monochrome pictures in the second half of the 1950s to his *Vide* [Void] exhibition at the Iris Clert gallery and blue illumination of the Concorde obelisk, by way of a number of air blown architectural and town planning projects, the range of techniques displayed by Klein throughout his artistic career stemmed from a single conception. In his eyes, the artist's role was to grasp beauty wherever it could be found and reveal it to others. For beauty already existed in invisible form, in the air, in matter or on the surface of his models' bodies.
The "Anthropométries" series stemmed from live performances by models, who pressed their paint-coated bodies, like "living paintbrushes", on to the surface of the medium. The artist stood back, leaving the human body itself free to create the canvas. With this technique, Klein paved the way for a return to figuration, but in a pictorial space in which the illusion of the third dimension had disappeared, in favour of a so-called "first" art form, in which subject, object and medium were intermingled. In *ANT 82...*, the literal imprint of the model's presence was therefore left upon the picture •

1960

ANT 82, "Anthropométrie de l'époque bleue"
[Anthropometry of the Blue Period]
Pure pigment and synthetic resin on paper mounted on canvas
156.5 × 282.5 cm
Purchased 1984 - AM 1984-279

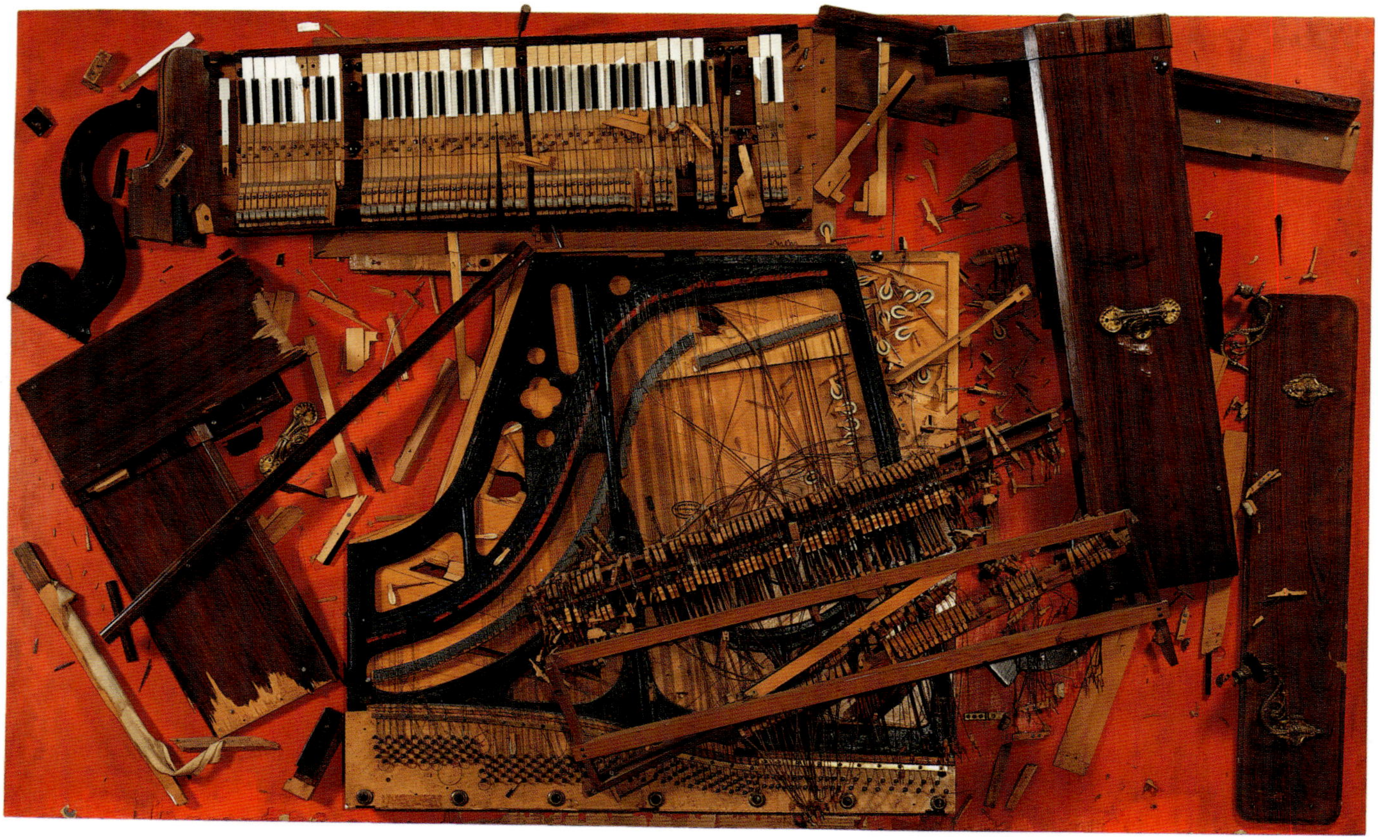

1962

Chopin's Waterloo
Fragments of broken piano fixed on to wooden panel
186 × 302 × 48 cm
Purchased 1979 - AM 1979-344

Arman

(born Armand Pierre Fernandez)

1928, Nice (France)
2005, New York, NY (United States) †

Arman first studied at the École des Arts Décoratifs in Nice and then at the École du Louvre in Paris. His friendship with Yves Klein led him to give up painting in favour of techniques using scrap elements and from 1959 real objects became the main component of works such as "Accumulations" and "Dustbins". Arman believed that the artist should be the witness of his era. Like production and consumerism, destruction formed part of the trading cycle of contemporary society, and his critical, ironic condemnation of this became the lynchpin of his work, linking him to other artists in the French New Realist movement. In August 1962, during his "Musical Rage" exhibition, held at the Swiss Saqqarah gallery in Gstaad, Arman carried out an action performance: he destroyed a piano with a sledgehammer and then fixed the shattered fragments on to a plank, freezing forever the role played by chance in the creative process. By petrifying the traces of a gesture launched against a symbol of harmony and culture, *Chopin's Waterloo* epitomises two paradoxical trends which cohabit in the artist's work: on the one hand, the need to preserve, illustrated by the 1959 "Accumulations" series, and on the other the need to destroy, particularly obvious in the "Colères" [Rages] performances he began in 1961. Over and above the spectacular aspect, the artist sought a grandiose dimension through destruction, but with a tinge of humour, as indicated by the title •

César

(born César Baldaccini)

1921, Marseille (France)
1998, Paris (France) †

In the early 1950s, unable to afford bronze casts for his plasters, César took a leaf out of Picasso and González's book and began welding scrap metal. Even at that stage, he managed to capitalise on the effects of these elements, which he picked up and reappropriated, thus lending the sculptures a remarkable, usually zoomorphic expressive force.
In 1957, the sculptor began compressing small objects but it was in 1960, when he came across a large American press at his scrap metal supplier's in Gennevilliers, that César really decided to make the most of the possibilities offered by this process and by the objects of our industrial civilisation, thereby forging links with other artists from the New Realist movement. It was at this point that César produced his first "directed compressions" from increasingly voluminous objects, creating a furore that same year when he showed his first compressions of cars at the Salon de Mai. *Compression "Ricard"* illustrates the attention paid to the shape of the compression, its play on proportions and the plastic qualities of its "skin", saturated with coloured folds and crevices. César managed to predict the end result through his choice of materials (nature and colour) and his knowledge of the process, restoring creative sensitivity into a seemingly impersonal mechanism.
César also created the *Césars* cinema trophies, which have been awarded every year in France since 1976 •

1962

Compression "Ricard"
Elements of compressed cars
153 × 73 × 65 cm
Gift of Pierre Restany, 1968 –
AM 1698 S

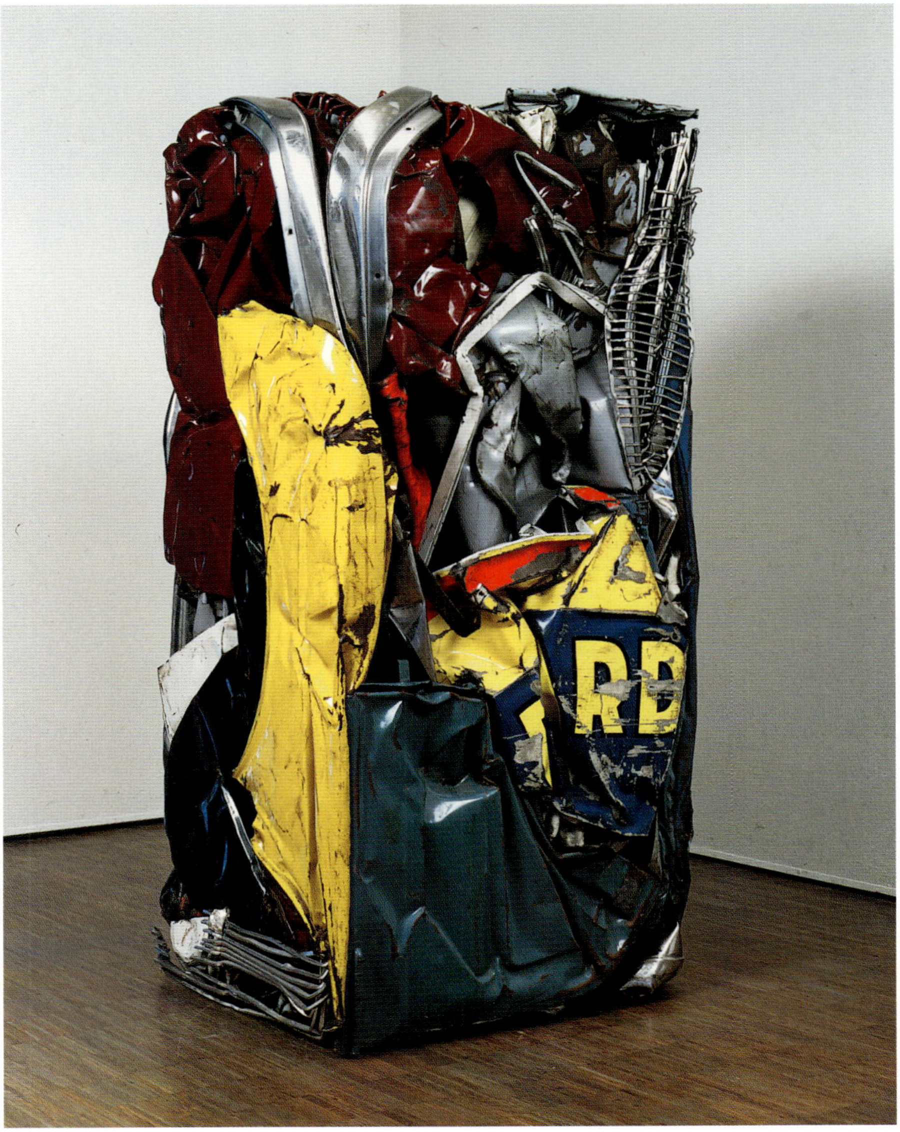

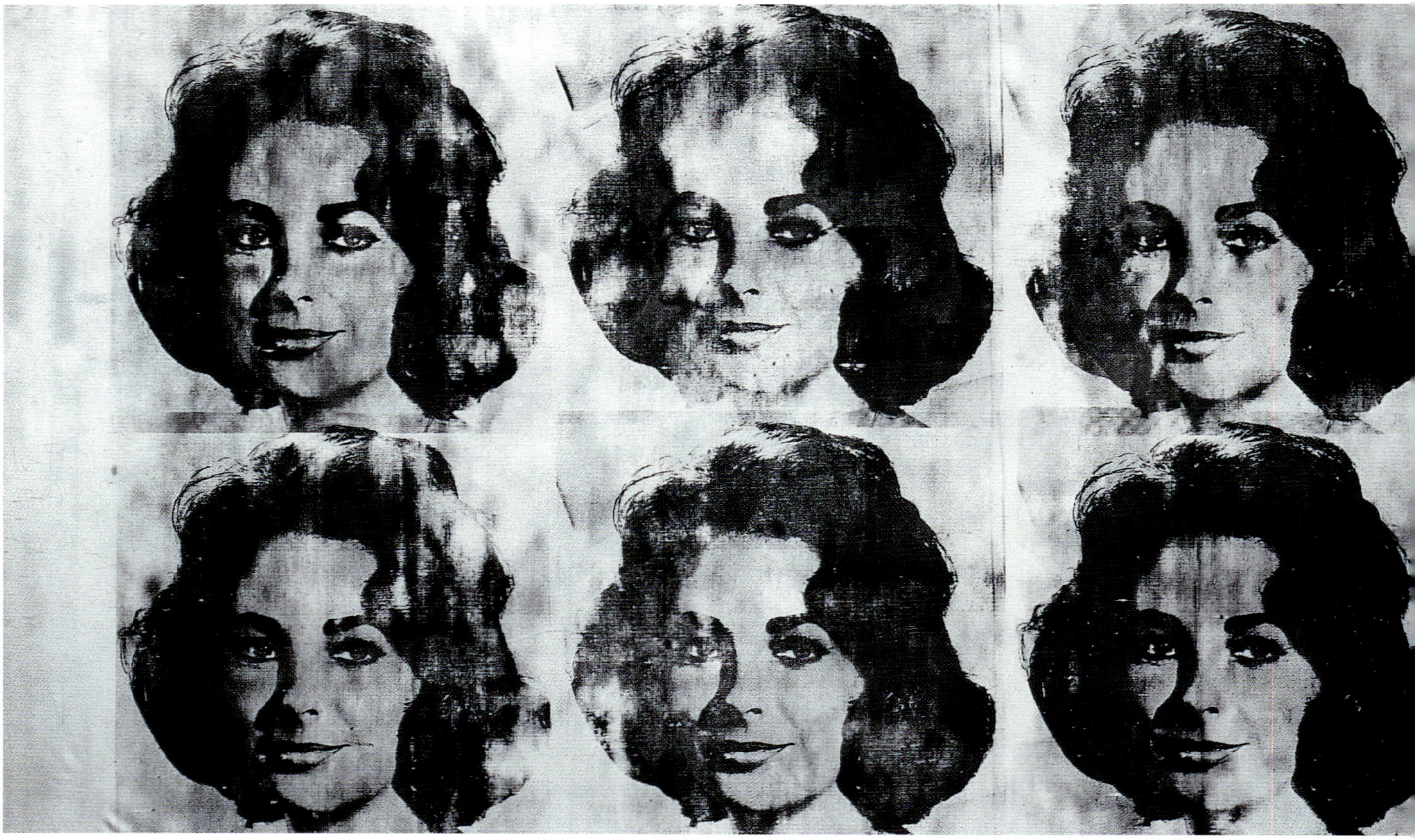

Andy Warhol

1928, Pittsburgh, PA (United States)
1987, New York, NY (United States) †

Following a highly successful career in advertising spanning around ten years, Andy Warhol took up painting full-time in the 1960s, producing works taken from strip cartoons. The deliberate choice of a mechanical process of reproduction (silkscreening) reflected an element of standardisation and mechanisation n his creative approach. In less than five years, Warhol managed to forge his celebrity image, surround himself with the leading names in counter-culture and become the emblematic figurehead of American Pop Art. Elizabeth Taylor, who was in poor health after playing the title role in Joseph L. Mankiewicz's controversial film *Cleopatra*, was an icon of the entertainment industry at the time, and Warhol chose to depict her, as he did Marilyn Monroe, on a canvas that was similar to a cinema screen in scale. These depictions of stars, rendered ambiguous by the poor definition of the process he had chosen, which elided their portrait with a ghostly picture, coexisted alongside symbols of pop culture (Coca-Cola bottles, Campbell soup cans) and media images (racial riots, car crashes, suicides, the nuclear cloud). Each one echoes like an allegory of a world dominated by the proliferation of images •

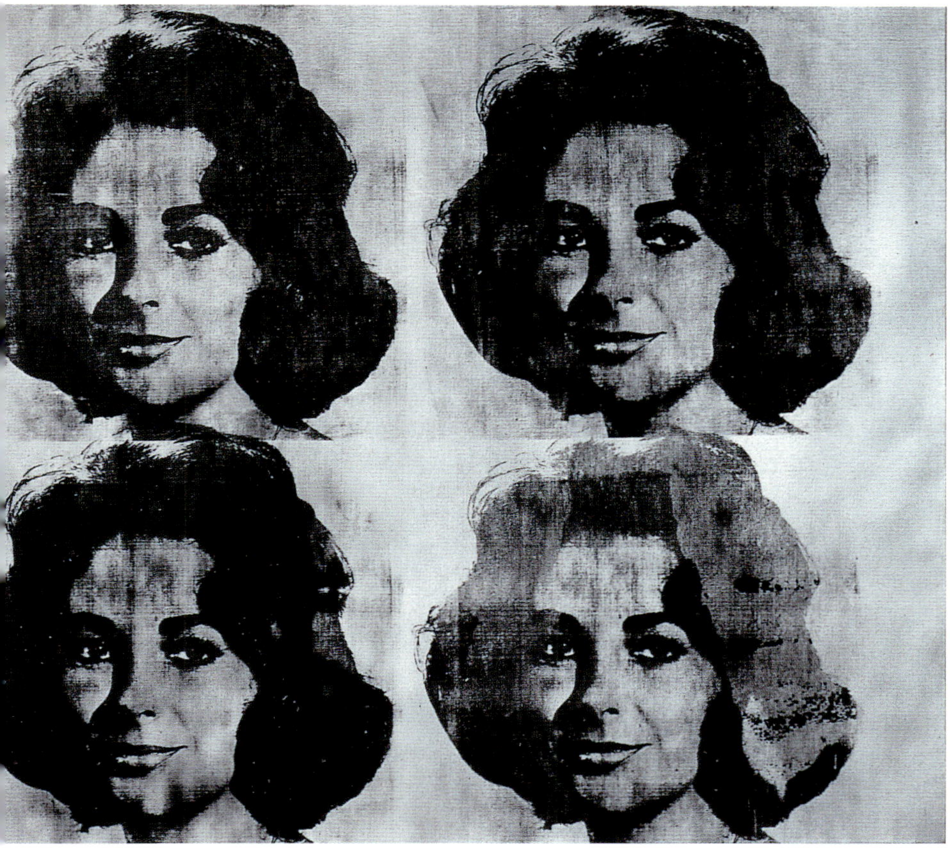

1963

Ten Lizes

Silkscreen ink and spray paint on canvas
201 × 564.5 cm
Purchased 1986 - AM 1986-82

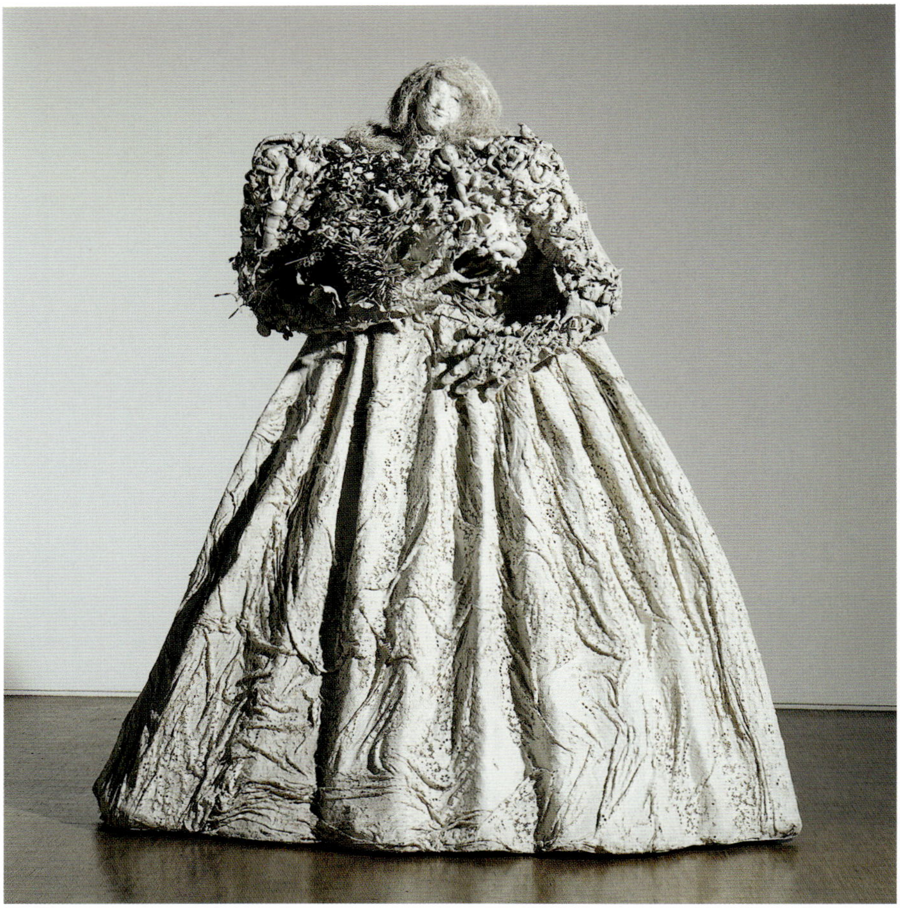

Niki de Saint Phalle was born in France but spent much of her childhood living in New York, before returning to France in 1952. At that time, her art consisted of naïve canvases inspired by Art Brut. Her meeting with Jean Tinguely, however, led her in a completely different direction, akin to the New Realists. In 1961 she staged a number of warlike performances entitled "Feu à volonté" [Fire at Will]. The public was invited to shoot with a rifle at plaster objects the artist had made, on which she had suspended sachets of paint. During the same period, in keeping with the spirit of the New Realists, Niki de Saint Phalle began producing human figures using scrap elements and everyday objects. These were all used to convey her sensibility and sense of revolt regarding the conventions and shackles imposed on women. Her *Mariée* resembles a large, mournful doll, somewhat discomfited by her tawdry bridal gown, a ceremonial outfit rendered burlesque by the miscellaneous odds and ends clustered into the plaster. The white dress, a symbol of purity, and the romantic vision traditionally associated with the bride are here turned on their head, in a castigation of the social constraints which hampered women in the early 1960s. Niki de Saint Phalle was later to design a great many sculptures for public spaces. Together with Jean Tinguely, she created the *Fontaine Igor-Stravinski* (1982), situated next to the Centre Pompidou •

1963

La Mariée ou Eva Maria
[The Bride]
Wire netting, plaster, pasted lace, miscellaneous painted toys
222 × 200 × 100 cm
Purchased by the State, 1967; attribution, 1976 - AM 1976-1016

Niki de Saint Phalle

1930, Neuilly-sur-Seine (France)
2002, San Diego, CA (United States) †

Martial Raysse

1936, Vallauris Golfe-Juan (France)

1964

Made in Japan - La grande odalisque
Acrylic paint and objects on photograph mounted on canvas
130 × 97 cm
Gift of the Scaler Foundation, 1995, AM - 1995-213

Following his literary studies, Martial Raysse launched his first "assemblages" in 1958, using everyday objects which he enclosed in transparent boxes. This reappropriation of totally commonplace elements linked him to the New Realists, such as Arman, Spoerri and Tinguely. In the 1960s, he became interested in the imagery of the consumer society and in the depiction of feminine stereotypes, taken not only from fashion magazines but also from famous paintings. *Made in Japan – La grande odalisque* actually belongs to a series of pastiches and reappropriations of old masters, which he produced between 1963 and 1965. Here one can recognise a fragment of Ingres' *La Grande Odalisque*.

The impertinent nature of this approach is typical of the rebellious avant-garde spirit that prevailed in the early 1960s throughout Europe and the United States. This iconoclastic gesture also represented a tribute, however, and went hand in hand with a sound pictorial culture. The title, a reference to cheap replicas, together with the materials used – spray-painted garish industrial colours and tawdry trinkets fixed on to the canvas – lend support to the artist's claim that "beauty is poor taste". Raysse, however, revealed a whole world of unimagined magic and emotion underlying this poor taste – or as he put it, the "dream of a beauty excessively desired" •

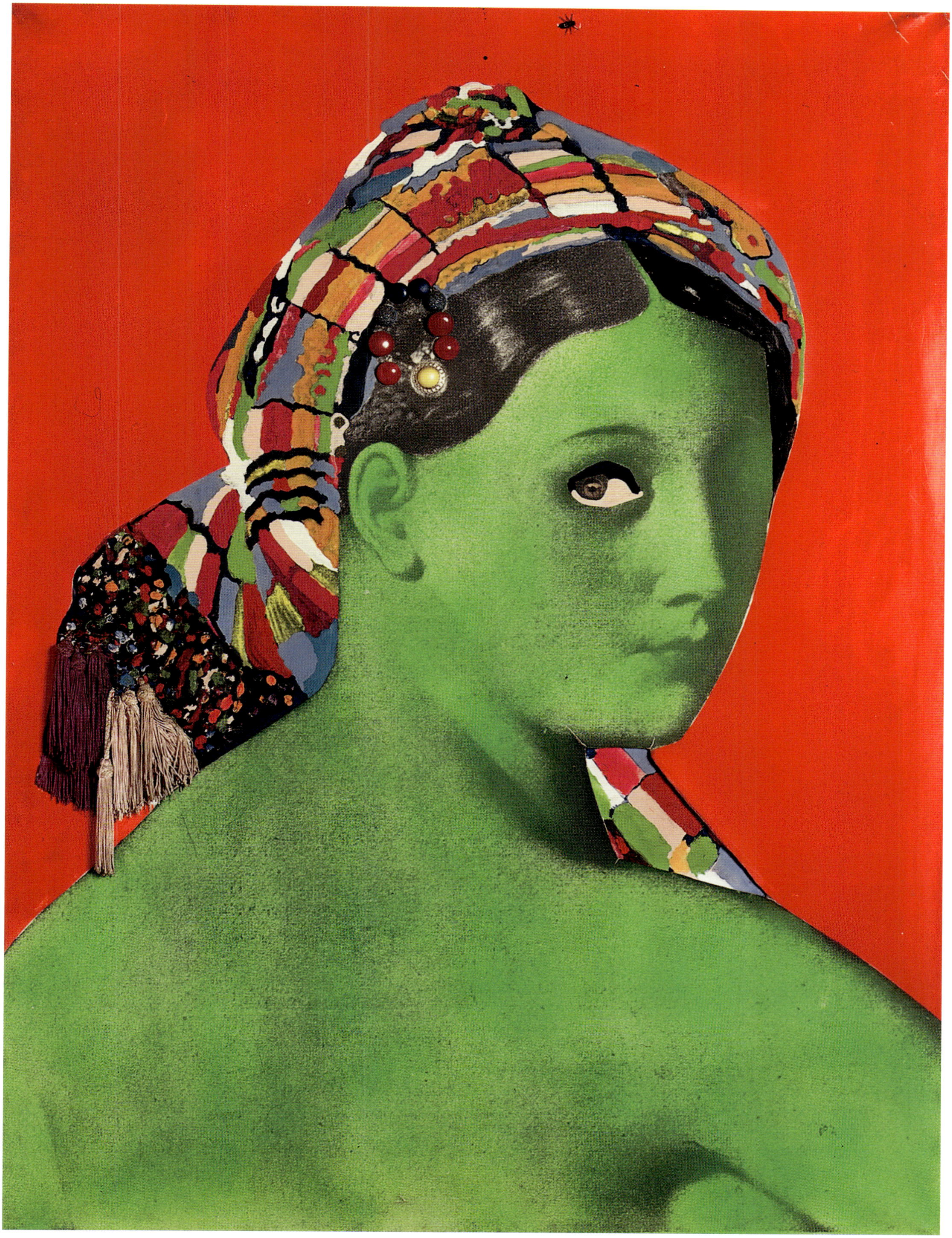

➔ 1963

Peinture
260 x 202 cm,
19 juin 1963

Oil on canvas
260 × 202 cm
Donated by the artist through the Société des Amis du Musée national d'art moderne, 1967 - AM 4409 P

Pierre Soulages

| 1919, Rodez (France)

Pierre Soulages, "painter of black and light", opted for abstraction from the outset; his first works, which bore no reference to either model or figuration, took the form of simple black or brown marks on a pale background. Following the astonishing *Brous de noix* [Walnut Stains], presented by Soulages in his first exhibition in 1947, came progressively elongated formats, verging on the polyptych, which encouraged a panoramic vision. By making his own tools, the artist freed himself of any kind of conditioned practice, designing his painting knives from bits of leather sole, rubber scrapers, broken planks and so forth.
In the mid-Sixties, Soulages started using more fluid paint, spreading it with vigorous brushstrokes on to large formats, which he laid directly on the ground. Careful to retain spacious areas of blank surfaces, he created monumental compositions in which the links between the white voids and marks captured the slightest gestural variation. These voluminous "fluttering[s] of forms in space", in which the tautness of line reflected a radical sobriety, betrayed the contained character of the energy.
To this day, the painter remains faithful to this paring-down of means, sometimes perceived as the expression of a serene solemnity and sometimes as a vital force stripped of sentimentality •

Mark Rothko

(born Marcus Rothkowitz)

1903, Dvinsk (Russia)
1970, New York, NY (United States) †

Mark Rothko was of Russian origin but emigrated to the United States in 1913, where he studied art. His first – figurative – period was mainly influenced by Rembrandt and the Expressionists. The early 1940s saw his painting glide towards a biomorphic lexicon, inspired first by Picasso and then by Surrealism. It was only in 1949–1950 that Rothko's art gravitated towards totally abstract works, making the ductile, shimmering, iridescent substance of paint itself the sole subject-matter of his canvases. Initially complex, the compositions were pared down until, in 1949–1950, they could be resumed by their formal, meditational nature, which was to become his "trademark". In monumental layouts, two or three rectangular forms with evanescent contours float in fathomless depths. This "ground colour", at once mythical and plastic, thereby emerged as the actual subject of the work. Right up to his suicide in 1970, Rothko continued to follow this principle, delving into a long process of graduation of colour, giving precedence to the gamut of red and to a gradual darkening of the palette •

1964

Untitled (Black, Red over Black on Red)

Oil on canvas
205 × 193 cm
Accepted in lieu of tax, 2007; formerly in the collection of Mr. and Mrs. Jean-Pierre Moueix - AM 2007-126

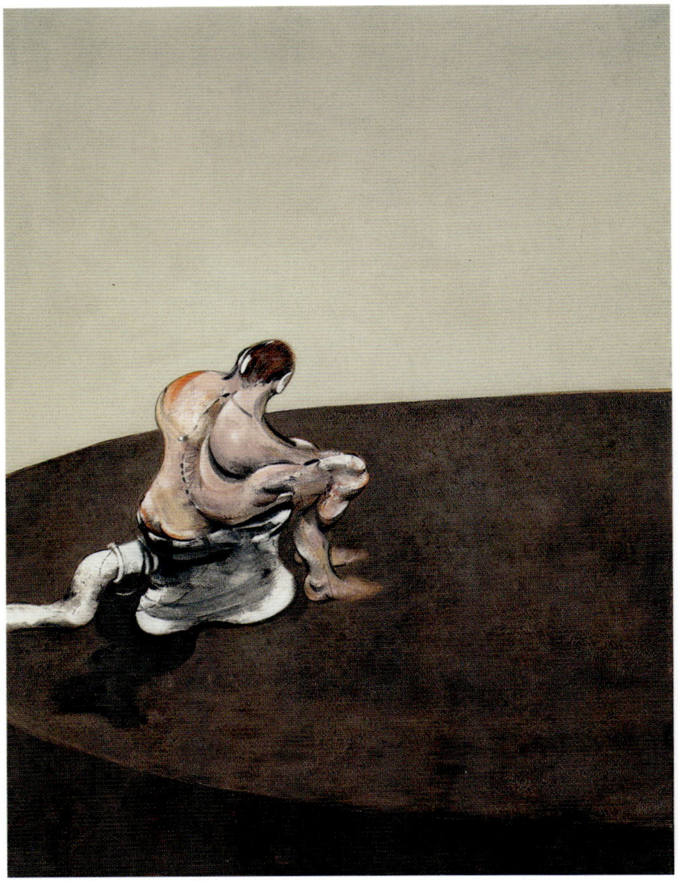

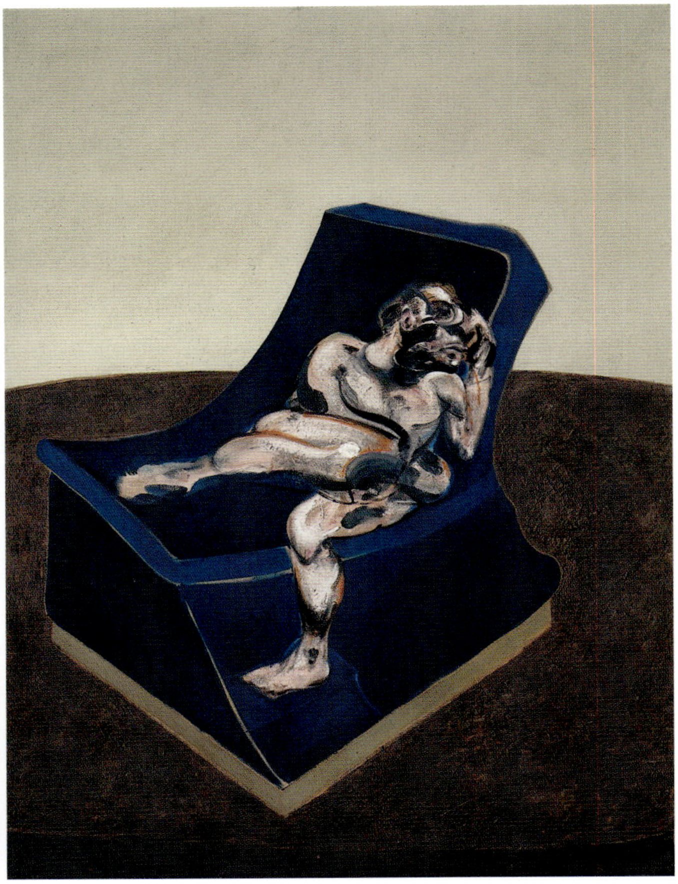

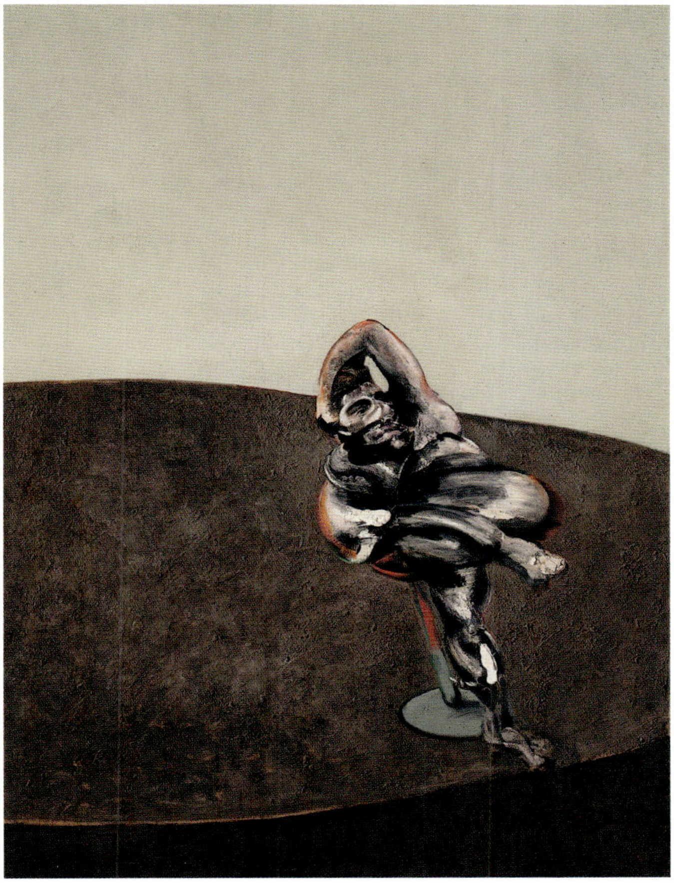

1964

Three Figures in a Room
Oil on canvas
198 × 441 cm
Purchased by the State, 1968; attribution, 1976 - AM 1976-925

Francis Bacon

1909, Dublin (Ireland)
1992, Madrid (Spain) †

It was only in 1944, after he had produced his first major triptych, heavily influenced by Picasso's late 1920s works, that Francis Bacon placed painting at the heart of his existence. He concentrated on several defining themes – Crucifixion, the nude, portraits and self-portraits – and from the 1950s, only painted his close friends (Michel Leiris, Lucian Freud etc.), always from photographs. The figures are cast into enclosed spaces, contained by a few contours and broad sweeps of colour. After 1962, Bacon often had recourse to the triptych. The painter viewed this configuration, a legacy of major religious art, as a cinematographic succession of images; above all it enabled him to carry out his analytical research into models. The panels of *Three Figures in a Room* form an adjoining space in which George Dyer is represented through three simultaneous views. Bacon's companion is first depicted from the back, sitting on a white lavatory seat, almost as though the body were excreting itself, then face on, sprawled on an armchair, his face contorted, and finally semi-recumbent on a swivel stool, in a spiralling movement. This work is characteristic of Bacon's merciless focus on lonely, tortured beings in which he sought, as he put it himself, to "paint the scream more than the horror" and to create "figures arising out of their own flesh [...], figures as poignant as a Crucifixion" •

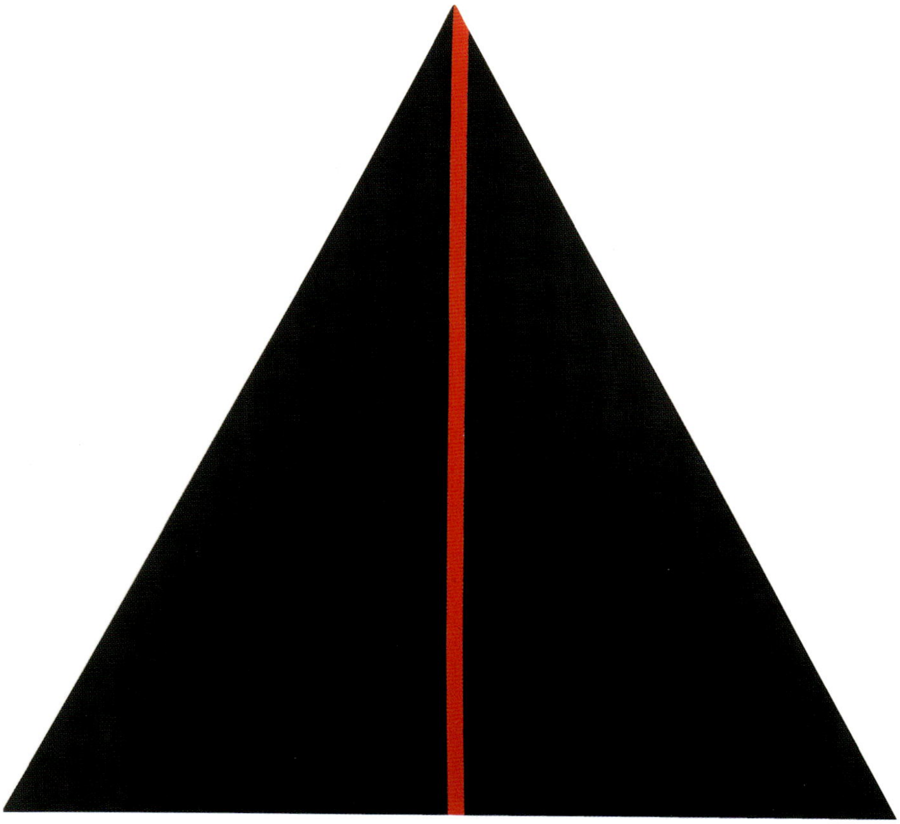

1968-1969

Jericho

Acrylic paint on canvas
268.5 × 286 cm
Purchased with the contribution of Basil and Elisa Goulandris, 1986 - AM 1986

Barnett Newman

1905, New York, NY (United States)
1970, New York, NY (United States) †

Barnett Newman was one of the leading figures in the post-1945 American abstract art movement. His paintings from the mid-1940s, influenced by Surrealism, were already characterised by bold vertical structures. The artist was to find his true lexicon in 1948, however, when he achieved radical simplification by dividing a monochrome surface with a vertical painted band, the "zip". Later, Newman's bands played with false symmetry, using subtle spatial shifts to create works imbued with a powerful rhythm. The idea of a triangular painting came to the artist as he was working on his only sculpture, *Broken Obelisk* (1963–1967), which was composed of a truncated obelisk placed upside-down on the summit of a pyramid. *Jericho*, along with *Chartres*, is one of the only two works produced in this geometric form. The monumental isosceles triangle is split into two parts by means of a red band, which veers slightly to the right. This shift is imperceptible in the bottom part of the painting but becomes more distinct as one raises one's eyes. The upwards surge of the "zip" shatters the closed form of the triangle, leading the eye towards an area beyond the image which cannot be rationally determined. The title, *Jericho*, is an allusion to the city in the Bible in which the walls crumbled to the sound of blaring trumpets and the war cries of the people of Israel. In both cases, a hermetic entity is ruptured by a force: the power of sound in the Bible and the energy of the intense red line in this masterpiece •

Louise Bourgeois

1911, Paris (France)
2010, New York, NY (United States) †

Although she moved to the United States in 1938, Louise Bourgeois retained strong links with France, where she was born and brought up. Her œuvre, which combines every creative form (drawings, engravings, sculptures, spaces) in a highly eclectic range of materials, does not fall into any of the classifications of art history. The path she followed in her art, featuring recurrent themes such as home, childhood, maternity and sexuality, appeared inextricably linked to her own personal history. She was already using flexible materials in her sculptures, such as plaster, latex or wax, in the late 1950s, lending them sensual, organic forms. When she decided to start working with marble, in 1967, she immediately went to Italy in order to work it *in situ*. She used this traditional material to produce a number of highly suggestive works. Comprising bulbs and hillocks, spherical and ovoid excrescences, they conjured up both breasts and phalluses, as in this series, entitled "Cumul" in reference to the convolutions of *cumuli*. Drawing her inspiration from the subconscious, Louise Bourgeois played a pioneering role in the emergence of a female autobiographical art form, which has become increasingly widespread since the late 1960s •

1968

Cumul I
White marble on wooden plinth in two parts
51 × 127 × 122 cm
Purchased by the State, 1973; attribution, 1976 - AM 1976-933

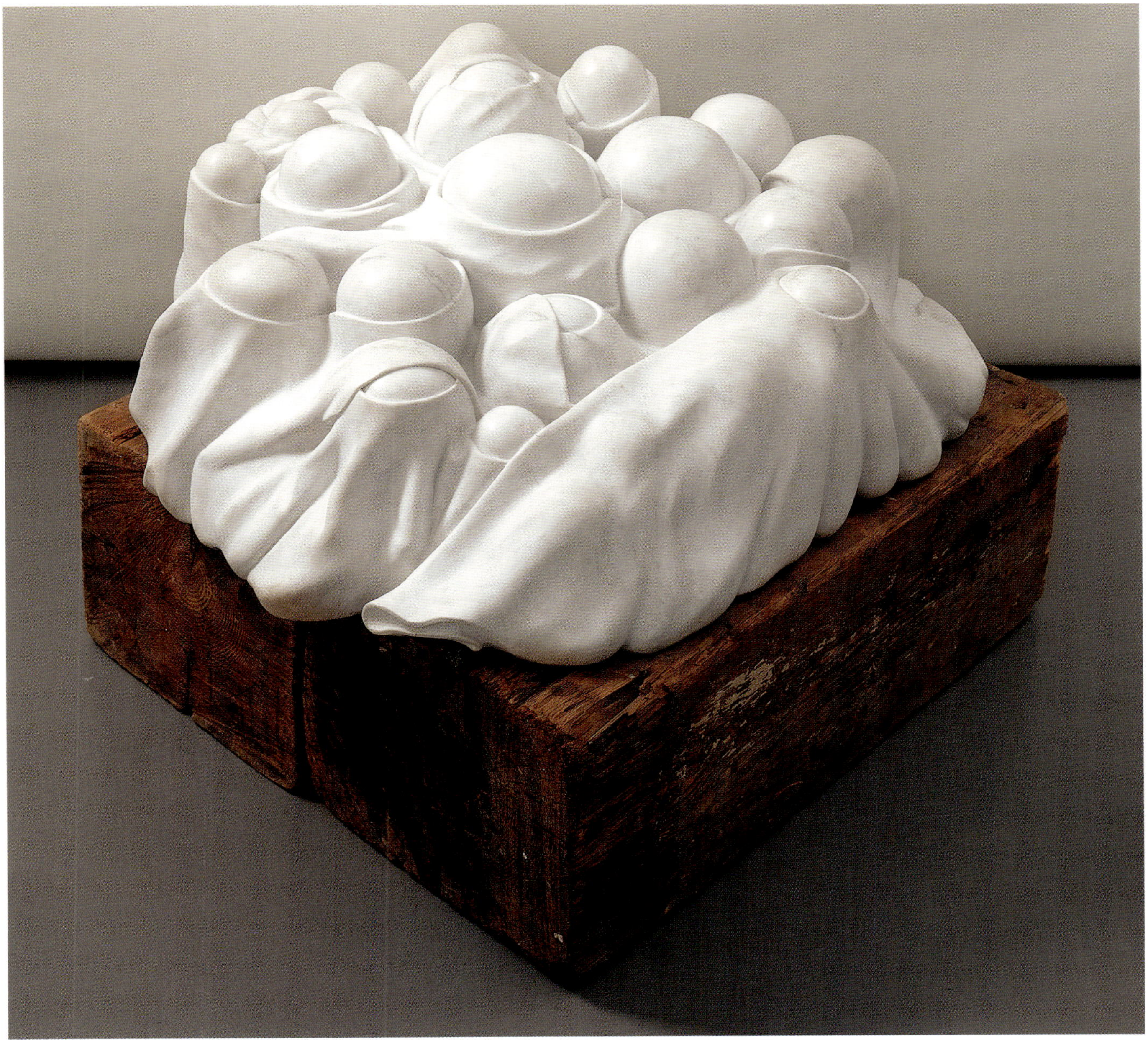

Yaacov Agam

1928, Rishon le-Zion (British Mandate of Palestine, now Israel)

In 1955, Agam took part in the exhibition "Le Mouvement", alongside Bury, Soto, Tinguely and Vasarely, among others. The exhibition, held at the Denise René gallery, launched "kinetic art", an amalgamation of technology, scientific theories and aesthetics, integrating movement into bi- or tri-dimensional works, either literally, by means of motorised machines, or by resorting to optical phenomena and plays on light. In the drawing-room he decorated for the Élysées Palace, Agam offered an emblematic example of a kinetic pictorial space, in which the walls, ceiling, ground and doors encourage onlookers to come up with different configurations as they wander through. The bevelled shapes with their countless hues play optical tricks in order to trap the attention and create an abstract composition, seemingly in perpetual motion. Commissioned by the President in 1971 and implemented under the aegis of the Mobilier National, the room was unfinished when Georges Pompidou died in April 1974. Although it was completed a few months later, it was dismantled and placed in storage following the election of Valéry Giscard d'Estaing, before being installed at the Centre Pompidou •

1974

Aménagement de l'antichambre des appartements privés du Palais de l'Élysée pour le président Georges Pompidou

[Redecoration of the antechamber leading to the private apartments of the Palais de l'Élysée, commissioned by President Georges Pompidou]
Installation: 3 walls, luminous ceiling, 6 sliding panels, sculpture and rug; coloured Transacryl, aluminium, painted glass and wood, Plexiglas, stainless steel, wool, paint and fluorescent tubes
470 × 548 × 622 cm (entire unit)
Purchased through State commission, 1971; attribution, 2000 - AM 2000-3

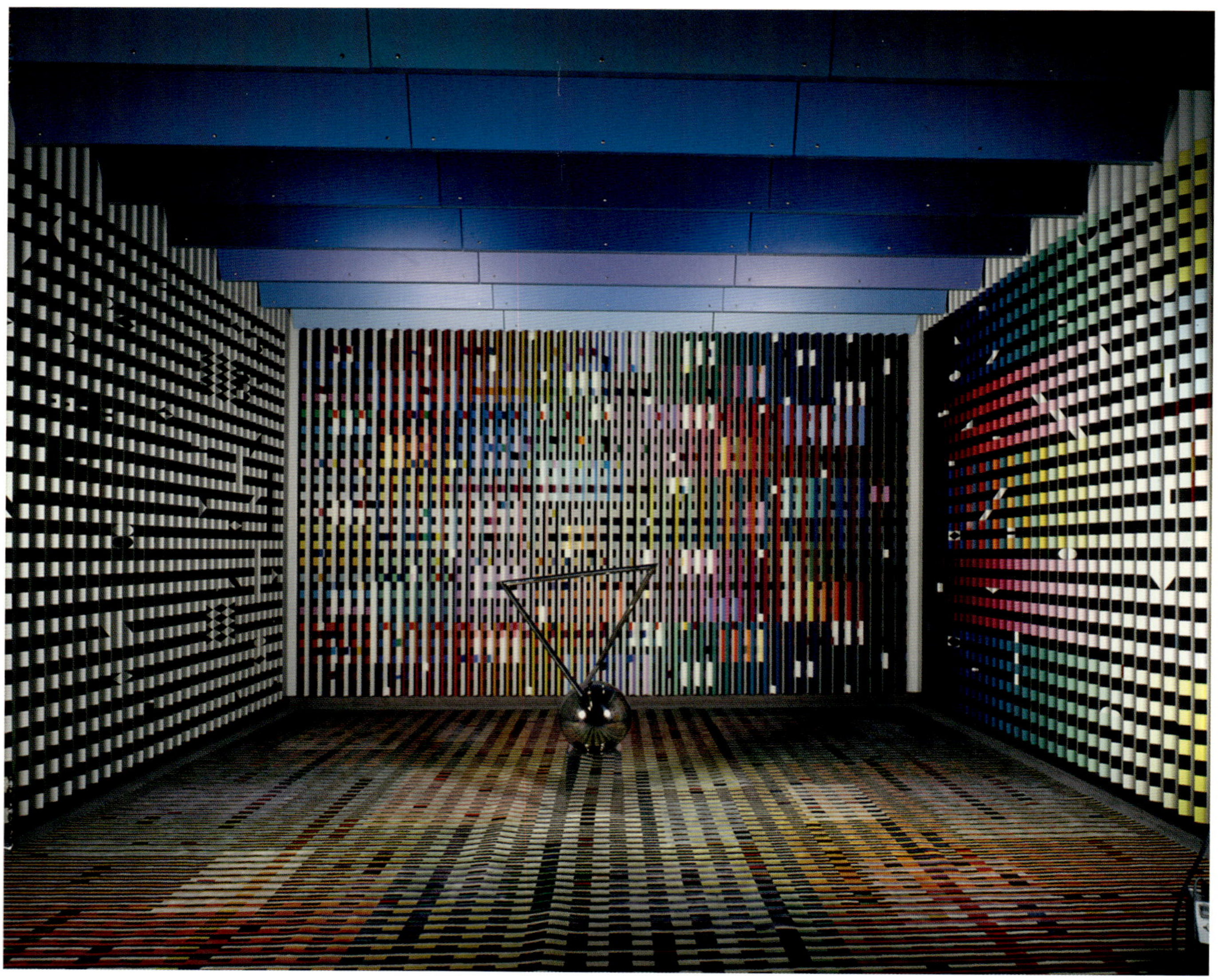

1976

Hommage à Georges Pompidou

38 aluminium profiles laid out vertically
500 × 400 × 6 cm
Donated by the artist, 1984 - AM 1976-1141

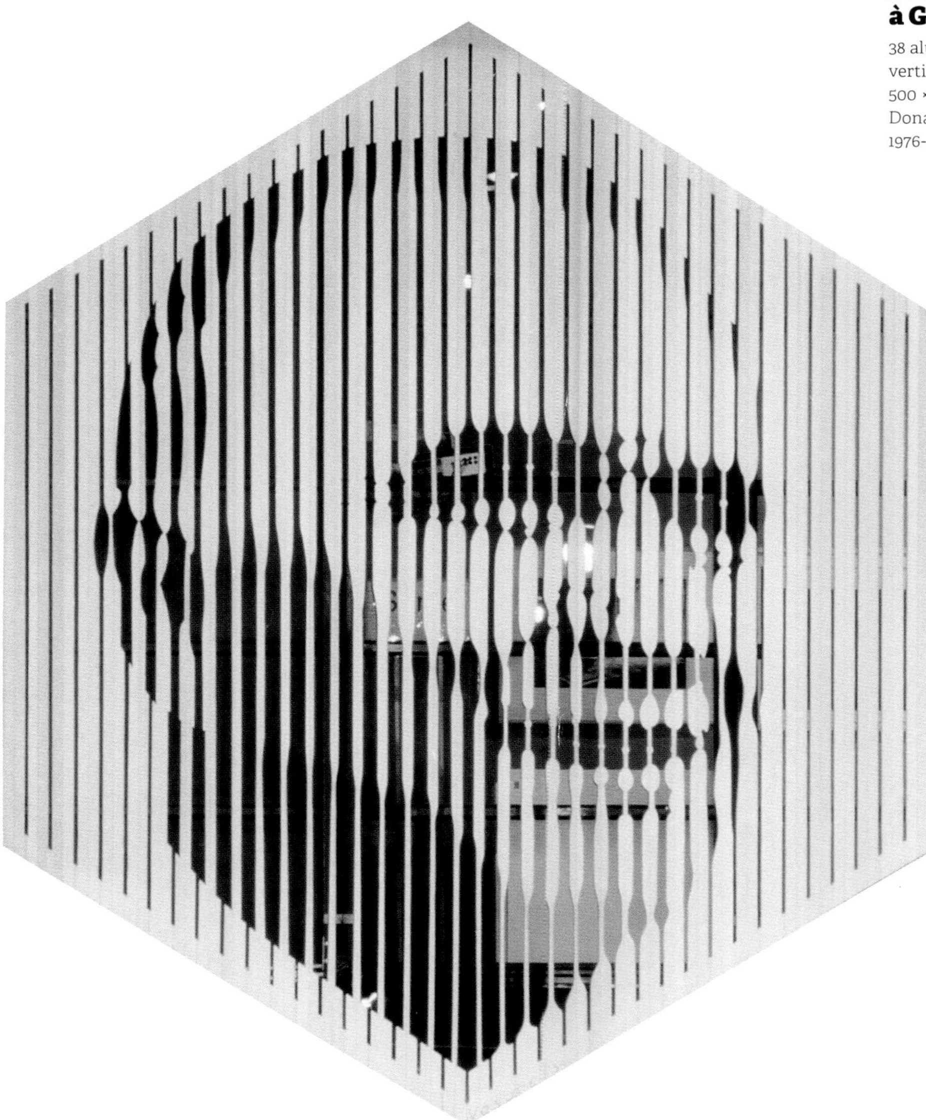

Victor Vasarely

1906, Pécs (Austria-Hungary)
1997, Paris (France) †

After studying art in Budapest under a professor whose teachings stemmed from the principles of the Bauhaus, Vasarely moved to France in 1930. He worked for several years as a graphic artist in an advertising agency, while continually developing his own work, inspired by geometric abstraction. In 1955, the artist took part in the exhibition "Le Mouvement" (Denise René Gallery), which launched kinetic art. Vasarely, however, did not opt for animating surfaces with mobile or mechanised elements. He explored the field of optical illusion, such as the vibrations emanating from retinal persistence or the difficulties encountered by the eye when having to accommodate simultaneously to two violently contrasting surfaces •

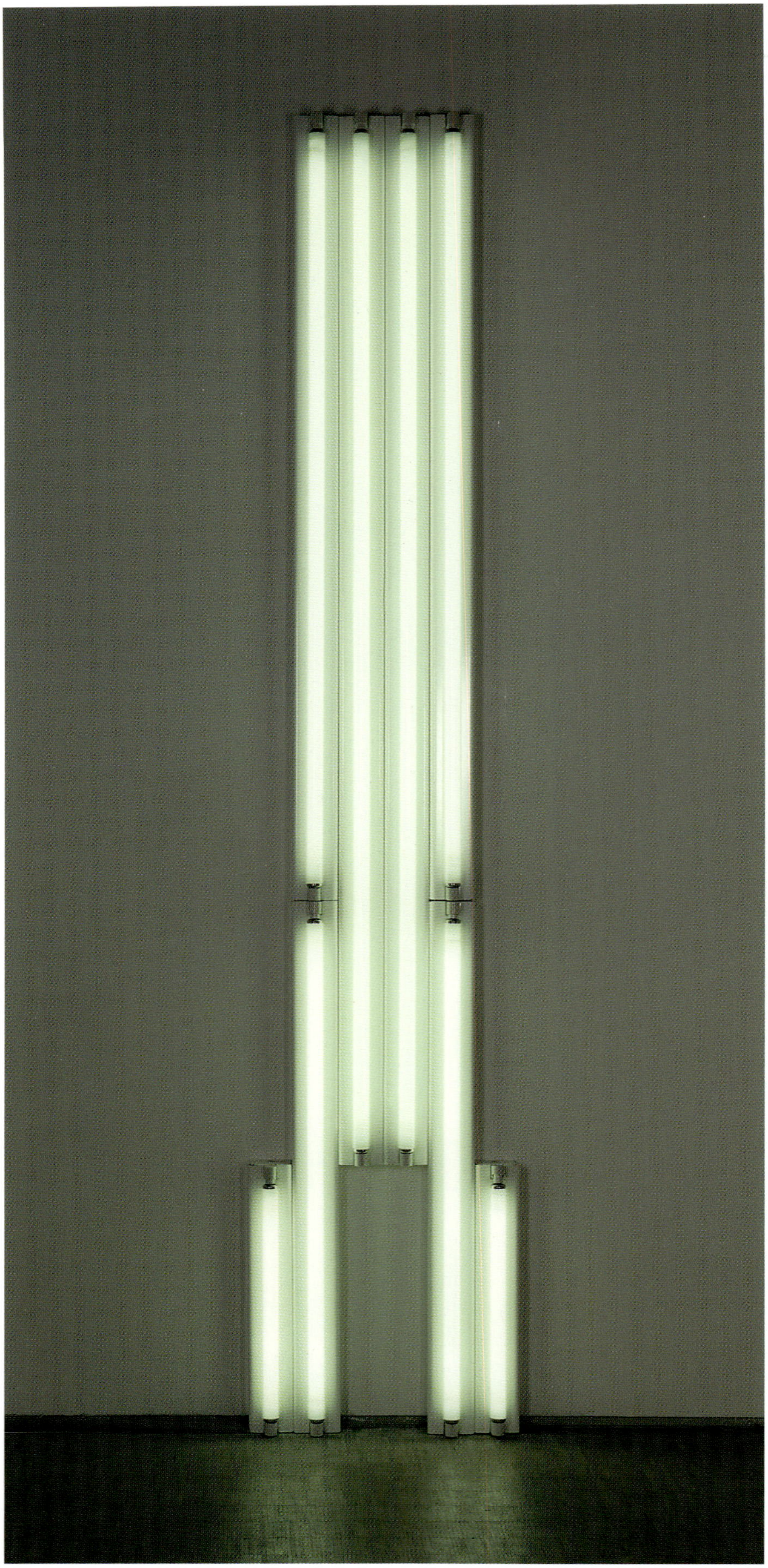

1974

"Monument" for V. Tatlin

8 cold white fluorescent tubes, painted metal structure
305 × 62.5 × 12.5 cm
Gift of Leo Castelli and the Centre Pompidou Foundation, 1992 - AM 1992-16

Dan Flavin

1933, New York, NY (United States)
1996, Riverhead, NY (United States) †

In the early 1960s, Dan Flavin moved away from painting and collage and from 1964 devoted himself exclusively to luminescent tubes. These come in a range of sizes and colours and are laid out in varyingly complex compositions which usually form the sole source of light in the exhibition venue.
Between 1964 and 1990, the artist produced fifty creations as a tribute to Vladimir Tatlin. Lenin had commissioned the Russian sculptor to erect a Monument for the Third International, a gigantic spiral construction theoretically designed for living in. Flavin's "monuments" are composed of several fluorescent tubes of varying sizes, vertical for the most part, which usually diffuse white light, as in this example. Although this does not signify an attempt to find any formal similarity, it does examine the links between American Minimalism and Russian Constructivism. Despite the decades that separate them, the two movements have a number of aspects in common, both at formal level and in their use of industrial components. They diverge ideologically, however: the Constructivists' goal was to participate in the creation of a new world by integrating all the fine arts into a holistic environment, whereas American Minimalism carried no political agenda. Only the visual impact of light is at issue here, radiating into space, its halo almost obliterating the physical presence of the object itself •

1977/2009

Le Baiser de l'artiste. Le distributeur automatique ou presque ! n° 2
[The Kiss of the Artist. The Automatic Slot Machine or Nearly! No. 2]

An element from the ensemble Action ORLAN-CORPS. Le Baiser de l'artiste [Action ORLAN-BODY. The Kiss of the Artist], 1977
Gelatin silver print under Diasec
155 × 110 cm
Purchased 2009 - AM 2009-141(1)

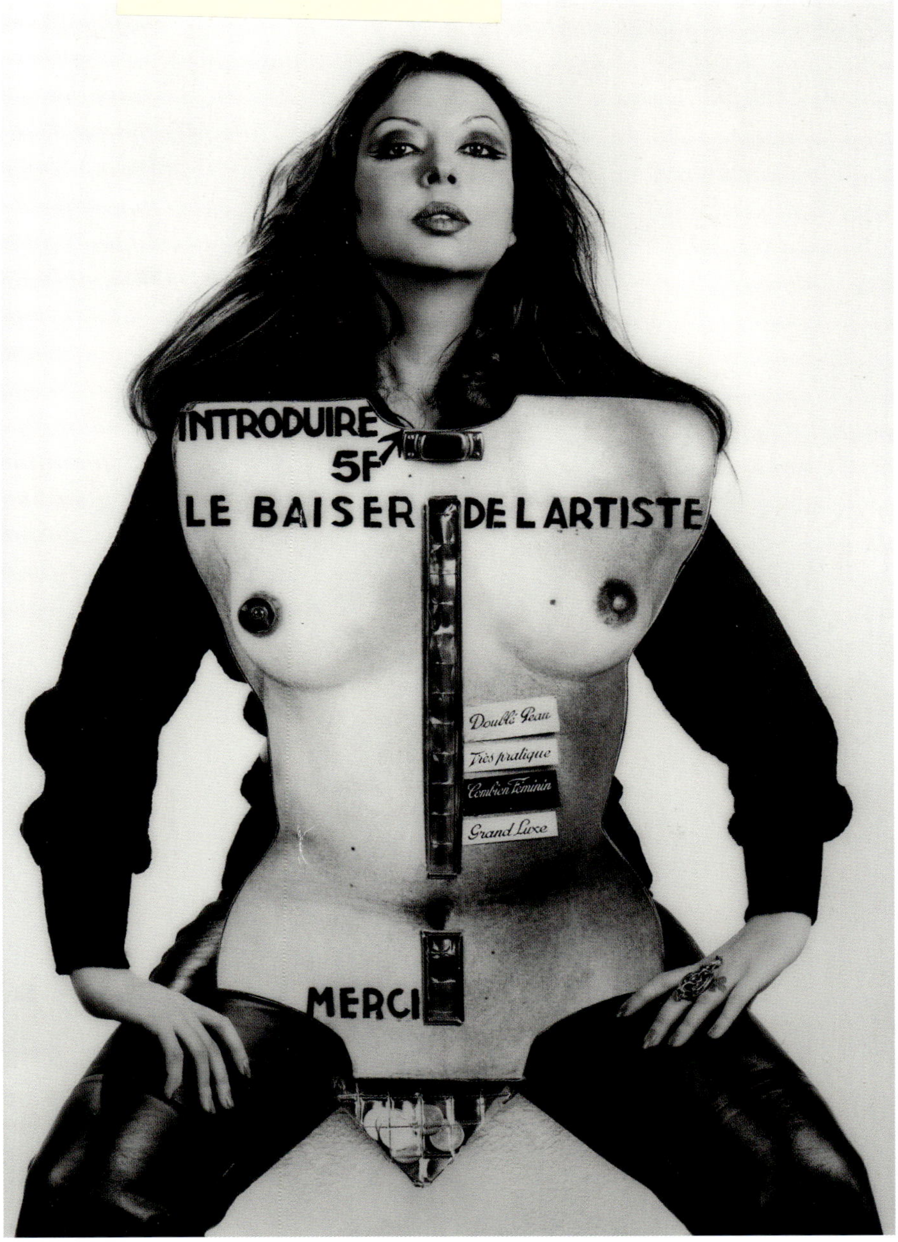

ORLAN

1947, Saint-Étienne (France)

"My life can be divided into before and after *Le Baiser* de l'artiste. The aftermath was my dismissal, the break from my family, people insulting me, the loss of my work and studio; it was a tragicomic period in my life." This is how ORLAN summed up in 2007 the consequences of the media scandal caused by her participation in the 1977 FIAC art fair. For many artists since the 1960s, the body has become a means of coming into direct contact with the public, even encouraging their participation. In body art, attitudes and acts prevail over the production of objects, which belong after all to the consumer world. In *Le Baiser* de l'artiste, ORLAN, sitting on a plinth behind the life-sized photograph of her own body, offers visitors a five-franc kiss, by means of a slot machine. By this action, the artist is proclaiming her right to use her body as she chooses but she is also questioning the nature of an artwork and the basic premises of the art market.
From 1990, the artist began putting her own face under the surgeon's scalpel, in order to move the goalposts of beauty archetypes, particularly those disseminated by the history of art and civilisations. Through this approach, she was determined to challenge both the constraints imposed by social norms of beauty and their arbitrary nature •

Georg Baselitz

| 1938, Deutschbaselitz (Germany)

1981

Die Mädchen von Olmo II
[The Girls from Olmo II]
Oil on canvas
250 × 249 cm
Purchased 1982 - AM 1982-19

Georg Baselitz first studied at the Academy of East Berlin before moving to West Berlin in 1957, where he completed his plastic arts course. Initially a proponent of lyrical abstraction, he soon took a radical stance against the prevailing aesthetics of abstract art. The painter's art is resolutely figurative, inspired by the intense expressivity of Antonin Artaud's drawings, art brut and all forms of primitivism. His provocative works with their powerful chromatics may make formal reference to early twentieth century German expressionism but the artist was trying above all to renew the ways of reading painting. From 1969, he concentrated on straightforward, everyday subjects (trees, portraits, nudes...) but he decided to counter their traditional representation by turning them upside down. This ironic, systematic reversal strips the subject of its value and implies both visual and mental gymnastics. Each theme must be regarded not as a subject but first and foremost as a *motif*. Three Indian ink drawings and a first painted version preceded *Die Mädchen von Olmo II*. The series features young women spinning round an Italian village square on their bicycles. The banal subject occupies the canvas, but without affecting the great freedom of the brushstroke. The painting, which is characteristic of Baselitz's approach, tempers the basic contradictions between figurative and abstract painting •

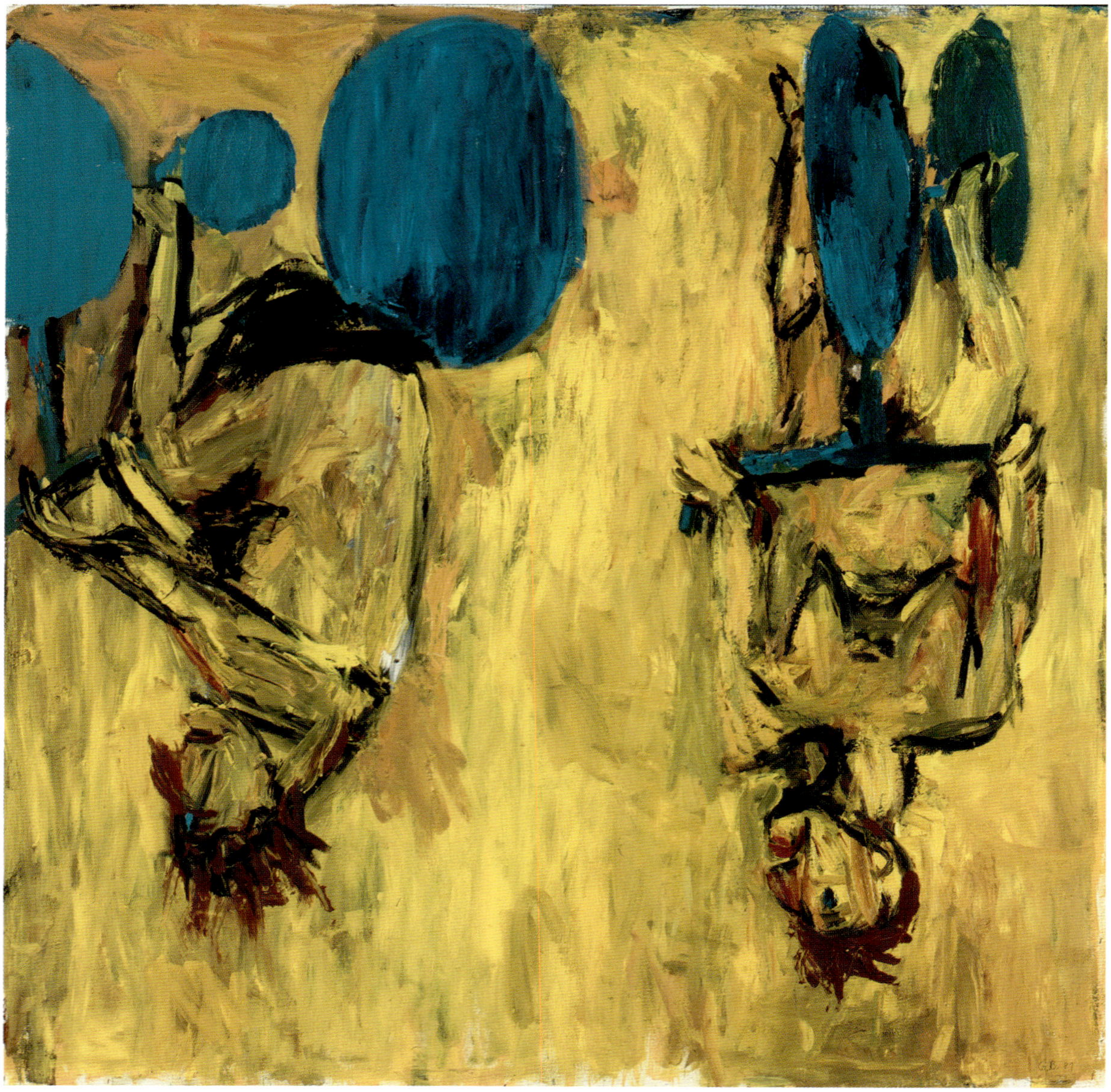

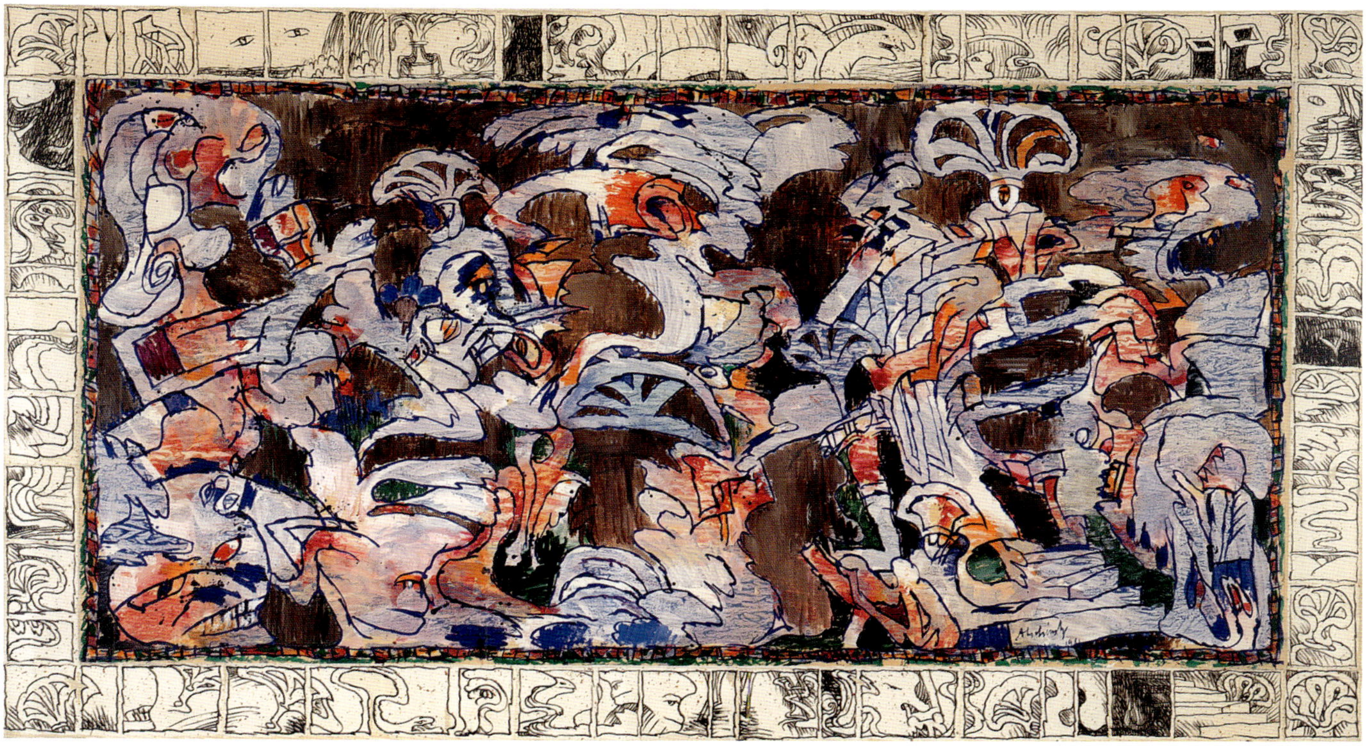

Pierre Alechinsky

| 1927, Brussels (Belgium)

1981

Le Passé inaperçu
[The Unperceived Past]
Acrylic paint and Indian ink on paper mounted on canvas
209 × 470 cm
Purchased 1995 - AM 1995-339

Determined not to confine his art to a single medium, Pierre Alechinsky has explored the realms of drawing, painting, engraving, writing and ceramics. He was linked to the Cobra group, which between 1948 and 1951 advocated collective and international experimentation within the fields of literature and plastic art, and he also got to know some of the masters of Japanese calligraphy, exchanges which proved to be seminal in his predilection for ink. Through the fluid, flexible nature of ink, Alechinsky poses questions, allowing the unknown to spring out from behind erratic lines conducive to the exploration of signs and forms. From 1965, ink began to be mixed with acrylic paint, bestowing a framework of little scenes to reflect the main scene in the centre of the composition. These characteristics can all be found in *Le Passé inaperçu*. In an exuberant turmoil of simmering abstract-cum-figurative forms, figures from the Binche Carnival leap out here and there, in their costumes bedecked with bells and tall feathered hats, recalling the artist's early years in Belgium. All around are the "marginal notes". These conjure up not only strip cartoons but also the small complementary scenes adorning the bottom of altarpieces in classic paintings, and even the notes used in printing in the margin of engravings, creating a range of prestigious and popular references that the artist has adapted to his own vibrant and impertinent lexicon •

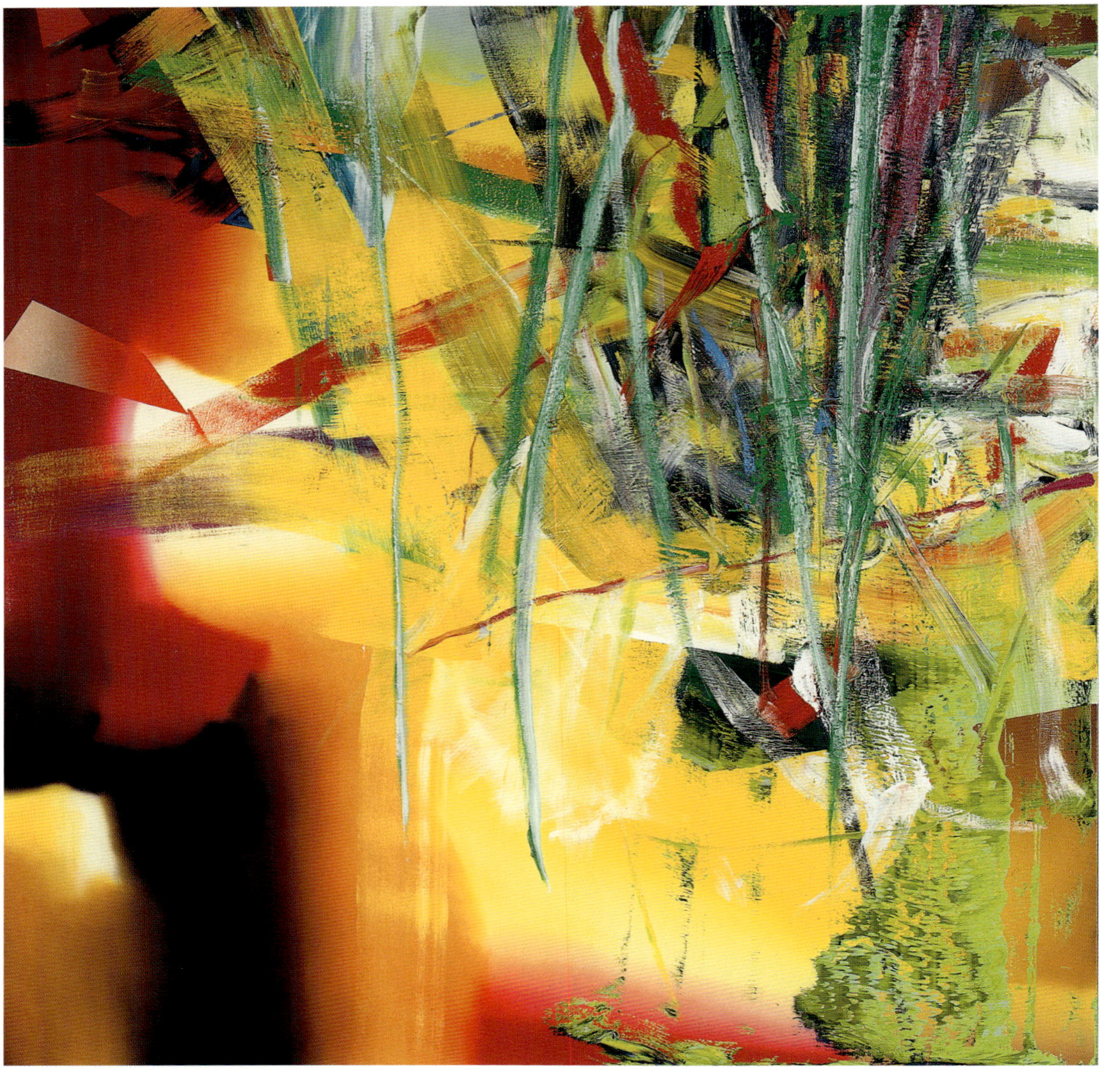

1983

Juni, 1983 (527)
Oil on canvas
251 × 251 cm
Purchased 1984 -
AM 1984-399

Gerhard Richter

1932, Dresde (Germany)

Gerhard Richter was born in East Germany but moved to Düsseldorf in 1961, where he discovered the latest avant-garde trends. In response to the announcements proclaiming the death of art, he tried his hand at all forms of painting in order to challenge it more effectively, rejecting any idea of a personal style. Going from monochrome to abstract painting, via photorealism, the artist did not adhere to any particular style, even tackling the most classic genres, such as landscapes, portraits, still lifes and personal or historic events. Between 1977 and 1979, he painted a series in which each work was invariably called *Abstraktes Bild* [Abstract Painting]. *Juni* belongs to this ensemble. On a formal level, the exuberant sweep of colours harks back to Abstract Expressionism. Here, however, it is not the speed of the brushstroke that leaves a trace on the surface of the canvas. A small sketch (about 20 centimetres high) was actually the starting point for this meticulously executed creation, using an airbrush on a broad swathe of canvas. The smooth pictorial matter, with its diffused effects, has broken away from any corporeal association. It is not the energy of the gesture that Richter is trying to express. As he puts it, "Painting reveals and enables us [...] to see the invisible, that which has never been seen before [...], and the pictures are all the better and more beautiful [...] when they correspond to this inconceivable reality."

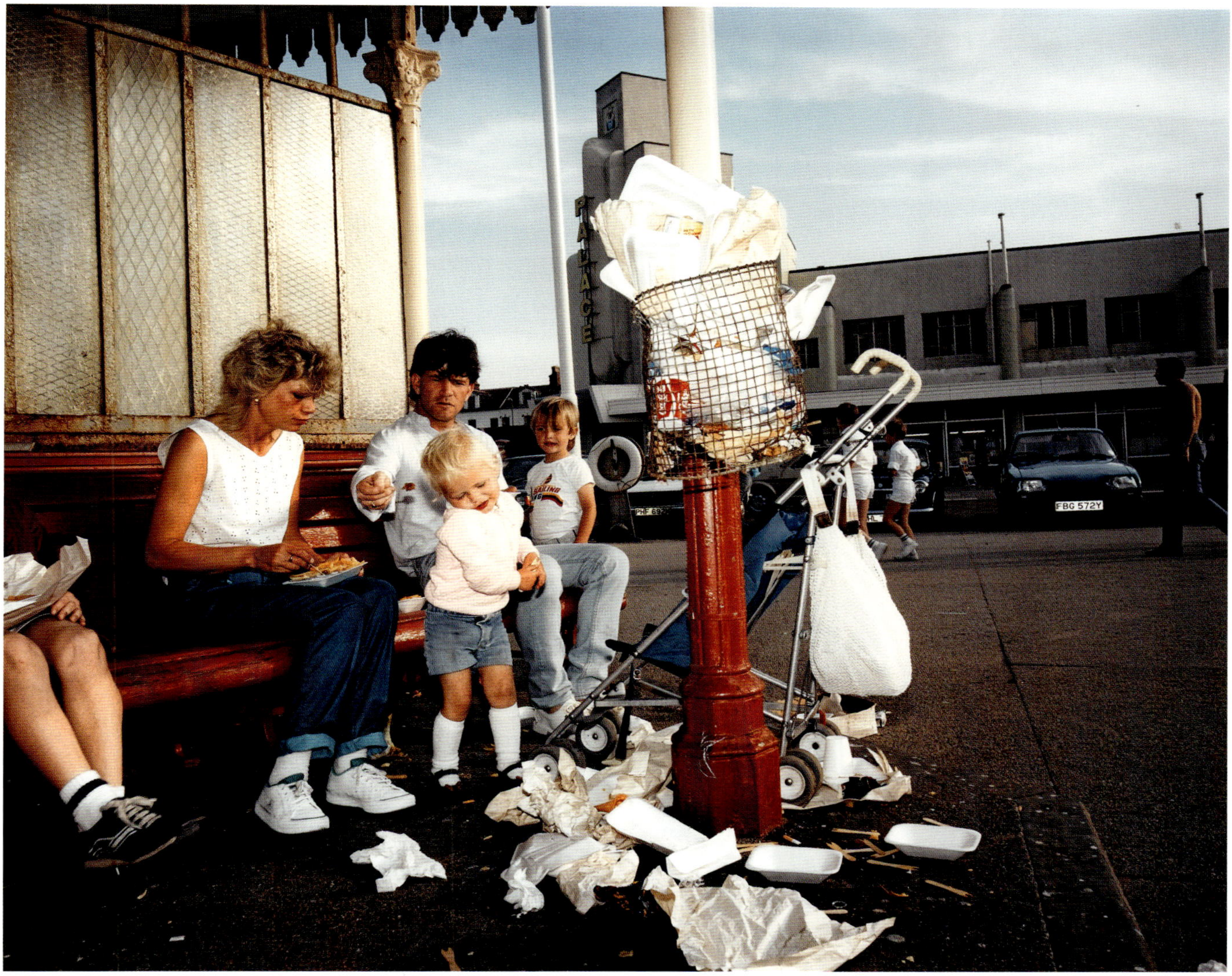

Martin Parr

1952, Epsom (United Kingdom)

Martin Parr became interested in photography as a teenager, taking a degree course in it at Manchester Polytechnic in the early 1970s. In 1982, the young photographer settled on the outskirts of Liverpool and began working in colour, resorting to flash even in broad daylight. The originality of his documentary approach, with its particular brand of wit, ensured him a reputation as one of the major figures on the new British documentary scene. The series entitled "The Last Resort" was undertaken between 1983 and 1985 and still remains one of his most emblematic works. It focuses on New Brighton, a popular sea resort situated a few miles from Liverpool and casts a not unironic eye on the leisure pursuits of middle- and working-class Britain under Thatcher. The caustic nature of the work and its lack of compassion triggered a fairly heated debate in England on the place and remit of the photographer •

1983-1985

New Brighton
The "Last Resort" series
Chromogenic print
50 × 60 cm
Purchased 2005 - AM 2005-135

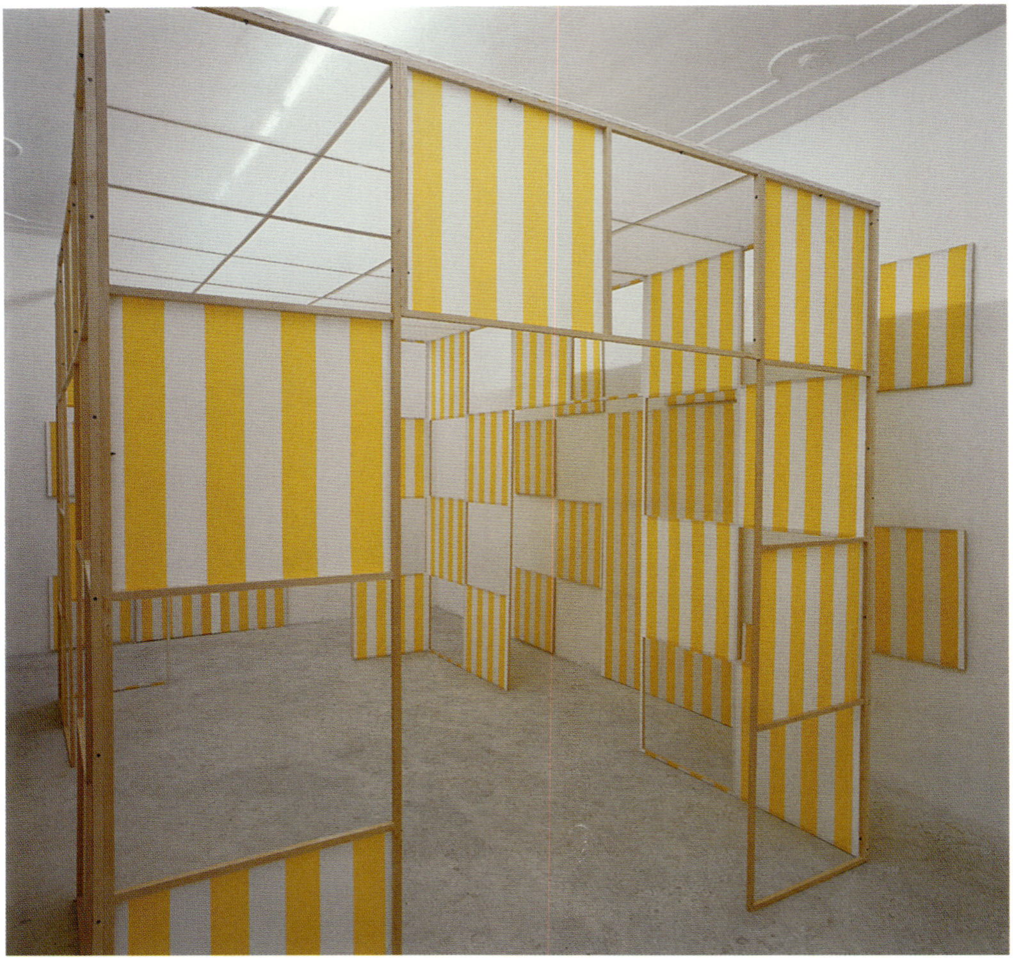

➔ **1985/1989/ 1990/1993/ 2001/2003...**

Cabane éclatée n° 6 : Les Damiers

[Exploded Cabin no. 6: The Checkerboard]

Situated work, created at Ugo Ferranti, in Rome, in 1985
Wood, cotton fabric with alternating vertical white and golden yellow stripes, each 8.7 cm (± 0.3) wide, paste, white cotton fabric, white acrylic paint
283 × 283 × 424.5 cm (before being exploded)
Purchased 1990 - AM 1990-87

(Souvenir photo: *Cabane éclatée n° 6 : Les Damiers*, in Ugo Ferranti, Rome, 1985, © DB-ADAGP)

Daniel Buren

| 1938, Boulogne-Billancourt (France)

In the late 1960s, Buren began creating in situ, calling on his favourite "visual tool": alternating 8.7 wide stripes. His "situated works" analyse and transform the venues in which they are erected, but never become inexorably dependent on them. This is the case with *Cabane éclatée n° 6 : Les Damiers*, which was created for the first time at the Ugo Ferranti gallery in Rome, in 1985. Since then it has been revamped several times, and on each occasion has been adapted to fit in with its new environment. The artist, who has no studio, and lives on site wherever in the world his project may happen to be, insists therefore on featuring next to the titles of his works the dates of each updated version. In keeping with the principles of this series, the premises of which date back to 1975 but which only really took off in 1984, the motif is projected on to the walls by means of square fragments that have been removed from the structure. The installation multiplies *ad infinitum* the viewpoints and sensations of the visitor, who is invited to step inside and move in and around this great volume, which has exploded in space •

Jean Nouvel

| 1945, Fumel (France)

From the moment he created his first agency, in 1970, Jean Nouvel stood out not only from the historicism of the "European city", but from the legacy of Le Corbusier and contemporary British technologically-inspired architecture. He came up with a different strategy for every project, tackling the context in its broadest sense, to include the location, culture, programme and client. The diaphragms of the south façade of the Institut du Monde Arabe in Paris, for instance, are taken from the moucharaby lattice windows one finds in Arab-Islamic architecture.
Here, Jean Nouvel has broken away from the transparency theme that characterised his recent creations in favour of an opaque monolith, whose abstract form evokes a musical instrument case but also a fragment of piano lying on its side. The shimmering polished black granite flank wavers between envelope, imprint and counter-form, hiding yet revealing beneath its streamlined exterior the smooth golden hues of the three auditoriums, which appear to be hanging in space. This effect is accentuated by the way the approach has been designed; the audience enters through a low door before emerging into a gigantic fifty-meter high lobby, into which spill the volumes of the three auditoriums. Two monumental openings provide a panoramic view over the skyline and city. Like an enigmatic signal-cum-object, Tokyo Opera forms an inherent part of this chaotic megalopolis, while providing a sharp contrast with the urban fabric, through its immaterial and metaphysical character •

1986

Opéra de Tokyo

Award-winning project, unbuilt; produced in conjunction with Emmanuel Blamont, Jean-Marc Ibos, Myrto Vitart and Philippe Starck
Scale model: black and gold plastic; 18 × 52 × 26 cm
Purchased 1992 - AM 1992-1-381

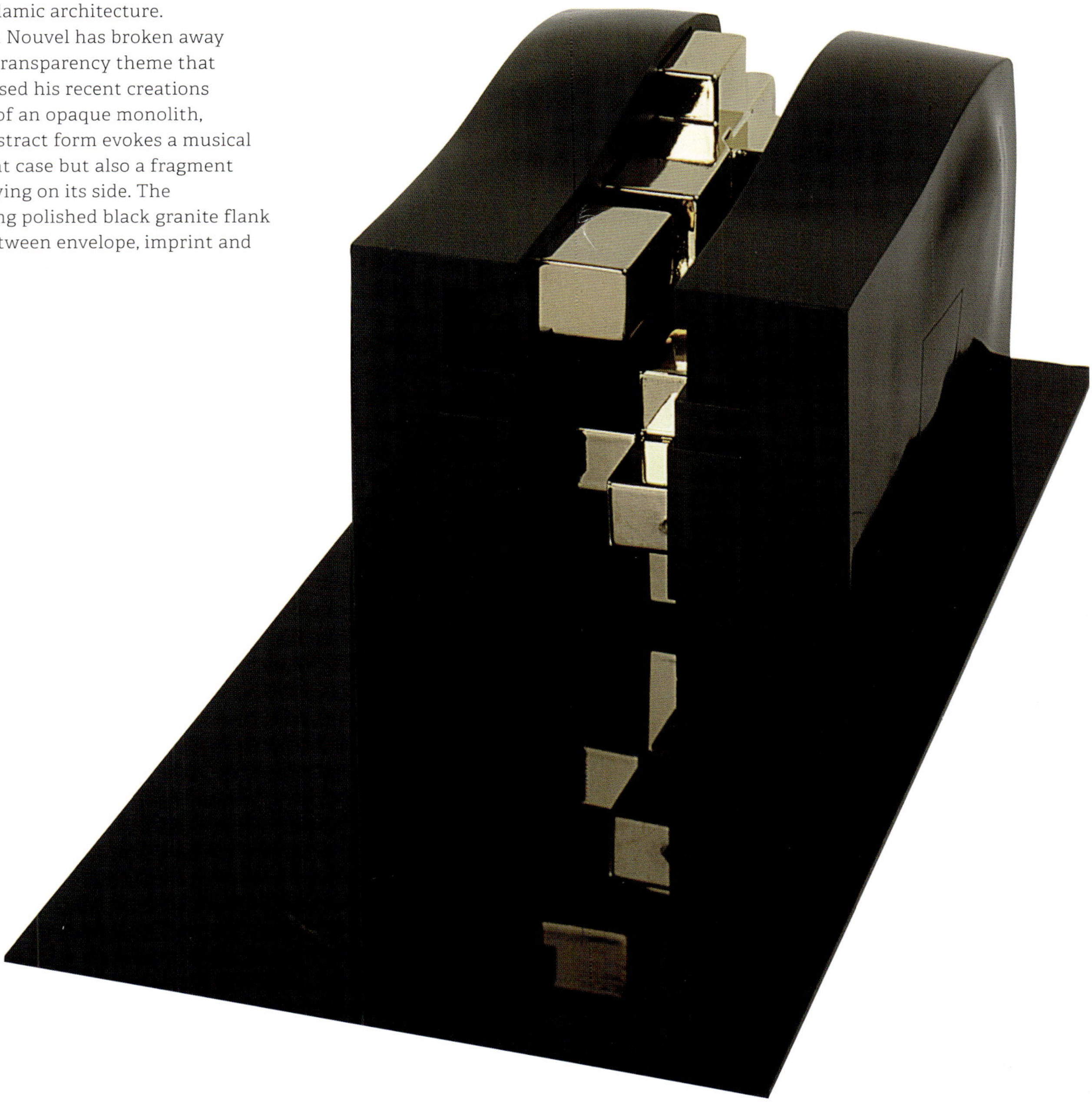

1985

Plight

Installation: 284 rolls of felt, a grand piano, a blackboard and a medical thermometer
310 × 89 × 1 813 cm (all together)
Purchased with contributions from Anthony d'Offay and David Sylvester, in memory of the artist, 1989 - AM 1989-545

Joseph Beuys

1921, Krefeld (Germany)
1986, Düsseldorf (German Federal Republic) †

During the Second World War, Beuys enrolled in the Air Force. When his plane was shot down, he was found by Crimean nomads, who healed his wounds by wrapping him in animal fat and felt. This seminal (though disputed) biographical event explains his use of real or symbolic sources of energy in his work, such as copper, fat and felt, chosen for their olfactory, heating or nutritional properties.
Shortly before his death, Beuys designed an installation for a gallery that was being polluted by noise. The artist, having initially joked that soundproofing was the only solution, covered the walls of the two rooms (recreated here) with rolls of felt. In the first space, a medical thermometer and a blackboard inscribed with empty musical staves have been placed on a closed concert piano.
The temperature of the room fluctuates according to the people in it. The visitor has to bend down in order to enter each of the rooms, which are both comforting and claustrophobic. The onlooker becomes the only source of sound in the whole installation, a situation which is conducive to listening and to reflection. Through this acoustic, olfactory, thermal and visual experience, he becomes physically aware of the depth and benefits of silence •

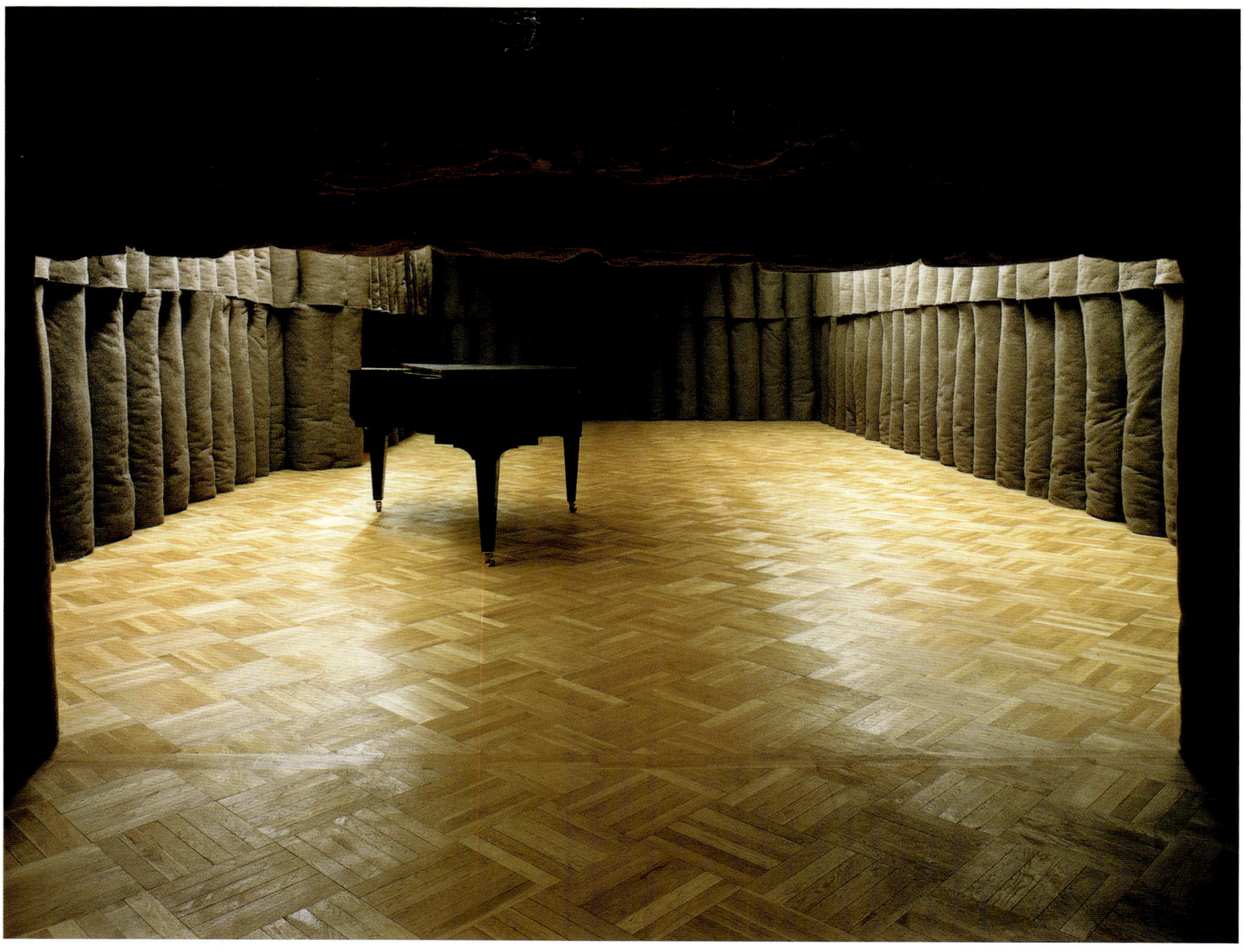

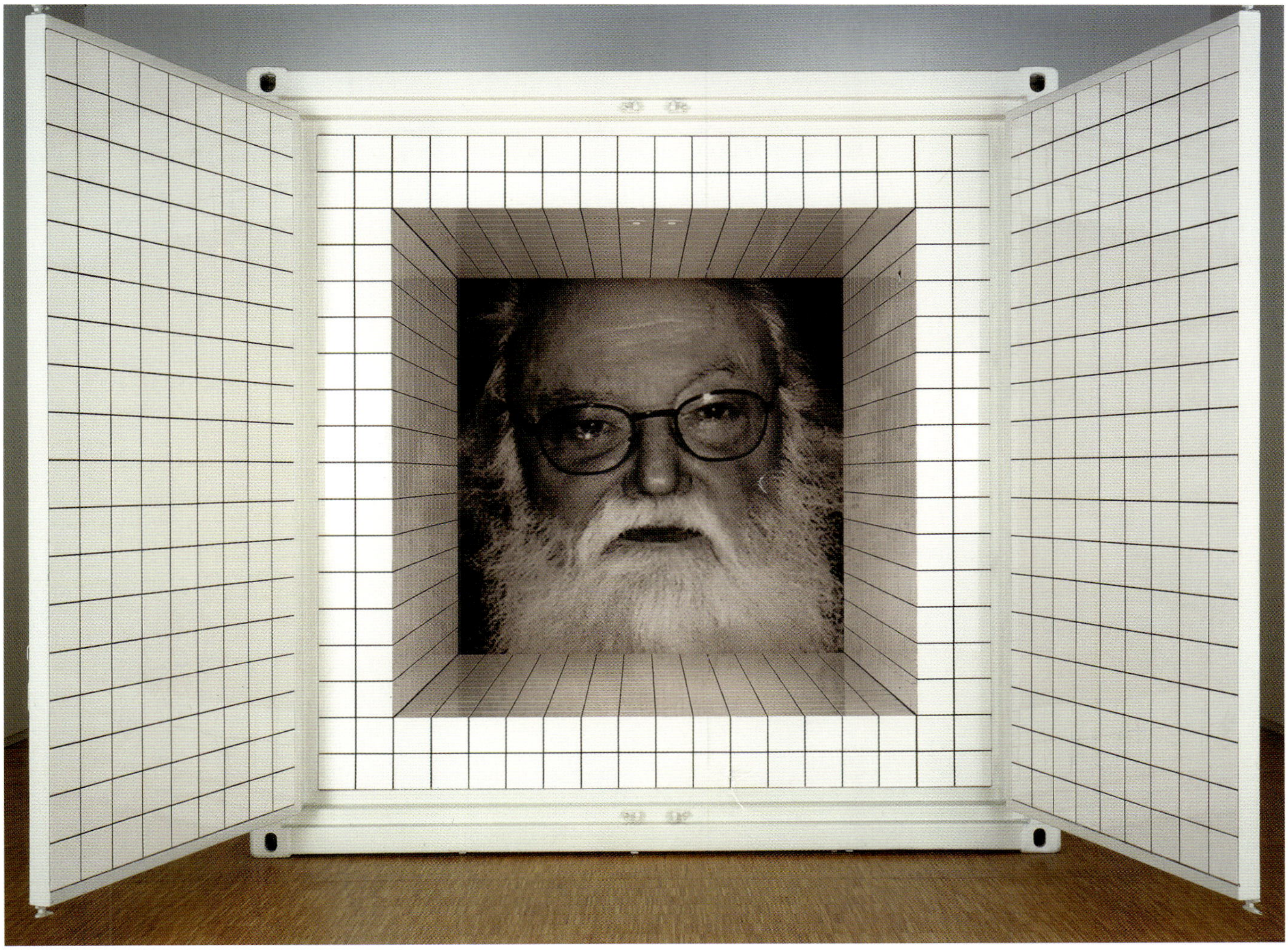

1988

Container Zéro

In situ creation: painted steel, tiles, lighting
330 × 330 × 330 cm
Commissioned and purchased with the contribution of the Centre national des arts plastiques, 1988 - AM 1988-2
(View of *Container Zéro* with *Hommage à Pierre Restany*, 2003–2005)

Jean Pierre Raynaud

I 1939, Courbevoie (France)

In 1962, on completing his horticulture course, Jean Pierre Raynaud filled a flower pot with concrete and painted it red. This instinctive reappropriation of an everyday object marked the beginning of a series of variations on a theme, illustrated by *Le Pot doré* [The Golden Pot], which was initially erected on the piazza of the Centre Pompidou and stands today on its terrace.
In 1987, the museum commissioned Raynaud to create a work in situ. The artist came up with a mobile, free-standing architectural structure, *Container Zéro*. The work was built on the same principles as the house which the artist closed in 1988 (and finally demolished in 1993), following a series of transformations carried out over a period of nearly twenty years. Like the house, the inside walls of *Container Zéro* are covered in white tiles, a commonplace material with simple forms. Inside the container, which is treated as an independent museographical venue, the artist has carried out works in the shape of manifestoes or tributes. In 1988, he conjured up the work of Yves Klein, with a square of ultramarine blue pigment; in 1991 he juxtaposed artistic and scientific vacuums by activating the physician Paul-Louis Fournier's ion pump; in 2003 he presented a portrait of Pierre Restany, the art critic who had defined and defended the New Realism movement, with which Raynaud was associated… The artist has decreed that these actions must end with his death. At that stage, his white tiled painting, *Numéro 0*, will be placed at the bottom of *Container Zéro* •

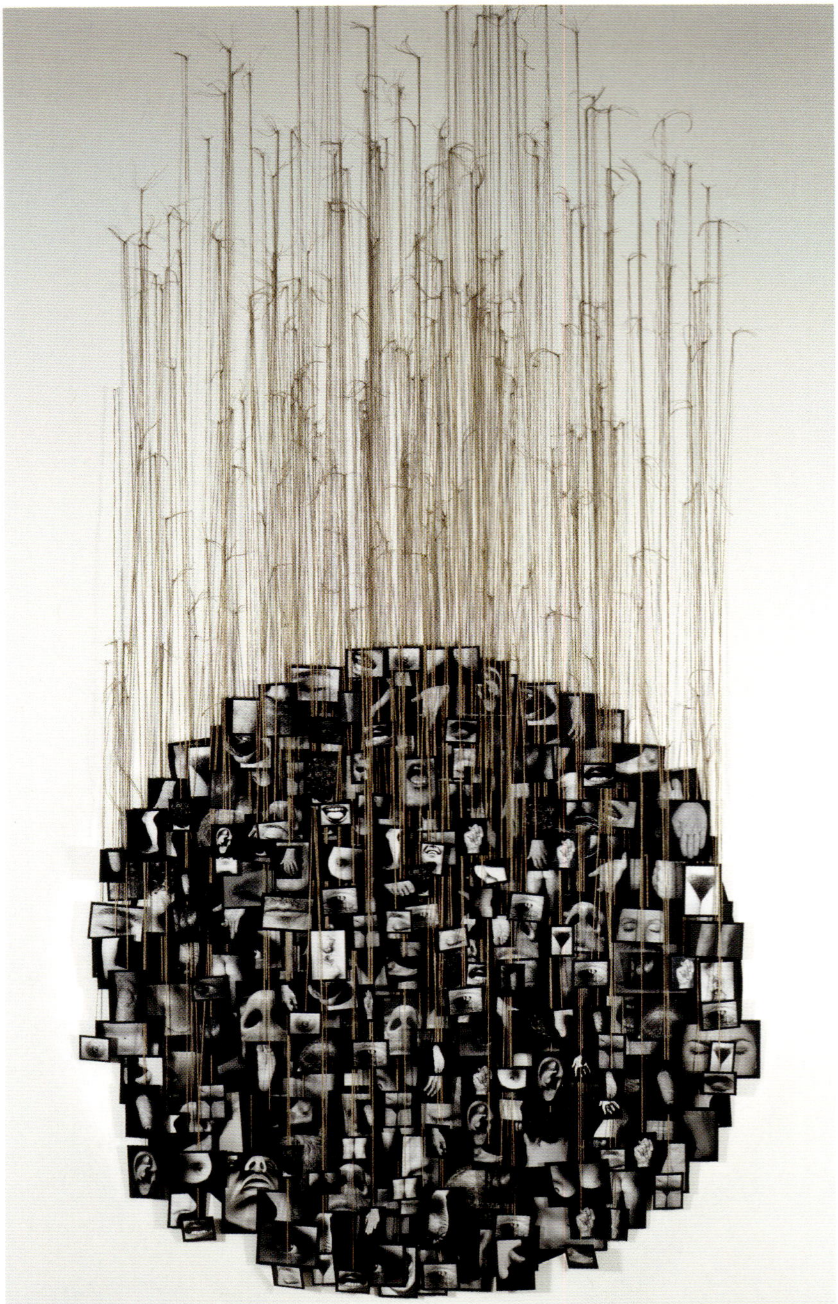

1989

Mes vœux
[My Wishes]
Mural installation: 263 black-framed gelatin silver prints mounted under glass in the shape of a circle and hung with string
H.: 320 cm; diam.: 160 cm
Purchased 1990 -
AM 1990-80

Annette Messager

| 1943, Berck-sur-Mer (France)

In 1970s Paris, Annette Messager, amid a circle of artists such as Christian Bolstanski, Jean Le Gac and Paul-Armand Gette, whose highly unusual approach to art had been termed "individual mythologies", insisted on the feminine dimension of her art. She incorporated into it the domestic universe to which women had been reduced by male attitudes. This criticism of the female condition is expressed through a plastic lexicon which includes needlework, precious personal diaries and beauty magazines. *Mes Voeux* illustrates the artist's predilection for fragments. Details of men and women's bodies, at all ages, are featured on dozens of black and white snapshots and placed in front of us, without any attempt at hierarchical organisation. The framed photographs, viewed objectively, are laid out in a circle and hung from strings, conjuring up ex-voto imagery. If the observer examines the frequently recurrent details more closely, he will see however that the presentation is really taking issue with identity, sexuality and the body itself. This whole intimate universe, while challenging the validity of taboos, seems to be expressing the vision of an artist with a visceral awareness of the contradictory movements of the subconscious •

Christian Boltanski

1944, Paris (France)

Humble materials, household objects, family photographs and worn clothes are the favourite medium of Christian Boltanski, whose work reflects existential issues and memory. The artist dwells endlessly on disappearance, oblivion, death... From his early, more satirical, works to his most recent creations, the story of his own life has always mirrored that of humanity, in a blend of reality and fiction.
From the 1980s, holocaust references gradually began to creep into Boltanski's work, as illustrated by Réserve. The space, its walls lined with used clothes, creates unbearable tension between the visible and the experienced. This is not merely a recreation of some cramped second-hand clothes shop – the visual and olfactory sensations, the saturation of the visitor's senses, jog the whole process of memory. For the "minor memory" of time passing in the *vanity* of clothes rekindles not only the memory of those who have been lost forever, but also the "major memory" of the history of the twentieth century. The accumulation of anonymous garments is echoed, in a ghastly hiatus, by the bodies of those who have disappeared. The work exudes a tragic sense of absence and silence. "We've fallen out with death" says the artist – and it is with death that this work is attempting to come to terms •

1990

Réserve
[Warehouse]
Installation: clothes and lamps
Variable dimensions
Purchased 2000 -
AM 2000-99

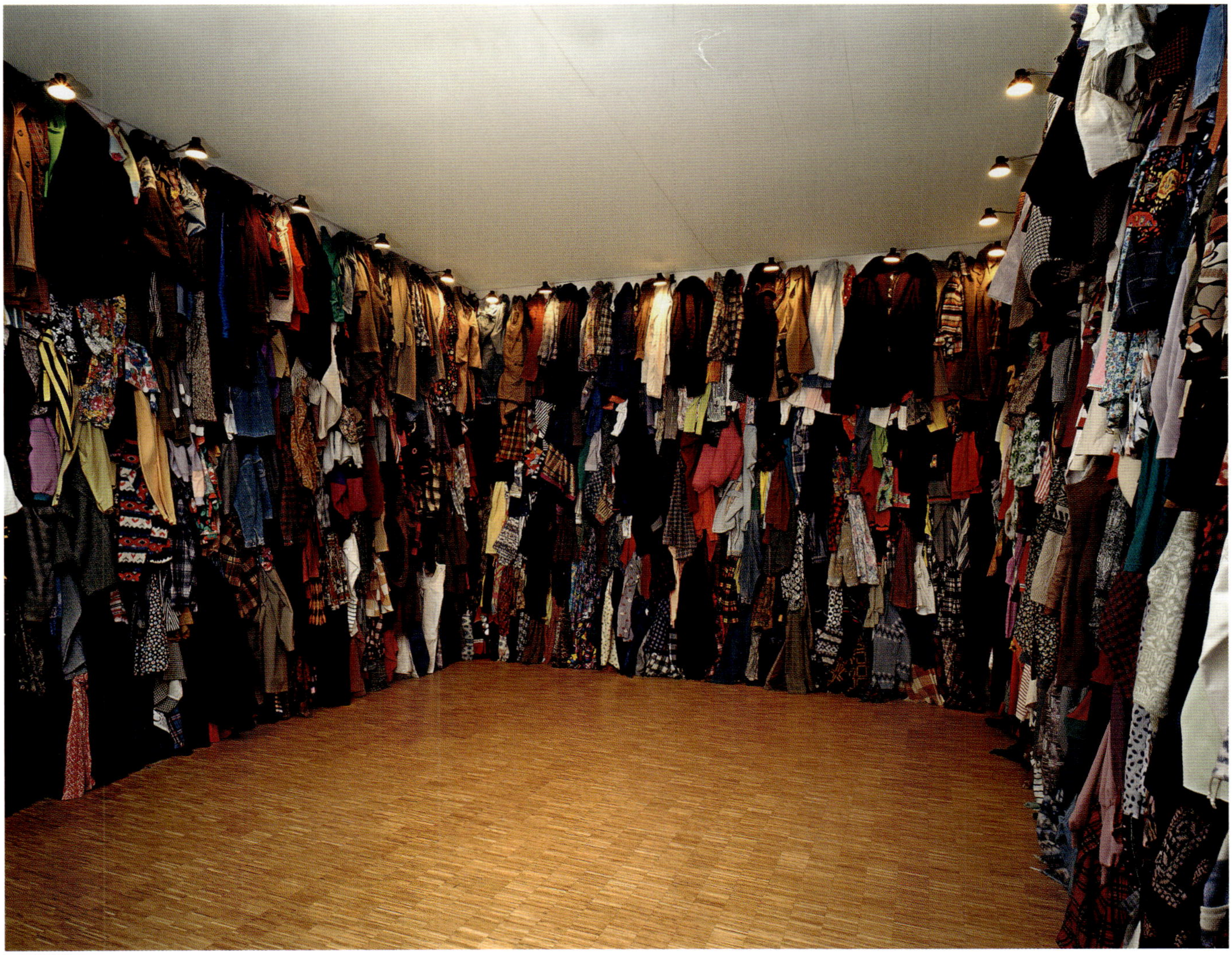

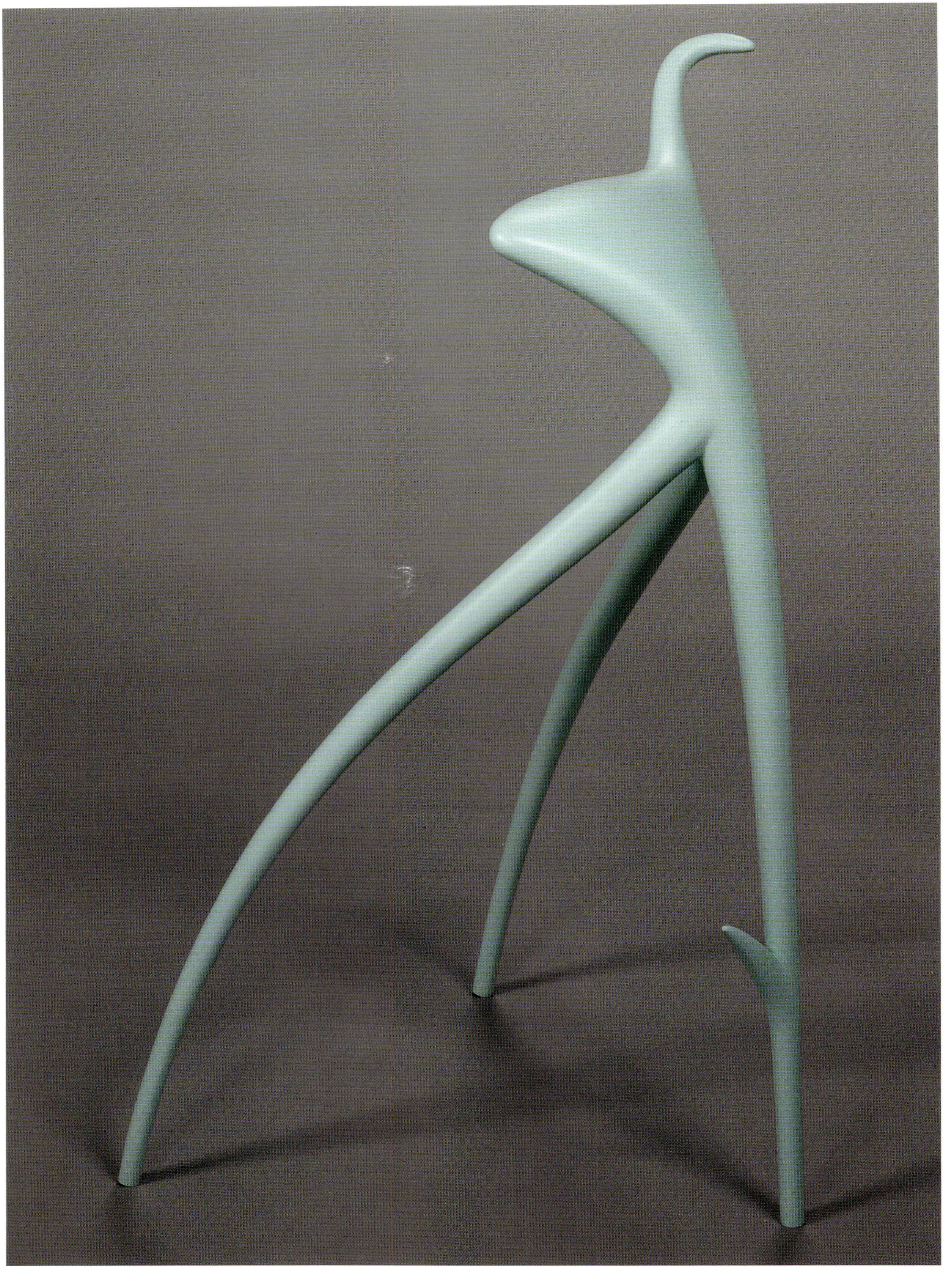

Philippe Starck

| 1949, Paris (France) †

Since the late 1970s, Philippe Starck's extraordinary inventiveness has been breathing fresh air into our everyday world. The son of an aeronautical engineer, he spent much of his childhood sawing, cutting out, pasting or dismantling objects on his father's drawing-board, and has used his consummate mastery of manufacturing processes and the resources opened up by new technologies to benefit new ideas and revolutionary forms, taking a new slant on the way objects function and are used, and challenging the very concept of "style". To Philippe Starck, design cannot be reduced to the mere production of objects. It is an act of creation involving passion, desire, motivation and questioning. Each of the objects he creates is accompanied by a written or spoken commentary, which places it within its context or destiny. *Tabouret W.W.* was designed for the study of German film director Wim Wenders. Not without humour, the stool, which challenges the conventional balance of the seat, was conceived more as an enigmatic sculpture: its clearly-defined yet ambiguous undulating forms are characteristic of an aesthetic derived from science fiction – particularly Philip K. Dick – a source of inspiration for the designer at that time. With its diagonal lines oscillating between those of a horn, a flame, the stem of a flower or a shard of wood from the trunk (illustrated in the wooden prototype), *Tabouret W.W.* conjures up a disquieting, unfamiliar figure striding forcefully into the urban arena, a powerful, recognisable sign, the imprint or signature of its creator •

1990

Tabouret W.W.,
[W.W. Stool]
Manufacturer Vitra International AG (Switzerland)
Painted cast aluminium
97 × 56 × 53 cm; donated by the Vitra Design Museum, 1997 – AM 1997-1-23

Vito Acconci

| 1940, New York, NY (United States)

1990

Convertible Clam Shelter
Sound installation: fibreglass, steel, rigging, shells, lights and 2 indoor loudspeakers, radio placed on a shelf
150 × 240 × 280 cm (each shell)
Gift of the Société des Amis du Musée national d'art moderne, 1994 - AM 1994-262

Back in 1969, Vito Acconci began to develop a work in which the body was to play a central role. A major figure in the realm of body art, Acconci is also a poet and cannot envisage words without putting a voice to them. Indeed in his works the sound of his own voice has gradually led to the obliteration of his physical presence. What secret is hidden within this giant shell, poised to shelter or trap us in its pearly embrace, like a womb? Vito Acconci's installation, which can be converted into a box bed, an alcove, an archway, a tent or simply a place to lie down, encourages the visitor to play an active role, to listen to the sculpture as he would listen to nature. After all, doesn't a shell epitomise nature itself sculpting? Two sources of sound blend together here: as the shell releases the sound of water, of the ocean – which passes from one shell to the other – a radio placed on a nearby shelf picks up and emits at the same volume. *Convertible Clam Shelter* is emblematic of the poetic language the artist has been tying in with architecture and design since the 1980s and reflects his preoccupation with the idea of shelter and its social implications. The work recalls the artist's fascination with the habitat theme and its links with furniture, the organic and fantasy •

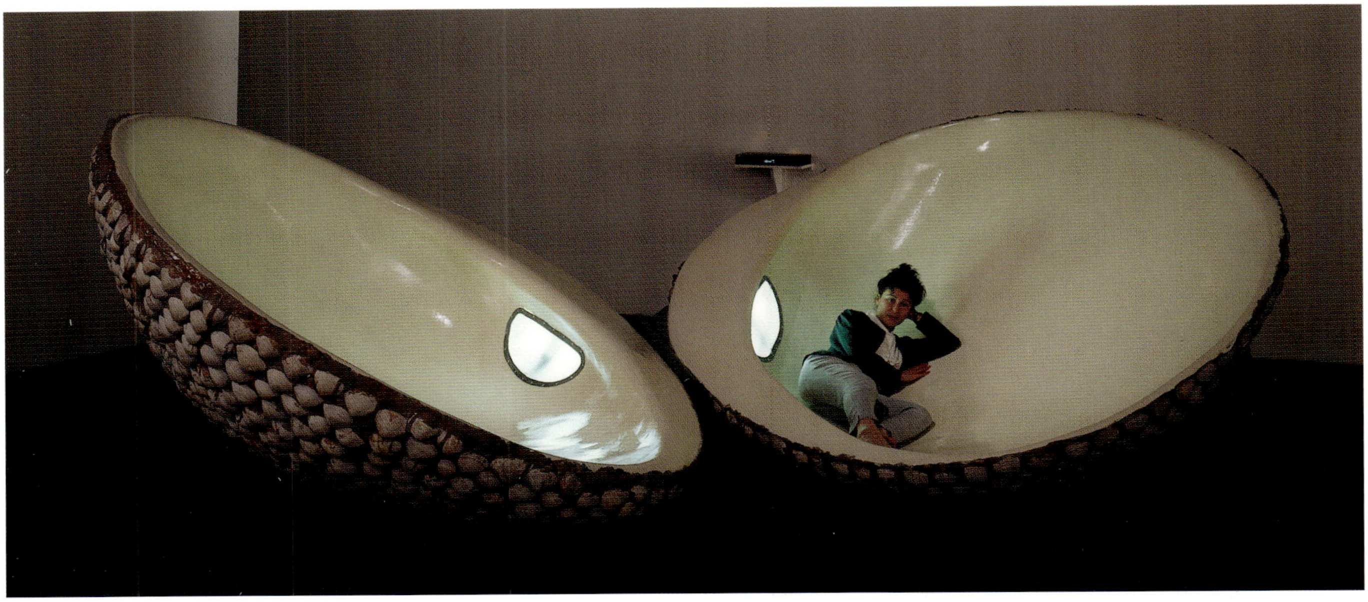

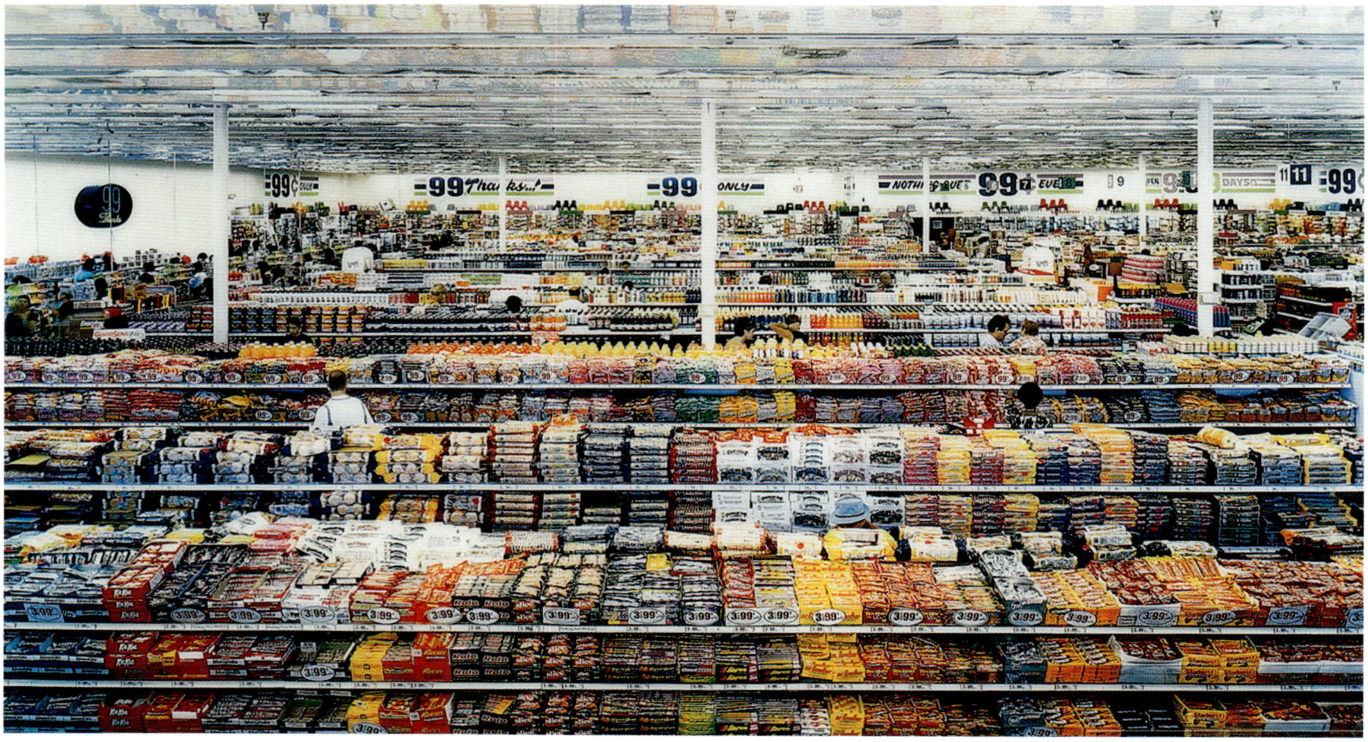

1999

99 ¢

197 × 326 cm
Chromogenic print (edition 5/6)
Purchased 2000 - AM 2000-96

Andreas Gursky

| 1955, Leipzig (German Democratic Republic)

Andreas Gursky, the son of an advertising photographer, took a course on "subjective" photography in Essen before going on to discover the teachings of Bernd Becher at the Fine Arts Academy in Düsseldorf. The latter was a proponent of systematic photography, designed to determine the integral nature of a phenomenon through an aesthetic, documentary approach. This principle was to influence an entire generation of artists. Unlike Bernd and Hilla Becher, however, who photographed industrial buildings in a systematic and serialised manner, Gursky attempted to explore the limits of realism in the context of autonomous images. His large formats are created from classic negatives featuring a number of shots, that he scans and assembles with software. This produces a new negative, which is then developed on traditional paper. Increasingly monumental formats and digital technology have allowed him to tackle phenomena affecting the contemporary world, in which individuals are swamped by environments they can no longer control (concerts, the stock exchange, supermarkets...). This is the case in this photograph of an American store in which all items are marked at 99 cents. Almost all the surface is covered in an infinite multitude of small coloured elements. So much so that the eye does not immediately take in the presence of a few customers The chimerical quality of this kind of image is, according to Gursky, a way of describing today's reality •

Xavier Veilhan

| 1963, Lyon (France)

Le Rhinocéros, which could be regarded as the heir to a long legacy of sculpted bestiary, delivers an immediate impact through its colour and material. Xavier Veilhan appears to have reversed the advertising cliché which inevitably associates a make of car to a fleet-footed animal (a horse for Ferrari, a lion for Peugeot etc.). In this case, the work, its red lacquer reminiscent of the bodywork of a car, attributes the speed of the vehicle to a ponderous animal. By reconciling craftsmanship and high-tech, objet d'art and consumer product, classicism (in its realism) and modernity (in its materials), *Le Rhinocéros* plays with paradox, entrenched in the tradition of history of art but also in the world of today. Xavier Veilhan is representative of a new approach to artistic creation, which integrates the latest transformations in post-industrial society. Thanks to the broadening and complexification of current techniques, whether in the field of production, documentation or communications, today's artists must inevitably call on other professionals. When he prepares his sculptures, Veilhan starts from a digital image, using software to create a model in 3D. This produces a maquette which is then enlarged. Each stage of the process takes place in the artist's studio, which he runs like a small business. The quintessential relationship between the artist and the world of work and production lies at the very heart of Xavier Veilhan's whole artistic practice •

1999-2000

Le Rhinocéros
Painted polyester resin
110 × 415 × 140 cm
Purchased 2001 - AM 2001-26

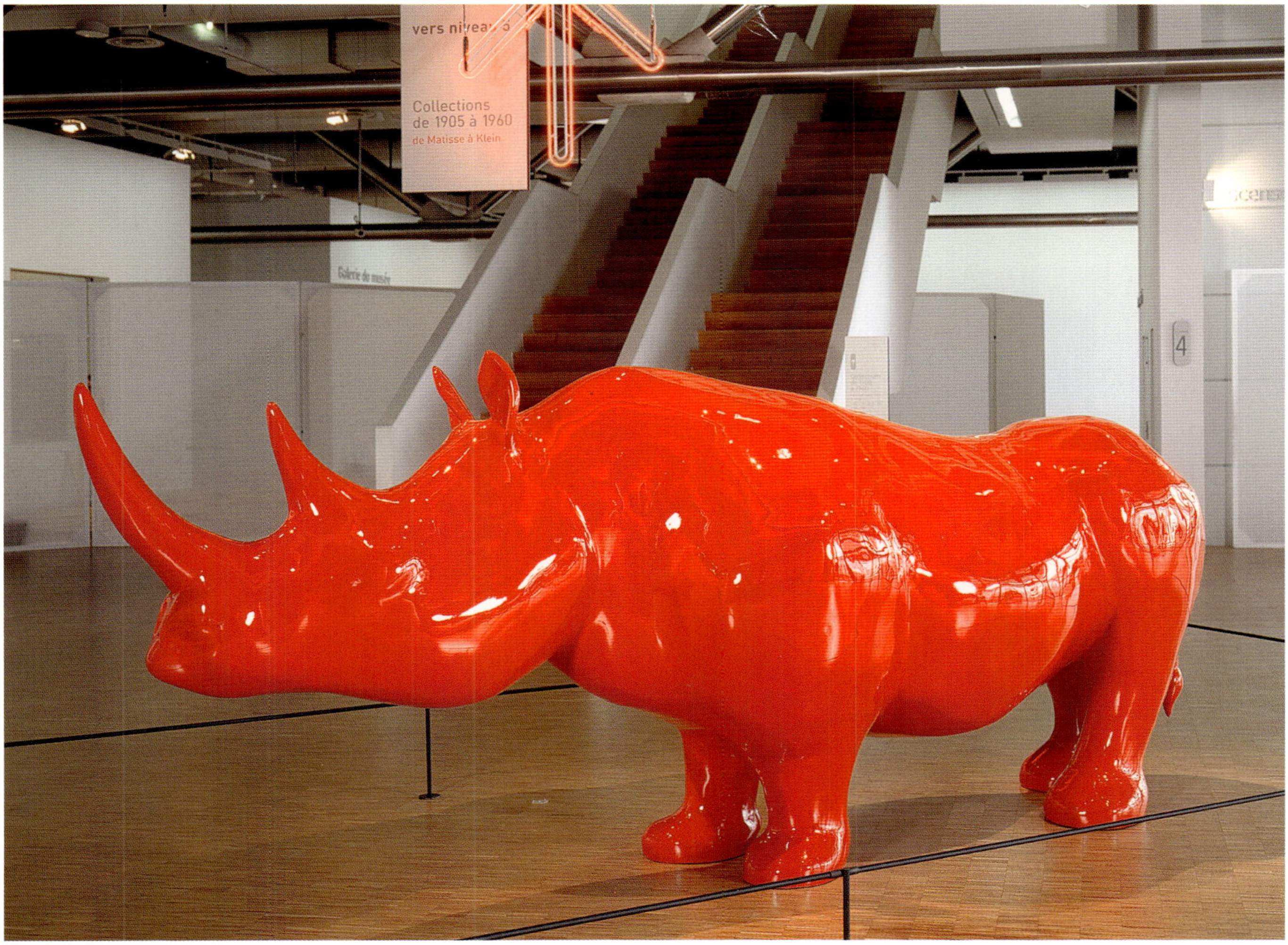

Bruce Nauman

| 1941, Fort Wayne, IN (United States)

In this vast installation, seven projectors broadcast forty-two video tapes simultaneously on to each wall. These were all recorded as static shots in the artist's studio, using infrared cameras, for one hour a night over forty-two nights. The images, which are virtually motionless, recall CCTV footage. Unlike *Mapping the Studio 1*, in which the artist did not tamper with the recording, here he has colourised the sequences. Some are reversed or upside-down, creating "flip-flops". The seemingly rudimentary subject-matter – the artist's studio by night, in his absence – is countered by this plethora of techniques. Although his choice may seem to belong to the realms of radical minimalism, an acute observer will actually detect a multitude of micro-events: the sound of mice, a cat padding past, fireflies... One can also spot material that may already have been used, or is due to be. Reminiscent of the approach of John Cage (to whom this work is dedicated), who encouraged one to listen to silence in order to discover its real depth, Bruce Nauman reveals the underlying existence of his studio, as it carries on, however tenuously, without him. The tapes enable us to discover a work consisting of almost nothing, which although it may be invisible to the naked eye is none the less crucial. The infinitesimal or potential activity of the studio, which constitutes the necessary foundation for his work to evolve, sheds light on the actual inception of a work •

2001

Mapping the Studio II with Color Shift, Flip, Flop & Flip/Flop (Fat Chance John Cage)

Audiovisual installation: 7 video projectors, 14 loudspeakers, 7 scripts, 42 video tapes, NTSC, colour, stereo sound, 5 h 45; version 2/4
Joint purchase by the Centre Pompidou, Paris, with the support of the Mr. and Mrs. William S. Fisher Family Foundation and contributions from the Georges Pompidou Foundation; the Bâle Kunstmuseum; and the Tate, London, with the support of the American Fund, Tate Gallery, 2004 - AM 2004-426

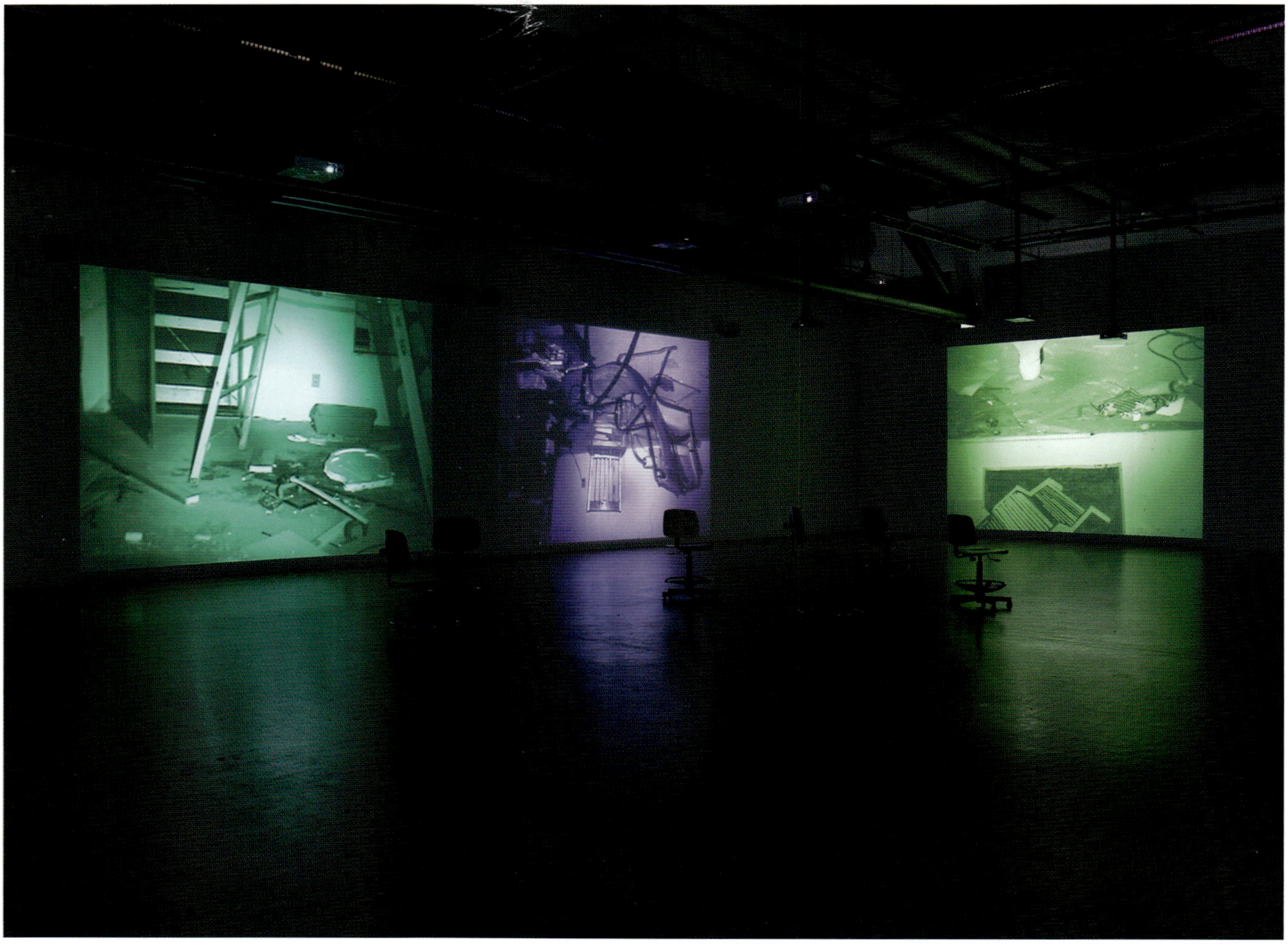

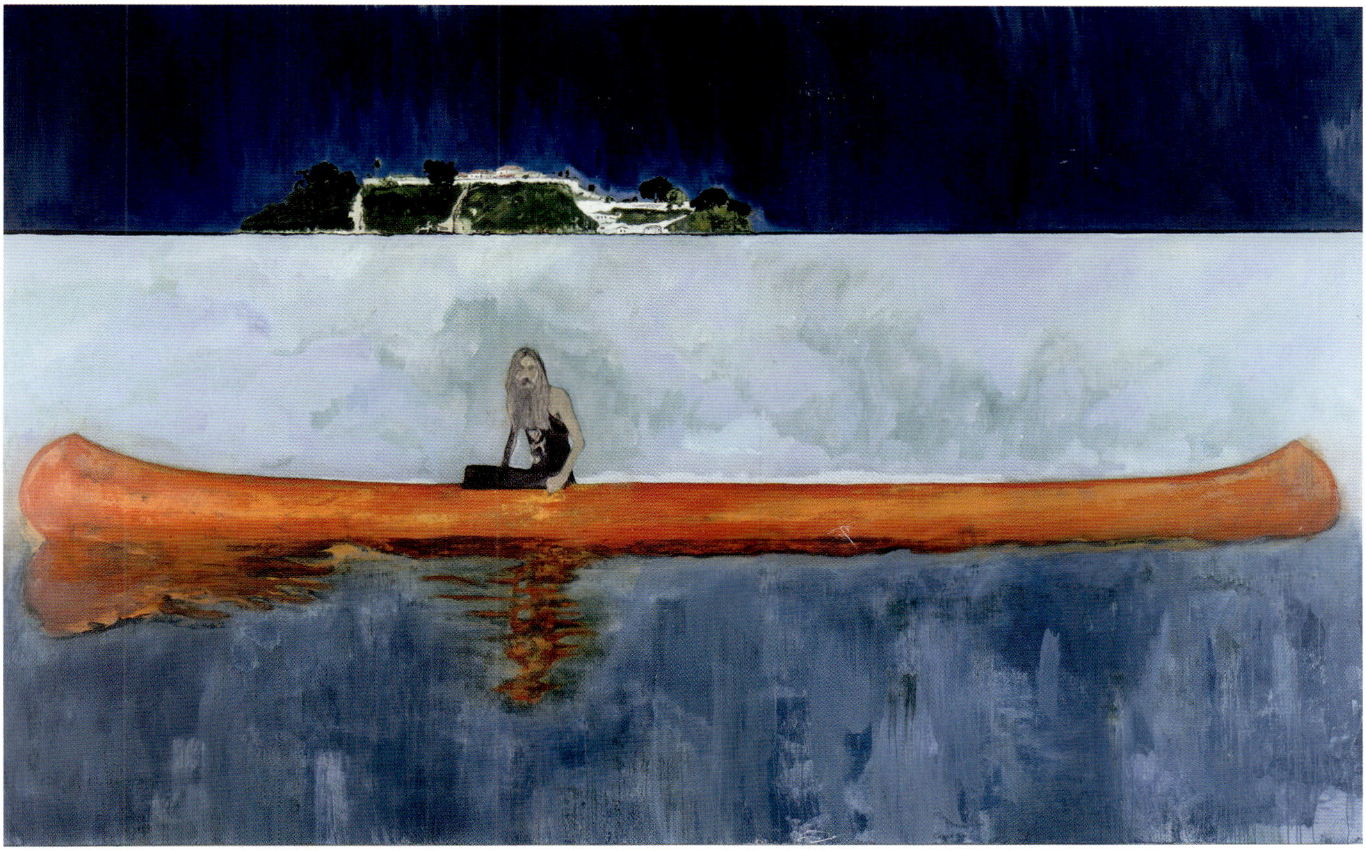

Peter Doig

| 1959, Edinburgh (United Kingdom)

Peter Doig was born in Edinburgh and then moved to Trinidad, before settling with his family in Canada. He studied Fine Arts in London, where he acquired a perfect mastery of pictorial techniques. This enabled him to create frequently large-scale works imbued with remarkable visual impact.
100 Years Ago, an iconographical blend of several references, is one of his most emblematic creations. The figure in the canoe, inspired by the sleeve of a 1970s rock record, is floating in a timeless pictorial space. The luminous fields with their saturated colours recall the uniform blocks of colour used by some modern painters, particularly Matisse, to structure the space of the canvas. In the background, set back and with no apparent perspective, stands a hospital. This building, its insular quality reminiscent of certain prisons, does actually exist, and is situated off the coast of Trinidad. The aquatic landscape and overall structure of the composition also echoes *Die Toteninsel* [Island of the Dead] by Arnold Böcklin (1880–1886). This reference adds to an underlying feeling of disquiet, nostalgia or melancholia, which seeps through the splendour of the waters, incandescent with the figure's reflection. The semantic wealth and pictorial force of this canvas, with its iconic purity, lend it a powerful evocative magnetism and a metaphysical dimension, buried in its unfathomable depths •

2001

100 Years Ago

Oil on canvas
240 × 360 cm
Purchased 2002 -
AM 2002-285

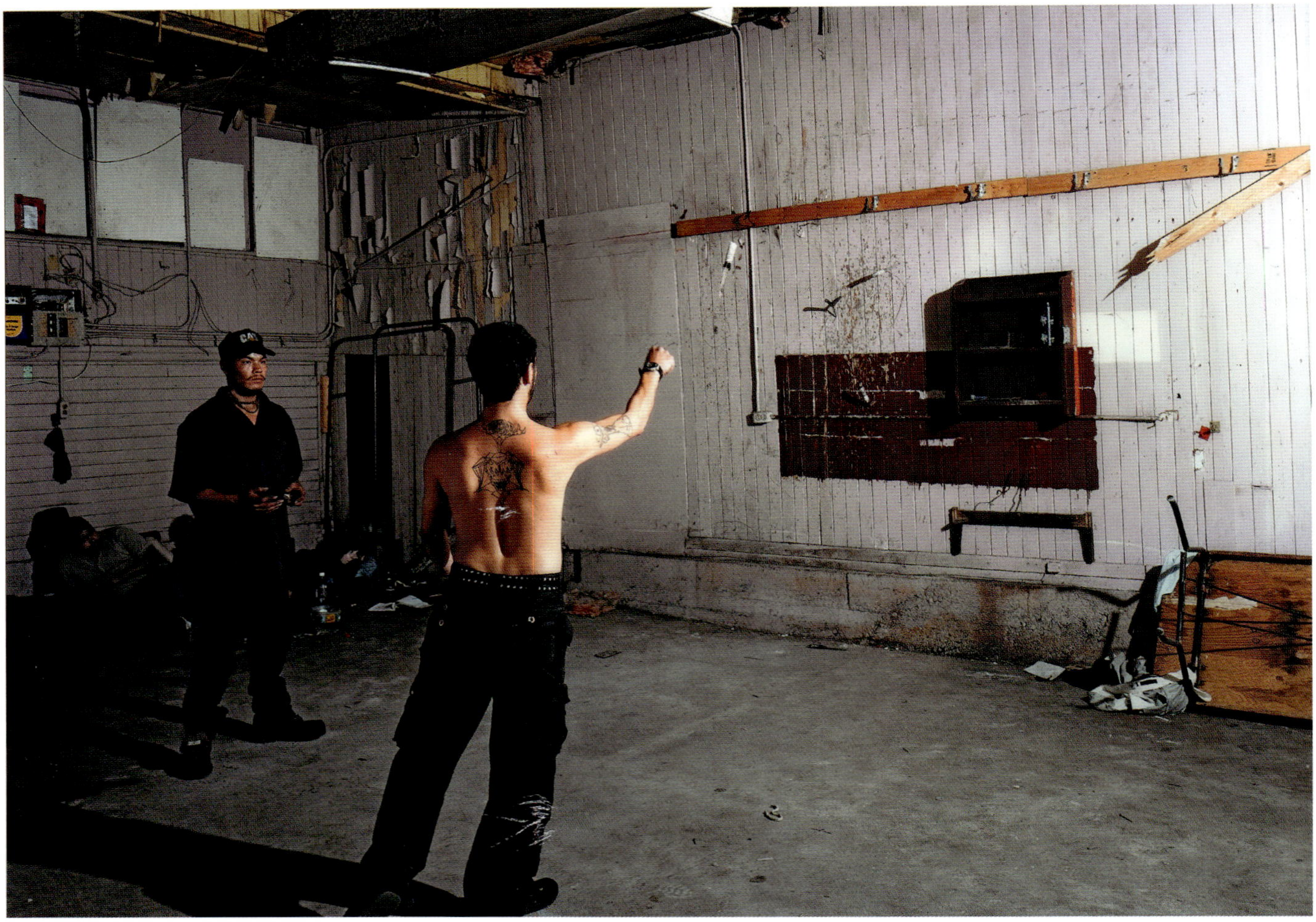

2008

Knife Throw

Inkjet print
Gift of the Société des Amis du Musée national d'art moderne,
2010 – AM 2010-3

Jeff Wall

1946, Vancouver (Canada)

For the last thirty years, Jeff Wall's photographs have reflected a special rapport with nineteenth century Western pictorial tradition (Delacroix, Courbet, Manet...). They also illustrate his interest in striking images derived from advertising and films, expressed through large formats and light boxes, which the Canadian artist was one of the first to use, in 1978. The complex images take a new slant on classic art works or feature characters (usually actors), ordinary men and women carrying out everyday tasks. In the early 1990s, the plastician reverted to a more d irect form of aestheticism, akin to a certain type of documentary photography. However, the theatricality of the characters, the acute attention paid to the sets and the frozen recreation of the instant undoubtedly reflect real life. In *Knife Throw*, a bare-chested man is throwing a knife towards a wall whose elements are reminiscent of an abstract composition. How has the artist managed to stop the knife in mid-air? By using video, as he has been known to do, in order to prepare and gain more control over the representation of the most minute details of the movement? What is the significance of the tattoo on the man's back and what role is the onlooker supposed to be playing? Oscillating between realism and artifice, *Knife Throw* is an elaborately staged counterfeit snapshot, its subject and technique emblematic of Jeff Wall's depiction of individuals in contemporary society •

2008

Untitled
Fibreglass, resin and paint
302 × 150 cm
Gift of the Société des Amis du Musée national d'art moderne, 2008 -
AM 2008-149

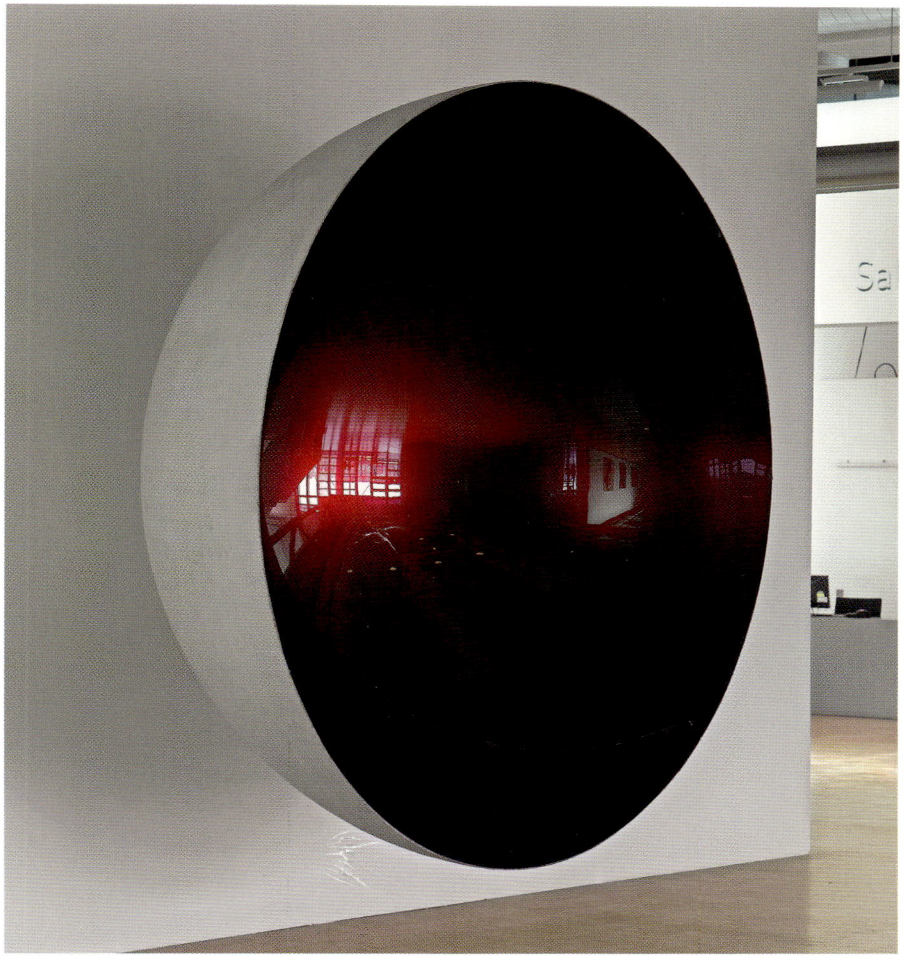

Anish Kapoor

1954, Bombay (India)

Anish Kapoor, who is of Indian origin, lives and works in London. For twenty-five years, his materials, forms and meanings have enhanced the world of sculpture, triggering a rewarding exchange between the philosophy of Indian culture and the conceptual references of Western art. The notion of perception is central to his work, which combines simplicity of form with a sensorial dimension, derived from the pure pigments he introduced into his work in the late 1970s. This technique was followed up by a meticulous process of sanding and polishing which enables the metal surfaces, whether concave or convex, to reflect and transform the space around them.
This vast mural work, with its simple yet imposing contours, consists of a curved reflective surface in dark red, a characteristic colour in the artist's palette. The sculpture, which epitomises his style and approach, plays on the contrasts between light and dark, visible and invisible, full and empty, inner and outer. Despite the industrial precision of its execution, it has great appeal, sending back an inverted image to the viewer, which seems to dissolve in a new space, as though the mysterious form has swallowed it up. Anish Kapoor, who gained international recognition in the 1990s, also creates sculptures and monumental installations in public spaces •

List of works

Centre national d'art et de culture Georges Pompidou

The Centre national d'art et de culture Georges Pompidou is a national public establishment under the supervision of the Ministry of Culture (law no. 75-1, 3 January 1975)

Alain Seban
President

Agnès Saal
Managing Director

Alfred Pacquement
Director of the Musée national d'art moderne - Centre de création industrielle

Bernard Blistène
Director of the Cultural Development Department

Jack Lang
President of the Association for the Development of the Centre Pompidou

François Trèves
President of the Société des Amis du Musée national d'art moderne

Musée national d'art moderne - Centre de création industrielle

Director
Alfred Pacquement

Deputy Director in charge of collections
Brigitte Leal

Catalogue

The entries on the artworks featured in this publication were drawn from texts by the curators of the Mnam-CCI.

Editorial Coordinator
Geneviève Munier

Translator and Copy Editor
Caroline Taylor-Bouché

Additional Translations
Dafydd Roberts

Graphic Design and Layout
les designers anonymes

Production
Martial Lhuillery

Publications Department

Director
Nicolas Roche

Deputy Director, Head of Editorial Department
Jean-Christophe Claude

Editorial Unit
Françoise Marquet

Sales Department
Sales Unit
Benoît Collier

Sales and Supplies Unit
Josiane Peperty

Press Officer
Évelyne Poret

Administrative and Financial Management
Expenditure Unit
Nicole Parmentier

Revenue Unit
Matthias Battestini

Iconography and Rights Department
Head of department
Claudine Guillon

Multimedia Department
Head of department
Guy Morvan

Internet publishing unit
Frédéric Nassar

Acknowledgments

Bénédicte Ajac
Jean-Paul Ameline
Quentin Bajac
Jean-Michel Bouhours
Laurence Castany
Clément Chéroux
Olivier Cinqualbre
Sophie Duplaix
Valérie Guillaume
Angela Lampe
Brigitte Leal
Necha Mamod
Camille Mansour
Isabelle Monod-Fontaine
Camille Morando
Camille Morineau
Évelyne Pomey
Cloé Pitiot
Perrine Renaud
Jonas Storsve
Marielle Tabart
Anne-Marie Zucchelli

Photo credits

Engraving: IGS-c.p.,
L'Isle-d'Espagnac

First printed in September
2010
by the Artegrafica-Graphicom
Group in Verona, Italy.